To Caral
with
wishes
Liz
Elizabeth Benney

The
LAST JUMP

Elizabeth Benney

MW01487606

Also by Elizabeth Benney

Reaching Summit Rock (1999)

Seventy-Something Acres (2006)

Published by Cape Catley Ltd

The LAST JUMP

Elizabeth Benney

CAPE CATLEY LTD

Dedicated with much love to my old friend Doff Gentry. In the face of devastating cancer, she is an exemplary example of how to cope with such an illness. Doff never complains. With grace and dignity she shows flawless courage and an acceptance that goes way beyond the grasp of her family and many friends.

First published 2011

Cape Catley Limited
Ngataringa Road
PO Box 32-622
Devonport, Auckland
New Zealand

Email: cape.catley@xtra.co.nz
Web: www.capecatleybooks.co.nz

Copyright © Elizabeth Benney 2011. The author asserts her moral rights. Except for the purposes of fair reviewing no part of this publication may be reproduced or transmitted in any form or by any means, electronic or mechanical, including photocopying, recording or any information storage and retrieval system, without permission in writing from the publisher.

A CiP catalogue record of this book is available from the National Library of New Zealand

Cover photograph: Kim Kordell
Typeset in Sabon 10/13.5
Designed and typeset by Kate Greenaway
Cover design by Trevor Newman
Printed in China through Bookbuilders
ISBN: 978-1-877340-31-4

CONTENTS

AUTHOR'S NOTE

I have two identities, says my editor Chris Cole Catley. There is the core 'me,' the complete New Zealander, and there is the 'me' that has been moulded by America for more than fifty-two years. Some readers will be pulled up short by many of the differences between the two countries, such as my usage of common Kiwi words and expressions. My truck has a tray, a synonym for a bed; train lines are supported by sleepers, (ties); I skite, (brag); a float is a horse trailer, and there are hundreds more.

American readers will constantly see the letter S substituted for a Z. Traumatised and traumatized, recognise and recognize ... And for Kiwi spelling, the letter L likes to be seen in its double form. Cancelled, travelled, pummelled. Americans sensibly save time by shortening words. Who needs the U in colour, favour, succour, or ME in programme? And as for jewellery – jewelry makes more sense.

I am so grateful to my editor who has spent above average hours working on this manuscript including my spelling and syntax errors. These were compounded by the fact that I had a very hit or miss education. Only in my last three years was I continuously in the same school when I was loaded off to boarding school in disgrace.

Something I can say for myself, however, is that I happen to have a good memory for conversations, particularly off-beat ones. As I like keeping an occasional journal and emailing family and friends, I find I have recorded a somewhat unusual oral history of daily life. Naturally I have changed the identities and names of certain people who feature in this true story.

My gratitude knows no bounds as I applaud my dear long-suffering, uncomplaining husband for the hours he has been neglected while I have been slouched over my computer. Meals have suffered or never materialised, my mood has vacillated between highs and the lows when nothing would come out of my head. And poor Dave has had to cope with the alarming times this SC – senior citizen – has fallen off her horses, with dire consequences.

My appreciation to Chris, Martin and Jenny Cole for their assistance in shaping my story.

In thanking all those who have helped me, I am flattered indeed to have renowned author Michael Korda give my book such a positive heads up.

Elizabeth Benney

Chapter One

The Beginning of the End

I check out my teeth. A top one is broken and the expensive brace that keeps the teeth Hollywood-straight has snapped in two. I manage to sit up in the muddy water and spit out grit, mindless of such vulgarity in front of all the onlookers.

Trainer Paul comes running over. "You okay?"

My wise mother's long-ago words race through my brain.

Rise above it, Elizabeth, and never complain.

"Yes," I mumble. He carefully pulls me to my feet and nothing feels broken.

Minty has cantered off and is standing at the arena gate. I call him my solid citizen, but he does fall short of perfection by never stopping the second he feels me lose my balance. Paul leads him over. "Let me leg you up and I'll lower the jumps."

"Thanks." It has to be twenty-five years since I could mount a large horse from the ground.

"Now you just sit there," Paul smiles, "and catch your breath."

He lowers four jumps to a humiliating beginner-rider height. I pat Minty, suck in an immense breath and try to ignore my left side, the wet itchy skin sticking to my underpants and my drenched breeches clinging to the saddle. I pick up a great rhythmic canter. Jump number one, two, three.

Faultless.

I turn the corner of the arena and head for the fourth jump. In the space of two strides, all the fresh adrenaline has emptied out of my system. I pull up my talented jumper and hold back tears.

A circle of silence.

Paul hurries over and puts his hand on my leg. "It wasn't Minty's fault, Lizzie. He was perfect. You just lost your balance when he arched his back so well over that big jump. You know I hate to tell you this, but you *are* losing a bit of your grip. Your heels weren't down enough so there was less weight in your stirrups to give you support."

But my body is full of arthritis, beginning at my toes. There's no way that my heels will go down any more. Paul gently caresses Minty's face. "You're a good old boy."

I spit more grit into a tissue and stare at Paul, my trainer for thirty-one years. "Right now I'm scared to finish the course," I mutter. "I'm sorry. I'll be okay to jump in a day or two."

He looks up at me, hesitates, and I can read his eyes. "Lizzie, we've agreed for several years that I'm to tell you when your jumping career should end. You've never been scared before. That time has come."

I exit the arena and Paul calls after me. "I'll get one of the help to drive you home." And that means two of his employees must come to our farm so my driver can return to the stables.

Dave's pulling weeds. When he sees me in the passenger seat, comprehension sweeps over his face. "What happened this time?" In almost fifty years of our marriage, there have been other such occasions.

"I went pitching off at the top of this oxer and landed in a muddy puddle."

"What's an oxer?"

"It's a jump with wide parallel rails. This one was three and a half feet high and about three feet wide. I can't believe that this darned fall has scared me."

"Otherwise are you okay?"

"Sort of. The bottom of a front tooth has snapped off and the brace is broken."

"I know you'll get over it. You'll soon be jumping again. Maybe just lower your sights." He puts Minty in his stall and I limp inside to struggle out of my mud-stained clothes. As I throw them in the hamper I think of the times I've bitten the dust, and the fright it has given my poor husband. And I think of some of my older horse friends whose husbands, unlike mine, have become intolerant of their riding.

This fateful day is 10 June 2006. I get the US Eventing Association's Omnibus for the summer horse trials, find a number and grab the phone. There's no way that in a week's time I can ride in the prestigious Groton House Farm Horse Trials, the best eventing competition in New England. "I have to withdraw," I tell the secretary. I don't want to go into the details, but I can't help myself.

I'm disgusted with this old body letting me down.

I hate being a Senior Citizen and to heck with all the accompanying discounts for SCs.

I'm mad that I was *scared* to go over a *tiny* jump.

I'm mad that I've had to withdraw from Groton House. Last year Minty was a splendid third in his classy division and I've had this dream of winning it this year and maybe ending my eventing career on a high note … and not supine in muck.

Stuffed with painkiller and a large dose of self-pity I lie in bed and think about my many idyllic years of jumping and the wonderful horses that have carried me. Of course there have been the inevitable falls, and I grin when I think of the broken bones, the rotator cuff injuries and the three concussions. But these accidents never really bothered me. I'm seventy-two now and I refuse to accept this unforeseen fear.

I can conquer it. I *will* jump again and I *will* compete again.

The phone goes. It's Paul. "You okay? You must be pretty sore."

"Yes, a bit. And thanks for ringing. I'll get over today and I *will* jump again. I've been thinking that I'll ride without my stirrups and do lots of exercises. That will definitely strengthen my legs."

"Lizzie, you're –" he pauses for quite some time. "You're getting on in years, you know. You've had a great innings and my answer is still no. *No more jumping.* Quit while you're ahead. Remember last year how I had you jump a line and then immediately stop? Minty was so obedient that you kept on going over his head?"

"Oh, that was nothing."

"It was a warning."

"Of the impending end?" I let out a false laugh.

"You know," Paul chuckles, "why don't you concentrate on dressage? You'd be good at riding all those figures in an arena." And he hangs up.

Dressage? No way, Paul. I'll show you how I can still jump Minty.

When I was a child I regarded old age as something like a myth, so far removed from reality that it would never happen. But it's certainly no myth. I'm arriving there and I'm encountering some of the classic symptoms.

I prattle to myself.

It takes ages to remember a common word.

I walk out of shops without my purchases and yesterday I rushed out of the grain store without my *wallet*.

I find one of last night's gourmet dishes still sitting in the microwave.

I need more and more time to untangle myself first thing in the morning.

And I'm falling off my horse.

But ...

I don't dribble.

I don't have frequency.

I can see and hear well.

I do have a broken tooth, but I've got most of my original ones, even if their surfaces are sporting a deepening yellow.

I have surprisingly good recall of my exotic youth and even a lot of the batty conversations of those days. As for current recall ... hmmm.

And horrors, sometimes I find myself drifting into my second childhood or my dotage. And how I despise that word.

As I lie in bed tonight, I'm back in my horse-crazy New Zealand youth, heedlessly jumping anything and everything and experiencing falls. But I'm never scared and I'm never hurt. And I never wear any sort of headgear except for my grandfather's old soft bowler hat, required when hunting or showing.

Mother always has horses at Tupare, our home outside small and provincial New Plymouth. I can ride and jump them quite well. (And today I wince at my ignorance and conceit.) Then out of the blue, I'm given my very own pony. I'm a skinny ten-year-old and a bit small on Monty, but to me he's faultless in spite of his massive draught-horse genes. I'm jumping him, or trying to, a few days after his arrival, and Mother scolds me. "Elizabeth, please stop this reckless jumping. Neither you nor Monty is up to it." At first I sort of heed her words, as things are a bit difficult for her right now. She's recovering from months fighting tuberculosis in the Chest Block of our local hospital, followed by months far away in the Otaki sanitorium near Wellington.

Dad hasn't a clue about reckless riding and takes an 8-millimetre movie of me trying to jump Monty. Three times he refuses the little hedge full of prickles the size of hat pins. I whack him, present him yet again and he leaps over it. I get hopelessly left behind in the saddle and seriously grab Monty in his mouth. But I don't fall off.

I'm jumping in a skirt, as there's never enough time to change into my one pair of overalls and Mother thinks it unseemly for little girls to wear pants all day. I can't wait for my jodhpurs to arrive from Great Britain. You can't buy them in New Zealand. As it is wartime, 1943, any order takes weeks to arrive. The boat must zigzag across the Atlantic to avoid being sunk by Nazi submarines. Then crossing the Pacific Ocean it becomes a target for the Japanese. If my jodhpurs don't make it safely to New Zealand I suppose I can still ride in a skirt. I shock Dad when he thinks that I'm more worried about my jodhpurs' safe passage than any passengers or crew members.

I think back to that day and Dad's reaction. Why did I speak with so little regard for the crew and passengers on their hazardous journey? I spoke selfishly and so impulsively. I should have followed my lovely mother's example – always so thoughtful and putting others first.

I might have surprised Dad but, looking back to those days, I see in many ways we were very alike. He was the youngest of ten and very spoilt – (all the family said so). Although he denied it, he often put himself first and liked to get his own way. I am the eldest, and I too like to get my own way, which, egotistically, I consider is the *correct* way. I'm ashamed to say that, like my father, I have a self-centred streak that can come boiling to the surface first. Did I unconsciously copy my father's traits? Or did we have a similar gene pool? I'm also built just like Dad, right down to the bandy legs. I have his energy level and positive opinions. I'm not always considerate of others, but

I like to think that in very important matters a side of Mother comes out in me.

As a ten-year-old, I was unaware of my failings way back then. And Dad did have moments of compassion and consideration of others. "You girls please do more for your mother. She's looking so tired and you know she's recovering from a difficult illness." But help her himself? No way. The culture of 'manliness' in those days seemed to make that impossible. On the other hand, he had great qualities ... and how we hated them at the time. The importance of hard work was always uppermost in his mind, fiscal responsibility and the appreciation of art and music ... and add to this list, manners maketh man!

Dad also had a soft side with animals. He could never slit the throat of a sick sheep, he could never wring the neck of an injured hen or drown a sick cat. He dealt with them at a distance. Out came his 22 rifle. Only his beloved dogs were ever taken to the vet for euthanasia.

Unlike Mother, Dad, at that time, takes my reckless jumping and falling off for granted. Someone tells me that it takes seven falls to become a good rider. To be on the safe side, my friends and I keep upping that number by deliberately falling off ... more honestly, we would half-jump off at the canter and roll when our feet hit the ground. I'm now at the count of eighteen and as the numbers increase I will become qualified to ride in the Olympics. I will enter the jumping competition and proudly represent my little country.

I've had Monty for two years and I keep hearing that my pony has no jumping talent. Reluctantly I have to add that neither does he have any jumping enthusiasm. It takes days for me to get over the disgrace of *elimination* in the jumping competition at my very first Taranaki Agricultural and Pastoral Show. To think that we didn't even get over that first jump! Three very naughty refusals and we were disqualified. I start yearning for a new pony, one that can *really* jump, so every day I scour the newspaper advertisements in the *Taranaki Daily News*.

At last.

For Sale. Rising three-year-old chestnut gelding, 14.00 hands high. This is the consummate pony for the luckiest child alive. Phone 975R.

I have to own him. Dad has vaguely given me permission to get a new pony, but he's away on business and poor Mother has had a tuberculosis relapse and is back in Chest Block. I tell our new housekeeper I'll be back late, borrow money from my grandmother and take a bus to Waitara.

It's overwhelming love at first sight. The pony's name is Mischief and I gasp at his beauty. I ride him at a walk and he gives me a very laboured trot, but in spite of my efforts he refuses to canter. Mischief has come off the papa or clay land, the poorer remote area beyond our mountain's rich volcanic pastures.

Of course the papa pony has had a rotten start in life. "I know you can improve him, Elizabeth," the seller tells me. "Once he's fattened up and turns three, there's nothing around Taranaki that will beat him." And by jove I *will* fatten him, and I'll give him so much love. I buy him on the spot. I knew Dad would say it's okay. I am now twelve years old.

Several months go by and in spite of all my love and care, Mischief still lacks energy and any willingness to canter. "I just have to forget about jumping right now," I tell myself impatiently. I'm riding along a country road just outside New Plymouth and there's a ditch beside us. "Golly," I think, "maybe Mischief will enjoy going *across* something and not *up and over* something. "Okay," I implore him. "Please jump over this." He pricks up his ears and tries but misjudges the ditch's width and depth. His legs bang against the opposite bank, he falls on to his knees and off I pitch into the hollow. I clean break my right thumb.

After the fracture has healed I'm riding down the same road. I've put a leather crupper strap on Mischief, going from the back of the saddle to a loop under his tail. It stops the saddle from sliding perilously up his neck as we ride down the steep hills around high Mt Egmont that dominates our province. I decide the crupper needs tightening and I lean around and pull on the strap, but the buckle is stuck. I kick my feet out of the stirrups and do a sprightly turn through a hundred and eighty degrees. Now I'm facing backwards and have leverage.

I haul on the buckle's strap. It's frozen with rust. I yank on it, really hard. The strap releases.

But – I am still riding backwards as the buckle gives way. It causes a small jerk on the rolled leather under Mischief's tail. He humps up his back, starts to trot and I accidentally yank on the crupper to keep my balance. The pull makes Mischief buck and I can't help yanking on the crupper again. Buck, bigger yank, bigger buck, bigger yank … a pattern is established. Our acceleration becomes a canter and then a gallop down the hill.

The pasture fences blur. Trees become indistinct. Utility poles grow together. How on earth can I stop him? How much longer can I hold on?

Help!

By now we're approaching the bottom of the hill and the town's outer suburbs. We're at maximum speed, in fact the fastest that I've ever been on a horse. It's time to bale out while there's still grass on the side of the road.

I let go.

The arc of my dismount is brilliant. I'm an Olympic gymnast, executing the perfect landing – until I hit the grass, peppered with stones. Mischief stops dead and starts to eat. I gather my wits and look up to see a man standing over me. It's Ernie, the town's sad simpleton. "I've seen everything now," he drools, shakes his head and continues pushing his bike up the hill.

And sixty years later I'm still falling off.

Yes, I will ride without my stirrups.

I will get fitter and stronger by running up and down the hills at our farm.

I will place my toes on the edge of the stairs and force down my heels.

Of course I will jump again. And I *will* compete in the horse trials once more.

Chapter Two

Coping with the Damage

Two days after my fall, Dave helps me out of bed. I pull up my nightgown and stare in the mirror.

My accident's black statement is spreading all over the left-hand side of my body. I don't remember any bruising after my gymnastic crash from Mischief. Next I stare at the aging contours of my body. It's losing its tightness and there's this ugly growing flab, especially down from my waist. The skin over my triceps reminds me of over-ripe passion fruit – I'd better start wearing long sleeves.

I make it into the kitchen and swallow prescription pain pills from a previous injury. They've passed the use by date, but they're all I can find. I can't stop looking in the mirrors throughout the house. My face doesn't look too bad, but there's an increasing black bruise around the forehead where the peak of my helmet met the ground.

I think of Mother.

Worse things happen at sea, Elizabeth.

I've still got life ahead of me.

The reflections will look better if I get my hair done, and my hairdresser has a cancellation. I should turn that noun into the plural. My hairdressers. The number of people at the Dawn Salon who work on me is endless. Today, the minute that I enter the salon, my face gives away my fall. Without the need of embellishments, I relate what happened. Then the repeated response, "Liz, don't you think you should give up all riding?"

First to work on me is John and he colours my thirty-five-year-old grey. Then Maria washes my hair and Tony combs it out and places clips in different places. Chris brings me tea and cake and finally Bonnie the boss cuts and dries it. One doesn't need to tip the owner, but she intimidates me into insincere generosity. Give me New Zealand where there's still so little tipping.

Every time that John works on my hair, I get another chapter of his personal life. And at each of my appointments his astonishing tales pile up. No, that's a euphemism for his outright compulsive lying. He has classy good looks and I guess is around sixty years old. At first I believed everything he told me.

John was born in Hollywood and his parents also had a house in New York City and summered in a family mansion in Newport, Rhode Island. "Our house was located in the middle of the famous seaside cottages as they're called." He rummages in a drawer and brings out an old newspaper photo of a grand entrance hallway. "This was my home," he boasts. There is no caption.

His education was at a fancy private school that I've never heard of and then a finishing school in Switzerland. "Do you speak French and German, John?"

"Of course. Both."

"Are you married, John?"

"I was. To a famous film star but we're divorced." He gives me her name and I look her up on the Internet. No man called John is listed anywhere under her numerous marriages.

I ask John what he is doing for Thanksgiving. "Oh, I'm going with my girlfriend to New York, also for Christmas. We stay in this dear old friend's fabulous penthouse in Manhattan. She's a famous writer and second only to, you know, that woman who writes the Harry Potter stuff. Our friend only cooks two meals a year, Thanksgiving and Christmas. She likes to give her staff a break. She's also," he catches his breath and hesitates, "a great friend of the Queen of England. They got to know each other through breeding Corgis. Every Christmas Day the Queen phones my old friend and they talk on and on about dogs and I get to talk with Her Majesty."

Yeah?

Bonnie's now ready to cut my hair. She was recently widowed, but lacks any sign of mourning. She's one of the skinniest people I've ever seen except for an immense protruding stomach. I give her credit for loving her little poodle, albeit excessively and obsessively. He does get under everyone's feet but he gives Bonnie her biggest interest in life. It's all about how the dog is professionally trimmed at Boston's leading dog salons. Every time I'm in to improve my own appearance, Bonnie is primarily concerned with Sweetheart's new unsatisfactory haircut and she is looking for another notable canine salon. I have a great suggestion. "Why don't you trim him yourself, Bonnie?"

"Liz!" my name explodes from her mouth and the whole salon comes to a momentary standstill. "How could you suggest such a thing?"

How?

I fling tips in all directions and drive home.

On Monday I phone my dentist and make an appointment to have my brace and front tooth fixed. It shouldn't be too difficult or too painful. At some point I bet the dentist and hygienist bring up the same old words. "It worries us to hear that you're still riding ..."

I wait for it.

"... at your age."

That evening I lie on the sofa and begin feeling very sorry for myself. Dave makes me a drink and my mind drifts way back to New Zealand.

"This won't be too painful," the school dental nurse tells me. She's substituting for the dentists who are overseas with the troops fighting in the big war. I'm at the little Mangorei Primary School outside New Plymouth and one by one, over several months, these two hastily trained dental nurses are checking every pupil for cavities. The middle-aged woman who's about to work on me has tiny eyes, a bun and no wedding ring. I'm in a makeshift dental clinic that has been built on the school's front lawn and is about to be blown over by the winds from nearby Mt Egmont.

A prong, that looks like it's from a farm's pitchfork, is poked all around my teeth and I spit into a kitchen bowl. Drilling begins. If only she would stop. I squirm, cry in a high pitch and get a rude punch on my shoulder. The equipment looks like my grandmother's sewing machine, but the drill is twenty times the size of her needle. The nurse huffs and puffs as she keeps telling me that I'm such a boob. And the drill never pauses as the nurse's foot pumps away at the machine's treadle on the floor.

During my four sessions the nurse drills deeper and deeper agonising holes in all my back teeth, fills them with amalgam and sends me red-eyed back to class. A friend tells me that her father heard that these dental clinic nurses are incompetent. I complain to Mother, who is never critical of anyone.

They're doing their best, Elizabeth.

Meanwhile my teeth are also growing in all the wrong directions, as if I could care less. An appointment is made with an orthodontist in Wellington and by myself I take an all-day train ride to our capital city and stay with an aunt. Lucky for me the orthodontist says he's coming every month to an office in Hawera where I can be checked. It's only a one and a half-hour train ride from New Plymouth and the outings will be great.

I know that very little pain is involved. I will miss a day of school. And gorgeous Michael, who's in my class, is scheduled to travel with me on the same train. His appointment will be after mine.

The train pulls out of New Plymouth's station at 8am and very soon we're chugging through Taranaki's luxuriant countryside, dotted with grazing Jersey cows. At Tupare we get fresh milk delivered every day from our next-door neighbour, and the Jersey cream on the top is so thick we have to spoon it off. I press my face to the window and gaze up at Mt Egmont's high, jagged slopes. Of course the views of the mountain are stunning if it's not raining. Dad says, if you can't see the mountain it's raining and if you can see it, it's going to rain. He tells us that the mountain is still very young and there's no doubt that it will erupt again. The most recent volcanic activity was the production of a lava dome in the crater and it collapsed down the side of the mountain in the mid-1800s. Before that, a violent ash eruption occurred about 1755.

Michael and I reach Hawera and gorge on cake and ice cream at the station's cafeteria. The train steams off to Wanganui and we walk the short distance into town. Michael is ahead of me and I must say that his strut looks a bit showy off. He's wearing shorts and I notice that his legs are getting covered in curly blond hairs. As we reach the small shopping centre we pass a Chinese greengrocer's shop and lining the footpath are many wicker baskets overflowing with fresh fruit and vegetables.

In an instant Michael has grabbed a luscious-looking pea pod and looks around at me, challengingly. I snatch one too, and, copying Michael, quickly scoop out the crisp peas and shove them into my mouth. By now we're walking outside the Hawera branch of the Bank of New Zealand and it has the typical open windows, high above our heads. Michael throws his empty pod through one of the windows and I follow suit. Oh the disturbance inside … We race off down the street.

That pod is the first and the last thing that I've ever stolen. And from that moment I dislike Michael, and my obsession with horses becomes full-time once more. Mind you, I persuade myself, it was only one pod, worth way less than a penny.

On our return ride to New Plymouth, Michael has sensed that I'm pissed with him. We say little until we're travelling beside a stretch of the main road near Inglewood. I'll impress him. "You know Michael," I grin to myself, "see that straight stretch of the road beside us? I can tell you a true story about how my parents stopped the main trunk line train to Wellington from this spot."

"Yeah? Why?"

"Well, they missed the train in New Plymouth when they were starting out on their honeymoon in 1932. They absolutely had to get to Wellington to board a boat to go overseas. A wedding guest whipped them back into his car and they caught up with the train right around here. They pulled up level with the engine, tooted madly and waved to the engineer to please stop."

I've really got Michael's attention. "The locomotive creaked to a halt and, dragging their luggage, Mother and Dad pushed their way through bracken fern and gorse on the edge of the road and hopped aboard as the passengers cheered and clapped."

"So what," he says. We ride the rest of the way in silence and I obsess about that one pea pod.

I hear Mother's words.

It's not the amount but the principle, Elizabeth.

I'll never tell her.

It's a week later and my tooth is fixed. The brace is also mended but the insurance company won't pay up. "Mrs Benney, we understand that the brace had been in place for many years. We feel that it was due for a replacement. In our opinion a dismount from a horse would hardly snap it."

"Excuse me," I find myself shouting, "you call my fall from a very high horse, already towering above a very high jump, a *dismount*?"

"Don't get so excited, Mrs Benney." And he hangs up.

Dave tells me to calm down and forget it. At least I have good news about the discolouration of my teeth. There's no denying that they're now a polluted-yellow and my dentist has taken a mold for a type of plastic clamp. Into each 'cup' that lines up with each of my top teeth I'm to put a bleaching substance called Opalescence and leave all in place all night. And voilà, by the morning my teeth will appear snow-white and youthful again. Am I being vain? Yep. And I don't care! I'm not bothering with the bottom teeth, which never show unless my laugh is totally out of control. At least my bruised skin from my fall is looking better and the swelling has started to subside.

Of course I haven't jumped, yet, and as I mend that moment is getting closer but I keep it to myself. "Let's go to bed," I say to Dave.

It's nine o'clock and pitch-dark outside. The phone goes. "This is the police. Mr and Mrs Benney, please stay inside your house and double-lock all your doors. Hurry. There's a warrant out for the arrest of a very dangerous man, and he's currently hiding on your land."

Holy smoke.

We jump out of bed. At that very minute a police car, lights flashing and siren wailing, comes speeding up our driveway. The car swings around the stable and tears halfway back down the drive and stops. More police cars and an ambulance burst on to the farm. Everything parks beside our hay field and a cruiser bounces across it, mindless that it's ready to be cut and baled when we get a stretch of fine weather. The car reaches the edge of the thick woods.

More police cars arrive and officers are running across the field. We hurry to our upstairs spare bedroom windows and with all the vehicles' lights on full beam we have an even better view. Eventually the men saunter back to the ambulance and all the vehicles remain parked. Dave gets a torch and decides to walk down to check things out. He's told that the criminal was apprehended while trying to flee into our woods. Dave can just see him lying in the ambulance. The officers won't give out any more information.

Forty-five minutes later they all start to leave, gouging the soft lawn on either side of our driveway. Someone we know on the police force rings us and relates what happened. A man had been riding his motorbike and had collided with another man on a second bike at the bottom of our dead-end road. The police arrived and did a scan on one of the men, to find that there was a serious warrant out for his arrest. Meanwhile he had bolted up our road. The police soon caught up with him and he veered across our hay field. The man was so violent the officers had to beat him and use pepper-spray before they could handcuff him. Then came decontamination in the ambulance. Dave is reluctant to relate the rest of the conversation but I get it from him. "The police believe when the accident happened the criminal had decided to make a run for it … and to our remote house at the end of the road. He would have forced us, at gunpoint, to give him the keys to one of our vehicles."

Do other Senior Citizens have as much ongoing drama in their lives?

We get back to bed, but I know that I won't sleep. There's one big difference between Dave and me. He grew up in the middle of Wellington and everything was locked up. I grew up four miles outside New Plymouth with a population of a mere twenty thousand people. Any crime was so petty it barely made the *Taranaki Daily News*. We would go away on holiday and leave Tupare unlocked. I don't think we had a key to any outside door of the house. Dad did lock his study, mainly to prevent little fingers taking pens, paper, stamps or delicious sweets from a special jar. And our house was hidden from the road by a long driveway that snaked into the valley. "Liz," Dave breaks into my thoughts, "from now on, please lock the doors to the house whenever you go out and I'm away." I will try, of course, but old habits are hard to break.

A few years ago Mother moved from Tupare into New Plymouth after Dad died. I arrived one summer and she said to me, "We lock our doors now, Elizabeth. Don't forget the bank hold-up around the corner." She sighs, looks out the window at her beloved Tasman Sea. "How times have changed – and sadly there is crime now in this town."

Mother really did witness a bank hold-up in the suburb of Ngamotu. She was sitting in her car in the small shopping centre when an officer banged on the window and yelled, "Quick, ma'am, lie right down this minute and don't you move out of your car." Lying down was not an easy task for an eighty-five-year-old woman in a car with bucket seats. The hold-up was on the other side of the street in a small branch bank and Mother wasn't going to miss it. Of course she was right back in her days of reporting for the *Taranaki Daily News*. She did stay in the car and was glued to the hold-up, declaring that it was a little difficult sorting out the good guys from the bad guys. If I had her fearlessness I'd be jumping again tomorrow.

Chapter Three

We Find the Farm

For years Dave and I lived in a pleasant Boston suburb with what we thought were excellent schools but the high school turned into a disaster for our boys, Richard and Paul. There was no discipline, no motivation, they were bored and soon were kicking over the traces. And slowly the town was also turning into yuppie-land. There was an influx of the hoity-toity and they wrote negative horse-letters to the local paper.

We didn't move here to look at horses.

Try walking in the trails when riders come bombing along.

How about avoiding all the manure?

Think of the smell.

And the mess horses make of the snow when we want to cross-country ski.

I was mad and decided to write a response to the paper. I would give these unwelcome newcomers my rider's point of view. How those on ATVs heedlessly swore at us as we quietly rode the trails on our well-behaved horses. And how the trails were 'grandfathered' for riders, whether we were enjoying them in the summer or when they were covered in snow. I would also ask how many of those people constructing their show-off McMansions had defied the law and illegally fenced off riding paths that crossed the back of their properties. Horse owners had the right to sue them.

But Dave said to forget it. No horse-owner had the time or the money to take these affluent newcomers to court. Of course Dave was right. He saw the situation so clearly while I was incensed and having a fit ... the compulsive fool who rushes in where sane people fear to tread! Thank goodness for Dave's reasonable influence.

Then the final straw. I was invited to a women's elegant luncheon in the most desirable part of our town. It was right down to the guests arriving in hats and long white gloves. Well, I turned up in my best attire, sans gloves and hat and driving my three-quarter-ton pick-up truck. My car was being serviced. The truck was old and badly needed a wash. It really stood out among the fancy ego-cars.

I was mingling with the other guests when everyone's attention was caught by a high-pitched voice. "Oh, look!" The elderly guest of honour, platinum blonde and white wine in hand, was pointing through a plate glass window. "Oh my goodness me," she bellowed, "Someone drove here in a *truck*!"

I was still in my late-fifties and didn't have the nerve to admit that I was the one who'd driven that old vehicle to the luncheon and I was not ashamed of it. Now I find to my satisfaction that as a Senior Citizen I can usually say what I think and get away with it.

Along with the complaints and the wrecking of the trails, that luncheon did it in for me. And Dave agreed. It was time to find a farm and take our dogs and horses to live in the country. It was 1989 and fortunately our three children were leading very pleasing and independent lives ... the two boys *finally* making it after very, very shaky starts.

Richard barely graduated from the high school ... why work at your studies when you are bored stiff and there are no consequences? Life is for having fun. He did get into university and dropped out after one term, getting an F for the 8'oclock lecture, a D for the 9 o'clock lecture, and so on up to an A for the final lecture in the afternoon. We did tough love and Richard became a Boston taxi driver, getting no help from Dave and me except warm clothes for Christmas and his birthday. Of course he was always very welcome to come to dinner whenever he had transportation. He also paid back all the money that had quickly hit the limit on a credit card we'd given him for emergencies.

Those years certainly had their high and their low points. For me, I was constantly worried, slept little, ate little and at least was spared the common middle-aged spread. Often I would bump into acquaintances around our changing rural-to-snotty suburban town. One of the conversations would include my asking after two of Richard's contemporaries, such as, "And how are Johnny and Jennifer doing?"

"Oh, Johnny is flying through his medical degree at Harvard and Jenny's doing law and finding it *so* easy. She's is in her third year at Yale, you know. And how is Richard doing?"

"Well, Richard is driving taxis in Boston," I would gulp.

Silence!

After two years of driving, Richard was held up and thought he was going to be killed. He quit the company that very day and decided he'd better get an education after all. It blew Dave and me away as we watched him knuckle down and pass exam after exam, year after year.

At other times I'd bump into the mother of one of Paul's friend's. She would be brimming with self-centred news. "Oh by the way, it looks like James is getting into Stanford to study philosophy." After trying my best to be enthusiastic, the predicted question arrived. "And how's Paul doing?"

"Well, you may have heard from James that Paul dropped out of school before finishing the eleventh grade. Presently he's pumping gas on Speen Street in Natick."

Paul had legally left school and we patiently waited out his maturing process. Let him kick over the traces and have a taste of the real world with the minimum pay of a high school dropout.

As we expected, Paul got sick of pumping gas in the freezing winter weather and we enrolled him in a private school where he streaked ahead academically. "Man, I can't wait to get to school," he exclaimed at the end of his first week.

"Wow! How come?" I asked him in stunned astonishment.

"Mother, they really care, and are so interested."

Sweet Tonia saw the headaches that her brothers had given us and she chose to grow up more traditionally. But taking no chances, we also enrolled her in the private school and further tightened our belts. Miracles do happen ... the children all continued through university and between them have six degrees, in engineering, business and science. Dave and I were so thankful and proud that I just had to announce our first success, which was Richard's, in our local suburban newspaper. I would show those snobby locals. I made the snippet sound like the ones that sometimes came straight from the university. There was no mention of Richard's address, that he is the proud son of so and so and that he was summa cum laude ... One can always guess when the parents have submitted the news as it reads so flowery.

Richard Benney of ... has graduated in engineering from Harvard University.

How I relished the retribution, but modest Richard and Dave were absolutely appalled and very angry with me. So I never announced Paul's and Tonia's graduations. Dave really meant it when he said to me, "Absolutely no!"

Why did I want the snotty neighbourhood to hear some good news about our boys while Dave and Richard were so against it? For a long time I felt I'd failed as a parent. And yet I myself had had the consummate mother and I too did poorly as a teenager. I could not have cared less about school rules and about learning and I flunked at New Plymouth Girls' High School during the two years I attended. Along with my unruly behaviour it culminated in my expulsion. My boys' errant ways had to be genetic!

After looking at forty-eight farms we found our present one, seventy acres that had been abandoned for twelve years. With it came a 1912 neglected converted two-family house and a couple of two-hundred-year-old collapsing barns. It was nothing to photograph home about. The old cow pastures with their crumbling stone walls were smothered in regenerating native trees, bittersweet, briars, poison ivy and weeds. Actually, in another twenty years, the new struggling native trees might have held some New England forest charm. Compared with some of the farms we had viewed, at least this one was only a fifty-minute drive along the nearby Massachusetts Turnpike for Dave to get to MIT where he taught. And our new land had privacy, a view and *potential*.

Oh how hard people tried to agree when we pointed out the land's potential. But we could read the doubts that clearly showed through their expressions and shallow words. When friends visited us in the downstairs apartment of the old farmhouse they were rendered speechless. "We won't be here for long," we explained. "We're putting an apartment over the stable that we're building in the middle of the farm."

The farmhouse had never seen any maintenance. All the attic windows were broken, and there was a three-foot leap to the ground from our back door. The heating came via a very old converted wood system and we could never get the heat up to anywhere near 70 degrees. When both burners came on at the same time, it was as if two old steam locomotives were barrelling through the building.

Our windows were tightly closed for the winter and the curtains swayed wildly when the wind blew. The out-dated electricity and plumbing caused us major problems with the insurance company, and large holes in the roof invited rain and snow. It leaked through the attic floor into the upstairs apartment and of course the tenants we inherited were people who grumbled. Whenever their illegally installed washing machine was on spin, everything vibrated in our kitchen below. We did have superb well water.

We called our new farm Tahuri, the Maori word for starting over, or set to work. And how true that has proved to be.

So began years of hard work, designing, creating and making a ton of mistakes, combined with the hit or miss stresses of hiring and firing contractors. We got quite adept at analysing the skills of workmen, measuring their integrity and their loyalty. Ninety percent of them were splendid as they built the long driveway, the stable for my horses and where I planned to board horses, and the apartment above. After enduring six months in the farmhouse, we rented its ground floor and Dave and I made an upscale move into the thousand square feet above the horses. Our four dogs squeezed in as well.

The first spring arrived with a massive effort to clear the land, plough, seed and begin the arduous task of fencing. On and on it went over several years. We were really savvy planners by the time we built three-sided run-in shelters in the fields, then our house and a detached three-car garage for all the essential farm equipment, and finally an indoor riding arena. Now, some fifteen years later, with Dave and me in our seventies, we plan on turning the *creativity* years into the *maintenance* years of the seventy acres, with forty-five of them left in woods. Well, here and there we did build some rough riding trails through them and a track on which I could gallop. More upkeep.

With the *maintenance* period has come some relief for me. I have no big complaints, but with all my arthritis I can no longer work strenuously. There's no way that I can help build fences any more or drive the tractor that is designed for men with long legs, and the days of lifting a hundred pounds with ease have gone. The total weight that I can lift slowly has decreased over the years to a sixty-pound bale of hay, then to a fifty-pound bag of grain, and, more recently, half a bag of grain.

This morning I had to take one of the cats to the vet for his annual physical and I just managed to lift his sixteen pounds into the cat carrier. No longer can I touch my toes or reach behind my back to do up my bra, and my knotted fingers are striped with thick blue vein tassles. I marvel they haven't blown out like a tyre. My fingers won't close completely, so I've twisted big knots onto my bridle reins for grip. Of course I gripe … it's maddening, until I remember how much worse things could be.

I'm also trying to take my doctor's warning to cut down on my activities. "You've had three rotator cuff injuries, broken bones, concussions, and you have that problem with L5, that fifth lumbar vertebra. You *must* be careful." Still, I've lived with the L5 injury for more than sixty years and it's so hard to change one's set ways.

How well I remember every detail of that foolhardy accident.

Chapter Four

'Is Everyone Like You?'

I think back to New Zealand. My sister Jill is now twelve and also has her own pony. I'm fourteen and we're ecstatic that Mother is home again from the sanitorium in Otaki. She has just sold Mischief from the papa land and bought me a sweet and much more accomplished pony called Pollyanna. Jill and I are galloping along the wide grassy verge of the New Plymouth to Wellington highway. As we approach the turnoff to Mangorei Road on which we live, we come to a walk and start crossing the road. In the middle of it I say, "Hey Jill, stop a minute. I have this great idea. Let's swap ponies without our feet touching the ground."

"Well," Jill hesitates, "you go first and get on behind me." I prepare to launch myself in back of her and suddenly there's no steed beneath me. Pollyanna has spooked sideways, flinging me out of the saddle and I land flat on my back on the tar seal. And why didn't we try this manoeuvre on the grassy side of the road? Because the ponies would have dropped their heads to eat the grass, making the transfer trickier.

I struggle home, leading Pollyanna. When Mother's sees me her face loses its colour. "Oh my goodness, you look terrible, Elizabeth. Whatever happened?"

"I did something dumb. If I explain, you'll get all upset."

"We'll talk about it later. Now go and have a hot bath and lie down."

For once I don't have *to rise above it.*

No one thinks that I should see a doctor. Such visits are rare and only made for the highest of fevers or broken bones ... and only if you complain enough. When Jill falls off the swing and Mother is away in hospital, Jill keeps telling Dad that her arm hurts and he says, "Jilly, you *must* stop complaining. Think of the starving children in Belgium, or the poor London children being bombed to pieces by the Germans. How would you like to be living in the middle of a war in Europe?" It takes him three days to realise that it just *may* be serious and he bundles her off to the doctor. Her collarbone is broken.

I'm also taken to a doctor as an eleven-year-old when my recurring tonsillitis problem is taken seriously at last. I'm whipped into a private hospital and out come the tonsils. The busy nurses can't stand me. I'm constantly ringing my bell for the smallest reason. "I'm bored. Please can someone come and stay with me?" Three times I've heaved my bed across my single room so I can see all the activity in the parking lot. The nurses get mad when I insist I can only eat a plate of jelly if it has pepper sprinkled on it and I hide the clots of blood in my handkerchiefs instead of the sputum mug where they can be examined. So I'm sent home, two days earlier than the scheduled discharge.

Somehow Dad finds a nurse to stay at Tupare and watch over me but she's soon gone. Did I drive her crazy? Or was her contract up? I'm ashamed to say I was an awful brat and had become very self-absorbed. Was I looking for attention? Was it because Mother had been gone from Tupare for well over a year, fighting for her life in the hospital? And we were not allowed to visit her, as we were less than twelve years of age. I was missing her terribly and I was very afraid she was going to die. It was hoped that rest and fresh air would work wonders for the disease, but it was not a given. The wireless news was often full of the spreading tuberculosis crisis and the many resulting deaths.

With my injured back from the aborted horse swap, I take it easy at Tupare and eventually recover to a certain point. The pain goes, but every so often I'll be walking along and suddenly collapse into a heap on the ground, with no warning and no discomfort. Neither my parents nor the family doctor think much of this deviation from normal.

I live with it until I'm doing my O E (Overseas Experience) in London in my early twenties. I have a stunning aunt-by-marriage, who's into the Pygmalian thing.

She takes me under her wing to refine me. To try to.

"Darling," Elinor exclaims one day, "It is so *unbecoming* to collapse like that on to the floor. I'm sending you to the best orthopaedic surgeon in London. In fact he's the same man who attends the Queen."

Wow!

I take a bus to the appointment. Who am I? A very unsophisticated colonial girl with a colonial accent. The surgeon couldn't be more charming. He takes X-rays and diagnoses something with a big name in my Lumbar 5 vertebra. And says he bets I had a bad accident at some point. "Yes," I tell him and he can't believe how stupid I was. "Are all young girls in New Zealand like you?"

I'm to have physical therapy and it's doubtful that I'll have any major problems until I'm older. He sends me to a Danish physiotherapist and after many months of twisting and turning exercises, to the point where I could be on my way to a future in ballet, the problem goes.

It's not just a bad back that I brought from New Zealand. Elinor's appalled that I'm suffering from toothache and am trying to ignore it. I'm sent to her fancy dentist. He gasps and sighs and pokes and prods. Every filling in my back teeth, done with all that suffering by those wartime dental nurses, has brought me close to dentures. Below the amalgam, continual decay has had a great time reaching for the nerves. Every molar must be redone. And it is just in time.

Then it's my face. "Liz darling, your makeup is *so* backyard. And your clothes are *so* colonial. And those *shoes*! I can't wait to take you shopping. We'll hit Bond Street for a start." (Please pay, I pray.)

"Elinor, I have rotten bunions and a funky back. I can't wear fancy high heels."

"Well, we'll have to get all your new shoes stretched. You can learn to wear smallish heels. Now, let's start with how you wear your lipstick. In fact I'll shout you to a make-up fair that starts next week."

So boring.

The Queen's orthopaedic surgeon was right on, and I began having

L5 problems. In my forties I'm in New Plymouth and go to a radiologist who's a great family friend. After taking a ton of X-rays, Chum calls me back into his office. "Liz," he says shaking his head, but laughing a little, "you have the backbone of a seventy-year-old labourer. I also see that you broke your scapula at some point. Riding? In America?"

"Yes. I was jumping a horse for someone in a show and the mare caught a hoof in the top of a high picket gate. We both crashed to the ground."

"Well, you be careful now that you're getting, well, into middle-age and I'm afraid there's nothing that can be done for this deterioration and it'll continue to go downhill." He shows me the X-rays. "All this here," he says pointing at my spine, "is arthritis forming. See it weaving its extra bone deposits around L5. In time it will probably impact the spinal cord."

Chum was right, and now this genuine seventy-two-year-old labourer has added some more whopping falls off horses to the L5 area. It's no wonder that my spine is going downhill. I start taking glucosamine and chondroitin and MSM and it does somewhat mitigate the discomfort.

The backbone might be going to pieces but today I still have my original teeth, albeit I'm scheduled for root canals and fancy crowns on a couple of my molars. I bet all my old Mangorei School classmates are having the same problem. Or maybe they behaved in that wooden chair and the dental nurse drilled out every bit of their tooth decay.

We're eating dinner and Dave looks at me. "You know you're at an age when you need to slow down a lot more." He sounds so serious, and adds, "Let's make a pact and we'll sit back and really enjoy our old age."

"Okay, sure, but I'm darned if I'm going to sit back and just wait to arrive at the terminal. Let's thoroughly enjoy these so-called *maintenance* years, Dave. I want to ride and we'll travel more, lots more. New Zealand of course, and China, the Antarctic …"

"Not for me, thanks," says Dave with a broad smile and shaking his head. He's never so happy as when he's sitting at his desk and solving applied mathematical problems. "Honestly, I've done my share of travelling, and you know I enjoy living vicariously through your adventures. I'm just obliged to go to Hong Kong and China every year but just for three or four days." I know he has promised to help some academics with their problems. "I'm close to eighty," he grins, "and I don't have your stamina."

I think over our situation.

We actually decided three years ago to lessen some of the farm work by gradually closing down my horse-boarding business. We have thirteen loose boxes and I had great boarders for seventeen years, but the stable work was catching up on me and the breaking point was imminent. The cost of hay and shavings was skyrocketing and I found myself becoming a worn-down Senior Citizen even with excellent help. (Only two employees ever had to be given the boot, with their incensed departures leaving long strips of rubber on the driveway.)

I never asked any boarder to move her horse, but some were sold, died of old age or shipped to a retirement home in Florida in order to avoid our New England winters. Two girls left with their horses for college and we were finally down to one boarder, a great old German imported show horse called Jax. He came here to die, and it took him eleven years.

Now we just have my three home-bred horses living on the farm. There's Minty (In A Moment), retired Fancy, (Now Or Never) and Catch, (Catch Me Later.) She's my least accomplished horse, but the one with the most dressage potential.

So – will my remaining SC years now focus more on dressage, farm *maintenance* and travel? What about jumping?

Chapter Five

No Commitment

A fortnight has passed since my fall. The bruises and swelling are nothing compared with the sunken feeling that refuses to leave me. Whenever I'm around Minty I want to start jumping him again. And I will in a week or two. I rode him this morning and took my feet out of the stirrups but they were back in place within minutes ... not a good sign. That sudden fear of jumping has diminished, but it hasn't totally disappeared. How can I ever end my years jumping with such a demeaning finale?

Then, out of the blue, Dave walks into my study. "I've been thinking long and hard and I really beg you to forget about jumping Minty again. You're too valuable to the children and to me."

"Thanks," I smile warmly at him but I can barely hide my exasperation. I try to get my jumbled thoughts in order. I know he speaks the truth but the old self-absorbed and thoughtless me surfaces. "I've also been thinking a lot about it ..." I let these words hang with no commitment.

That night I can't get to sleep. Jumping again ... what do I have to prove? I've had a great innings, but the drive to jump and compete won't let go and it mixes with the compelling need to consider my family. I can't afford to fall off again and next time could be much worse. My independence, with its infusion of selfish moments, probably started way back with Mother's first bout with tuberculosis. At ten years old I had to make so many of my own decisions … not always considering other people. Who cared about pleasing the endless housekeepers who constantly bitched at me and often quit on the spot? Dad was a man trying to cope with these hit or miss women as he ran a business and worried about Mother. He was often away from his children who were trying to make the most of their parental separation. Was a self-absorbed pattern established way back in the 1940s? Now it's so hard to give up jumping when, without much athletic talent, I'd struggled for so long to become reasonably accomplished. But again, it has been only a hobby.

When Dave wakes up this morning I'm talking flat out before he's out of bed. "How about I promise I'll just jump very low stuff and I won't compete in the horse trials any more? Or of course I could drop down a level," I give him a weak smile, "and compete in the division with lower jumps. Minty just loves to get in the start box in the cross-country phase, and his anticipation is such a great feeling as he looks for the first fence."

I blow Dave a kiss. I know he is serious. But my thoughts keep going back to the same theme. Am I being inconsiderate? Am I being cocky? Or am I being realistic, knowing the skills are there and I just need my legs to become stronger again?

Hmmm.

I think about the challenge of a future in just dressage. First, neither Minty nor I is built for the task. Of course we've always had the dressage phase of the horse trials. We seldom won that phase, but we weren't too bad *if* I didn't forget one of the movements and had two valuable points deducted from my total score. But Minty was consistently perfect on his cross-country gallops and seldom brought down rails in the stadium part of the competition, so we would usually move up in the standings. His breeding is three-quarters thoroughbred and a quarter Hanoverian. The latter quarter does lend itself to dressage but he is built a bit low in front and his body is too long for us to be serious in this discipline.

Neither does my figure lend itself to dressage. I'm a shrinking five foot two and a half inches in height. I don't have long elegant legs that have a judge wowing whenever I enter the arena, so I'm already slightly handicapped in the judge's subconscious.

I'm also very round-shouldered. There's no way I can correctly sit up dressage-straight. When I was a sprouting teenager, Dad would make me walk around the house with one of his heavy volumes of the *Encyclopedia Britannica* on my head while I tried to shut out his constant reminders: "Shoulders back, Liz. Please try to remember to put your shoulders back. Think elegance. Think poise." Elegance? Poise? To heck with them. They were the last things I cared about. And how could I help being born with round shoulders? One time I told Dad *my* body was stuffed with genes directly inherited from *his* body. He laughed.

There is one positive as we ponder a dressage future. In one of my last horse trials, a dressage judge did write in the important space at the bottom of the score sheet, *Horse and rider have lots of potential.* My friends and I laughed like mad … the judge had to be cock-eyed. How much time is left for either of us to learn much more? Like pirouettes, tempi changes, piaffe, passage and the renvers and travers movements. When I think of the long time it took me to gain decent jumping skills …

Minty and I are actually at a dressage level where I must sit the trot for the whole of a test. But with my damaged Lumbar 5 vertebra, sitting the trot on a 16.2 hands high horse, with suspension and a huge stride, would race me quicker than ever to a wheelchair.

I must say there is one interesting incentive. When Minty's and my combined age reaches one hundred, we can ride a dressage test of choice at a sanctioned competition and achieve some sort of diploma. How I would love to get it at one of the top shows in this country, like Devon in Pennsylvania. I work out the timetable. Today, Minty is fifteen and I am almost seventy-three. That makes a combined total of eighty-eight. Six years to go!

No. That's too long to wait. Forget about dressage. I can still jump for a while.

I think about my two home-bred mares. They're both lovely movers and jumpers, and friends often persuade me to breed them. It's tempting, but I'm not sure if I could handle foals any more. I have to admit my energetic youth and reasonably productive middle-aged years are no longer with me. Of course someone else could break them in, but I'm stubborn and cocky about my own particular method, perfected after making many mistakes over many years. I bred my first foal when I was fifteen and broke her … well I tried to. I made such a mess of the job I had to send her to a fancy racehorse handler near Waitara. He charged me five pounds, telling me my precious mare was the worst-handled horse he'd ever worked with.

I've always planned to live to be ninety-seven, like my paternal horsey grandfather. But as I watch the terminal rush closer and closer I've upped my adieu to one hundred. I'm pretty sure I can make it as I have the genes, I have the attitude and I get much more than the recommended amount of exercise. Recently I heard some advice on the radio. "To maintain good health and to enjoy a long life, women in their seventies should exercise for thirty minutes at least three times a week." Ha ha.

If I fail to reach one hundred, I have a back-up in my daughter. Tonia has already assured me she will take charge of all the animals. That will put the youngest, Catch, around thirty-eight years old, an unlikely age for a horse. And no matter what I say to change his mind, Dave has convinced himself he'll die before me.

Fancy is Minty's half-sister. She's retired from a very successful career competing in the horse trials, or eventing as they're also called. While I competed Minty, my trainer Suzie rode Fancy. But little by little I sensed something was wrong with the mare. She started to object to the required positioning of her body for dressage, even though she was physically well prepared. And her stunning jumping style started to deteriorate. My great vet and friend Lol felt something was not quite right in her neck vertebrae and off Fancy went to Tufts, the nearby veterinary hospital. The work-up started with X-rays and they clearly showed advanced degenerative changes in five of her neck vertebrae. The doctor at the clinic told me that the vertebrae were so impressively impaired he was going to use the X-rays in his classes. He also asked me if she'd ever had a bad accident.

"Yes," I told him. "When she was three years old and I was breaking her, she stumbled badly and fell heavily on her head and neck."

"That would do it, Mrs Benney. No question about it. And of course over time it has just become worse."

Join the crowd, Fancy. That accident also injured my neck, and arthritis sprouted in yet another part of my body. I can't look over my left shoulder and now I have a hard time backing the horse float, or trailer as they call them over here. People stare when I start messing up. "Poor old thing, fancy learning to drive a trailer at her age." Of course I could always use the truck's mirrors, but everything is in reverse from backing with your eyes directly focused on the trailer. For me, using the mirrors is like signing your name with your left hand.

Then there's my beautiful filly, Catch. She's not quite fifteen hands high and is Minty's and Fancy's niece. Trainer Paul calls her the *hony* as she's in-between the size of a pony and that of a regular horse. But the size suits my shrinking frame. She's built for dressage and is doing well for me in all the movements and I can sit her smooth trot without impacting Lumbar 5. But Catch at ten years old hasn't been exposed to as much of the wide world as the other two horses. Occasionally she gets scared about something and over-reacts by crow-hopping or bouncing up and down and trying to bolt. She has dumped me twice. Even pitching off her small height is not funny for this SC. To be honest, I'm slightly nervous of her. Long gone are the days when I could ride with no apprehension.

As I ponder my future in dressage or in jumping, we receive an invitation for a wedding in the Dominican Republic. Dave's classes have started at MIT so he can't attend, but I am *on*. And my body has recovered enough from the fall to manage the travel.

The bride is Alexandra, Jax's old owner, and she's marrying a great chap, Camilo from the island. To increase my enthusiasm my friend Meghan and husband Jim are going and they've offered to keep an eye on me. "You're super," I laugh, "and thanks, but I'm not quite helpless. Yet." Jim is from Australia and we have our down-under roots in common. A couple of years ago he and Meghan were excellent tenants in our old farmhouse.

Jim has a broad Aussie accent which broadens even more when he's in the company of beautiful women. Last year Jim and three men friends flew to Australia for the Melbourne Cup. In his generous way he bought tickets for them to scale the Sydney Harbour Bridge. But it was not to be for Jim and one of the others. They had partied so hard on the flight and throughout their first night in Australia they failed the breathalyser test and were not allowed on the bridge. No refund.

With my lingering injury, I'm so glad we're flying just four hours to the Dominican Republic and not to Australia – seven hours across the USA and another fourteen and a half hours across the Pacific.

I start making my plans ... and better get my hair done before the wedding.

At every appointment I hear more and more stories from John. They're beyond belief – how his father was a diplomat and the family once lived in Moscow and St Petersburg. His mother had show horses and also rode to hounds in Virginia and his father had many racehorses. He also donated the orthopaedic wing of a famous New York hospital.

Poor John and his imagination. I realise now that he's a despondent gay man with a dog, a tiny rented apartment and no car. He gives me his mother's maiden name and it equates with the Rockefellers. "So, John," say I as politely as possible, "you've told me you live in a tiny apartment and have no car. How come when you're from such a famous and wealthy family?"

"It's a bummer. My inheritance is tied up in court and has been for over twenty years. My estranged sister got her lump sum way back because it came from our father. My money is from my mother's estate. But my sister thinks half of it also belongs to her. So who knows when the courts will resolve it."

Yeah?

I ask John what he's doing this weekend. "Oh I'm flying in a private plane to the Hamptons. My dog's going too. This posh area's on Long Island, you know. I have great friends who live there," he hesitates, "and they often invite me to stay at their ocean estates."

But he also seems a bit distracted today and I'm dismayed when he has finished. The results are tacky and the colour has come out all wrong. "John," I moan, "I look like a retired lady-of-the-night!"

"Wash it three times and you'll look terrific."

I tip him the usual amount. On the way home I look in the mirror and almost drive off the road. I'm really mad at the mess John made of my hair and I chastise myself for being such a tipping wimp. Isn't tipping for service and satisfaction?

As I march into the house the phone interrupts my thoughts. "Liz, how are you mending?" It's one of my best friends, Marylon, in Florida.

"Slowly, Marylon. The older I get the longer it darn well takes. And everyone's on my back to stop me jumping again. But more importantly, what's new with you and Doug and Tucker of course? I'm so envious you can still jump him and with such precision and form."

"Liz," Marylon falters. "I've had some bad news. I've got cancer. I'm in hospital and have just had both of my ovaries out, and a length of my intestines."

"Cancer?" I fumble for words. "I don't know what to say, Marylon. I can't believe it. I saw you so recently and you looked ravishing and full of energy. How serious is it?"

"It's not good. I have friends who can't handle the fact I'm so bad. But I know you can."

"Thanks." And I do so hope I can. "Is there anything I can do? And how's Doug taking it?"

"Well, he's pretty bummed out. Just keep on ringing and emailing me and come and visit soon. I've got to hang up now. Oh, don't worry about the jumping. You have nothing to prove. Try your hand at dressage."

"That's what everyone says. I'll call you soon."

I make a strong cup of tea, flop on to the sofa and think about our long friendship and about life. Why Marylon? Why cancer? She has always been in perfect health. An apprehensive thought flashes through my mind. I've also been so lucky with excellent health – could it happen to me? Or to others I love?

Chapter Six

The Wedding of the Century

I'm off to the Dominican Republic, and along with do and don't lists for patient Dave, I've employed a great new girl to work in the stable. Sue lives nearby and worked on a Maryland racetrack with her trainer husband until he decided to go into the dot.com world in Massachusetts.

I ring Marylon to tell her about the wedding and to say goodbye. She has begun chemotherapy and doesn't complain when I ask how she's feeling but I can sense her wretched suffering under her forced cheerful words. "Don't worry about me. Just have a great time on the island. Take lots of photos and notes so I don't miss out on a single detail."

Marylon's only three years younger than I am. I put myself in her place. Could I ever be so caring about other people as I faced such a bleak future? How would I handle her crisis?

Not well.

I know ovarian cancer is a hard one to lick and I'm so grateful my superb specialist doctor at the Massachusetts General Hospital removed my ovaries a few years ago. "Ultrasound shows something on the right ovary. I am ninety percent sure it's a cyst, but let's get rid of your ovaries and be on the safe side. You don't need them any more," he had grinned. The highlight of the operation was being in a preparation bed right next to famous Elizabeth Dole. I'd been told she was coming to the hospital and quickly recognised this former and notable US Senator. Her husband was with her – also a past Senator and the Republican Party nominee in the presidential election of 1996. He lost to incumbent Democrat Bill Clinton. Senator Dole looked at me and I could read his thoughts. "You think you recognise me and you're correct. I *am* who you think I am!"

It's very early on Sunday morning and here I am blooming with good health, albeit I do fall off horses. But I'm not fighting for my life. I'm off to the Dominican Republic.

Jim has ordered a limousine and it picks me up at 4am. Jim's already in great form. Crickey, mate, is he the consummate Australian! At the airport I get my taste of being an SC when Jim insists on pulling my bag along. I find it's one of those dichotomous situations. I love having someone fuss over me but it makes me very conscious of my older status, which I hate in spite of all the over-sixty-five benefits. I still *feel* about fifty years old, but those numbers on my birth certificate don't lie.

We fly from Boston to Newark and wait and wait to be called for our direct flight to Santo Domingo. Our departure is delayed over and over again. Heavy rain is falling but at last we're on board and the cockpit announces we're really on our way. Meghan counts eighteen planes ahead of us.

We're airborne; three Caucasians surrounded by ecstatic and restless Dominican Republicans. Their homecoming atmosphere suffuses the whole cabin and there's non-stop excited shouting in Spanish – until we suddenly hit some pretty impressive turbulence. The cabin instantly becomes speechless followed by the murmur of prayers and fingering of rosary beads. There are numerous glamorous women on board, many with breasts bulging immodestly over their low-cut dresses. Children wriggle over everything and men in new clothes preen themselves. As we land, their immense sighs of relief fill the cabin, followed by rousing cheers and clapping.

At the airport my bag is the last one to appear and I'm held up at immigration as an officer peers and peers through my New Zealand passport, looks at me, frowns, turns page after page, frowns and looks at me again and again. At last he stamps a page and I join Meghan and

Jim outside. We climb into the oldest taxi in which I've ever ridden. It's dented all around, has broken windows, no air-conditioning and it's summertime, half my seat belt is missing – and *hold on, folks.* Our driver accelerates to the car's maximum speed and who needs to brake before rounding corners?

All the way to Santo Domingo we have a sparkling blue untarnished sea on our left and many scattered, weary buildings to our right. They're mostly flat-roofed, stand with decaying concrete walls and are surrounded by littered yards. We enter the town at an alarming speed, but the narrow streets soon slow us. Many of the buildings lining our way are hundreds of years old and made from coral, shaped into blocks or bricks, pitted with age and repaired with concrete. This is where Christopher Columbus arrived in 1492.

We alight outside a large closed door in a very slummy street and our driver indicates we've arrived at our hotel. A sign says animals are permitted.

But through the door is the Old World, a truly beautiful Spanish-style squeaky-clean foyer of tiles and wood with the walls freshly plastered. Immediately an employee in uniform rushes forward and offers each of us a wet, very cold and great-smelling rolled-up towel. Moments later we're offered a tall glass of red liquid with a cherry and orange slice pinned onto a swizzle stick. Aussie Jim knows his drinks, takes a gulp and announces it's a bang-up rum punch.

I'm shown to my room, number 3005 on the ground floor. It's misshapen, cool and very clean, with a high ceiling painted cerise and criss-crossed with old adzed beams. I have a TV, two desks, three telephones and a small four-poster bed. My one high window looks on to the street, with the constant movement of heads hurrying by. There are no curtains, but I have inside shutters that I can close for privacy. Pamphlets are lying everywhere, extolling the virtues of the island and saying we're in the Colonial District which has just been made a World Cultural Heritage site. Several cigars are on one of my tables, plus a bottle of rum and two Chinese-made fans. Welcome to the hotel Sofitel Nicolas De Ovando, four hours off the East Coast of the United States.

Meghan, Jim and I meet at the swimming pool where most of the one hundred and thirty-five American wedding guests are lolling.

Thirty-five other guests are local Dominicans. I find it hard to sit still, so go onto the street to walk around. No one speaks English, but they certainly know how to follow and ply me with postcards, appalling art, jewellery, music tapes, small food items and liquid sugar cane in small unhygienic-looking paper cups.

At 6.30pm all the wedding guests collect in the foyer and we're taken by bus to an outdoor restaurant, the El Conuco. We've been invited by Camilo's parents, a delightful pair, speaking so-so English. They moved for a while to New York so their three boys could get a good education, and Camilo graduated from Skidmore College. The restaurant is full of tables scattered under pergolas, trees, heat and humidity. I sit with Alexandra's old black nanny and her fourteen-year-old son, Darwin. Nanny bulges all over her space and is a love and full of fun. She tells me how she's a widow and was born in Haiti, which of course is across the border on the western side of the island, and how her husband was one of 30,000 citizens killed for political reasons during the rule of terror by the corrupt megalomaniac, Duvalier. She has never married again. "But," say I, "Duvalier must have died over thirty years ago and Darwin is only fourteen." Giggling, Nanny tells me that he was born out of wedlock.

Many waiters serve beer, wine and the ubiquitous rum punch. The meal is buffet and the meat is goat so I decide to go vegetarian. I once found a tiny baby goat at Pukeiti, the famous rhododendron park my father and Douglas Cook established in the ranges near New Plymouth. We called the kid Nin and Dad assumed that trappers had killed her mother. It was in the early 1950s and the goats were denuding the bush. Apart from the fact that Nin wet my lap as we drove back to Tupare, she was a sweet and very smart yellow-coated goat. But she had one determined obsession. She refused to be weaned from the bottle, and learnt that commotion always brought results. Years later, when we children were all grown up and away from home, Dad gave Nin to a good home, bottle and all.

But back to the pre-wedding dinner, followed by a performance of brilliant local dancing. A very skinny man in white pants and a straw hat first dances the Latin meringue with a flamboyant girl in a flaming red outfit, her billowing skirt often showing her red underwear that clings immodestly to her thighs. The dance is thrilling for its energy, skill and accompanying music of a wooden drum and a tin drum beaten with a brush of long tin bristles, and all this to the accompaniment of recorded island music as the couple shift sideways and back and forth in a fast-syncopated rhythm.

Then, to top it all, out comes a bottle of whisky and the skinny man places it on the floor. The girl puts one of her feet on to the screw cap at the top of the bottle's stem and her partner twirls her around and around at ever-growing speed. She persuades everyone to clap and we cheer as she contorts and keeps her balance to the very end. The bottle hasn't moved.

Next the dancers perform with hoola-hoops, then invite the guests to try. No one moves so I decide to give it a go, for the first time in sixty-five years. I desperately persuade my old hips to wiggle and jiggle and they don't let me down for seven revolutions when the hoop crashes from my waist. This starts the ball rolling, but not for long.

Someone spies an enormous stout rat creeping along a low partition beside a number of the tables. The rodent is at least eighteen inches long. Some of the diners, transfixed, watch its slow progress, mindful that one slip will bring it right on to someone's lap. Suddenly the guests at the tables below it spy the creature, scream bloody murder, leap to their feet and stampede to the street where a row of specially commissioned buses is waiting. It's now 11pm and the traumatised hurriedly get on board. I decide to return to our hotel, too.

The next morning Jim tells me how he danced with the whisky bottle girl in the flaming red outfit, accidentally trod on her foot and broke a toe. I never knew if it was his Aussie exaggeration or if it was just a broken toenail. But the dancer did have to retire and send out her backup.

Saturday morning we enjoy a buffet breakfast and three of us decide to walk the streets. We're told we must please stick together. Without a man with us there is the possibility of being kidnapped. Foreigners, especially women, are grabbed and held for ransom. Was I lucky yesterday, out by myself on the old narrow streets?

There are three parked buggies with depressed old ponies standing in the shafts. One has his ribs showing like an advertisement for the SPCA and I have to turn away. The good news is that Lol's vet partner, my friend Jay, comes to the island twice every year to help the poor animals. With other volunteers, including veterinarians, veterinary students and assistants, these caring people aid many of the horses, donkeys, mules and dogs on the island. In the past there has been no worming or castration, and the tick problem on horses is everywhere and miserable for the animals. The owners come to Jay's 'clinics' from great distances and of course it is a pro bono service.

We visit the museum with an excellent English-speaking guide, and among the many artifacts I'm transfixed by the branding irons used on the poor imported black slaves. Then the power goes off and stays off but we can just see by the light coming through openings in the building, constructed in the 1500s. Later we visit a shop with a stunning display of local jewellery. The items are of amber or larimar, a semi-precious stone found only in one location in the Dominican Republic and nowhere else in the world. Of course I want a couple of pieces for Tonia and take out my Visa. It won't scan. I try to explain they can punch in the numbers, but no one understands. Someone shouts "Bank!" and I'm guided along the street. The bank is closed but there's an ATM machine. I'm not comfortable with the look of the old unit and everything is written in Spanish. I picture it swallowing my only card. But I decide to give it a go. It refuses my card.

How I take the sophisticated world for granted.

I'm now hurried to another shop and the attendant tries to slide my card through his machine. Success. Of course this shop is not into jewellery, but I'm handed my purchases back in the store where it all began.

Finally it's time to prepare for the wedding, purportedly the biggest social event in the Dominican Republic this century. I try to be ready to meet everyone in the foyer at 5.30 as instructed, but I can't get my earrings on. It's another frustrating moment. I've been slowly losing the dexterity in my fingers and should have taken some Advil. Finally I give up, toss the small gold Arrowtown nuggets aside and hurry bare-eared to the foyer. The buses haven't started to fill and I'm blown away by the collective elegance. Everyone is wearing gorgeous clothes right down to their shoes, and jewellery glitters under the strong lights. It could be a fashion show, with plunging necklines now being in. Oh so in, and so low.

At least I am wearing a dress and stockings.

We pile into buses and drive slowly through the narrow streets and up a steep hill to the wedding venue, the magnificent expansive ruin of the oldest building in the Americas. I climb up steps designed for people with very long legs. Fresh petals are scattered everywhere. Then a walk through an ancient arched gateway and into the middle of the ruins with its remaining archways and holes in the magnificent stone walls, and every part built with coral. Everywhere are waiters in tuxedoes, carrying tray upon tray of drinks. To one side is a small lively orchestra and potted shrubs, flowers in vases and flowers hanging in ribbon arrangements.

The building was begun as a fort in 1502, and has been a monastery, a hospital and an asylum until two earthquakes almost completely destroyed it. I meet up with friends, make new ones and sip rum punch while curious children peep through gaps in the old wall or through the cannon holes. After an hour we all move to a higher patio, and on the way I have to negotiate a huge ditch. The ceremony begins. Camilo arrives dressed entirely in white. He's so charming, warm and good-looking and sports the most impressive dread-locks I've ever seen. (He works in the art world.) Tonight the hair is all bunched into a ponytail with two intriguing, tiny, ten-inch braids hanging down below them.

Alexandra arrives on the arm of her proud father. She looks like a model and is regal in a stunning wedding dress with her hair pinned up with real jewels. Her delightful mother is equally elegant. The service is simple and sincere. An introduction to the couple is spoken alternately in Spanish and English and the couple says their vows, exchange rings and a kiss.

It's dark now and lights come on and the music plays on and on while we wait for the dinner announcement. Apparently there is some confusion as Camilo did the seating list for one hundred and seventy people, but forgot to write down the table numbers at which we're all to sit. Waiters keep bringing out great pyramids of shrimp, lots of raw vegetables with dips and plates of finger foods.

The toilets. They're all porta-potties in a secluded part of the ruins and are reached through an archway, almost sealed with decorative shrub branches. There's an attendant and she opens the door for you, and I stop short. There's no light inside. It is pitch dark!

We're ushered into a huge room with a dance floor in the middle and thirty superbly laid tables. A live orchestra plays smiling Caribbean beat music. I can't believe we're actually in the middle of the ruins as the whole area is normally open above us. Now it is completely sealed, way up high, with see-through plastic. This is so the whole dining area can be air-conditioned. I join a hearty group at my table, laden with silverware, crystal glasses and little treats on a double damask tablecloth, flowers galore and a throwaway camera for each guest.

A waiter comes and points to the three options on the menu. Lamb chops, fish or vegetarian. I order fish. By this time a lot of the guests are a little drunk. Aussie Jim is at his best and kindly invites me to dance. I accept and he is good and soon we're sitting back down to eat. Just as we finish our main course, everyone is ushered outside. Fireworks start up in an abandoned field next to the ruins. Then it is back into the air conditioning and another plate is put in front of me. I go to lift out what I honestly think is a folded cool white towel. It's a sweet and delectable dessert.

I take the wedding bus back to the hotel at midnight, and the next morning Jim and Meghan tell me they returned at 1.30 when several couples were still dancing on the tables. We're told some guests didn't go home until daylight and there were bodyguards watching over everything, all night.

Sunday morning and the three of us leave for the airport. We check in quickly and go through the usual procedure of shoes, purses and carry-on bags clattering along the X-ray belt. One local man's bag is pulled aside and an official takes out a very large bottle of rum. Of course the new liquid ruling is now in effect. The bottle should have been in his checked luggage. It's obvious this is all being patiently explained in Spanish to the traveller. The poor man looks heartsick.

But hey ho, no one else is going to enjoy his rum. He takes off the top of the bottle and hastily starts choking down the liquid. He's still drinking when I move away.

It is back to the United States and I can't wait to travel again. And it certainly doesn't have to be on the grand scale of this exceptional trip.

Chapter Seven

Stop the Train!

At home I go on and on about Santo Domingo and the wedding. "Okay, Liz," Dave laughs, "no more for now. I'm saturated!" I prepare for bed and stare in the mirror. My high spirits drop a bit. I check out two distinctive sags. They've been getting worse over the months and skin is now hanging below the eyebrows on the outside corner of each eye. My scrutiny moves to the rest of the skin around my eyes.

There's red everywhere, a winter sunset.

I'm over-ripening.

I'm the classic example of someone with advancing old age. Of course intellectually I accept it … I have no choice. Emotionally, it's driving me nuts.

I *am* a bit party-worn, but no rest will help my unsightly eyes, and as for my hair – as John instructed, I washed it three times in one day and it turned out worse than ever, and brittle, too. My current somewhat vain disposition is probably from dwelling on all the glamour at the wedding. Am I jealous? Not really. But I *would* like to look a little fresher, sport a bit of allure, a bit of flair. Advertisements plug plastic surgery but that is not for me. And like so many of the horsey guests at the wedding, I would also have loved to recount some of *my* recent jumping successes, immodestly of course.

"So, Liz. What are you up to these days? Are you still eventing that super horse of yours?"

Don't ever gloss over the truth, Elizabeth.

"Well, I may have to forget about eventing." And out comes the full story of *the* fall.

I must stop thinking back to the wedding. But recalling all the stunning fashionable clothes also gets me musing about my own wardrobe. My riding outfits are more or less in vogue, but my riding boots, with their squishy ankles, are designed for jumping and not for pure dressage. Too bad! My non-horsey wardrobe is very out-dated. I resolve to go into swank Wellesley to shop, while knowing I'll never get around to it. Catalogue shopping is so easy but it can be very hit or miss. I've ogled over pictures of glamorous clothes on glamorous women and the ordered garments arrive as flops, the colours screaming. And forget about the fit.

I phone Marylon. She sounds so dispirited and here I am worrying about my looks, about competing again, my sags and my clothes. I can't picture myself in the middle of chemotherapy ... no one would want to be near me. I can't even picture not getting on my horse to go for a quiet walk. In her typical thoughtful fashion Marylon asks for every wedding detail. "Wow, Liz, what an incredible time you had. Now tell me, are you completely over your fall?"

I respond lightly. "Yep, but I haven't got around to jumping."

"Of course you will jump again," she says, and in a fading voice, "I have to hang up now. Sorry. Doug's taking me to another chemo session."

I struggle for words. "Marylon," I falter, "you'll lick this thing. You have so much determination to fight this battle. You *will* win."

I barely hear her whisper, "Thanks, Liz." And the phone clicks. I drive off to my annual eye appointment, with a gnawing anxiety in my stomach. Deep inside I don't think Marylon is going to make it.

I bring up the insignificant sag issue with my ophthalmologist. "I was going to get to that," he says, "and I agree that the excess skin is pronounced but it can be cut out." Then he adds, "What concerns me more is it's interfering with your peripheral vision. The procedure is no big deal. Check in at the office and see when I have an opening."

A few weeks later my poor ophthalmologist drops dead, quite out of the blue. All his patients are referred to a woman eye doctor in the city. I make my first appointment. Her office provides no convenient parking, which makes me late as well as drenched from a heavy rainsquall. Dumb me forgot to bring my raincoat and I have to sit restlessly in the waiting room until a new slot opens up. I'm called an hour later and leave a curvaceous watermark on the chair's fabric.

At first a technician tests my sight and I struggle through a couple of rows of the large letters and numbers. "Guess I've failed," I say, and she says nothing. It reminds me of Dave renewing his driver's licence this spring. He was in the same room as several other applicants and he memorised the sequence of letters and numbers in the row each candidate was asked to read. "Read me row two, please," he was told when his turn arrived. Without seeing a thing, he passed the test and is not required to wear his glasses for driving.

I'm mad at him! But he still drives tolerably well and hasn't hit anything but a poor deer earlier this year. The animal just jumped out of the bushes and smashed into the front of Dave's nineteen-year-old Toyota. It wrecked one of the lights and, since the air conditioner didn't work, the radio didn't work, the clock didn't work and the passenger door wouldn't open, my non-materialistic husband actually decided it was time to buy a new car. And he ended up with a second-hand Toyota manual-gear-box truck with only 7,000 miles on the odometer.

I love how Dave is so understated but I recall an example of this characteristic that really got me pent-up. It showed what complete opposites we are … the understated man and his little show-off wife. We had been married about three years and Dave had just been made an associate professor at MIT. I was brimming with pride.

A woman, whose horse I sometimes exercised at the local boarding stable, invited us to a swanky party. It was very upscale, with the conversation swirling around the stock market, the country club, trips to the Caribbean, one successful child after another … No one appeared interested in Dave and me, and for a starter we lived on the wrong side of the tracks in this upwardly mobile suburb. After an elaborately served dinner we all piled in to a mini-bus to drive into Boston for a show. On the way someone finally turned his attention our way. "Dave, that's your name, right? What do you do?"

"I'm a school teacher." I could have shot him!

A few miles further. "Dave, where do you teach?"

"MIT."

Retribution. I knew the interrogator had been thinking of some little elementary school.

Now the technician sends me back to the waiting room and I finger through glamour magazines. At last I'm called into my new ophthalmologist's office. She seems over-burdened and doesn't do peripheral/sag operations. She gives me the name of a "bang-up" eye surgeon in the city, but she's really more concerned with my cataracts. "You're ready to have your lenses replaced," she says in an automatic voice. "Why is this?" I query her. "I've had them for years, but they never changed until now."

"I'm sorry, but change does happen and it's often quite sudden." She also hands me the name and number of an excellent surgeon to replace my lenses.

The sag operation is about to start. The worst issue is dealing with the effect of the prescribed tranquiliser pill. "Swallow it forty-five minutes before you arrive," I was instructed. I take it faithfully as we come to the tolls on Route 128. The pill works so quickly it nearly knocks me senseless. By the time we're at the doctor's address, Dave half carries me from the parking building as I loll against him and stumble up the steps. (He tells me later that people were looking at me askance and someone muttered, "Drunk.") The doctor takes me on time and the prick of the desensitising needle is painful in spite of the fact I'm a long way off this earth.

As the knife goes to work, the pill must have unleashed something in my supersensory zone. I become vaguely conscious of talking non-stop, and regaling the doctor and his assistant about my new stable employee's crisis.

"Now I'm going to tell you about Sue," I hear my voice start off way in the distance. I know I am trying to distract myself. "She has been with me for two months and is an excellent employee. I'm down to just three horses of my own now, but they're still a lot of work. Sue is very moral, very religious and doesn't smoke or drink. One day, she comes to work and is not her usual bright self. She thinks that Karl, her husband of fifteen years, has a girl friend in Warsaw. That is

Warsaw as in Poland.

"*Poland!*" I shout out the name again in case the doctor and his nurse don't get it.

"Karl has flown off to Warsaw a dozen times in the past year. He can go anywhere – he works on a laptop in the dot.com world. Sue thinks she'd better do some snooping. And because she's so moral and religious, this secretiveness bothers her, but her gut suspicions must be confirmed.

"When she arrived at work last Monday, Sue told me she had discovered credit card items from Victoria's Secret. Scanty clothing that you wouldn't buy for your mother or your sister and none of the underwear ever came her way. Next she found a *fake death certificate* saying Sue died a year ago in a terrible traffic accident. This really freaked her out. Finally she found copies of bank drafts to one Anna, bearing Sue's surname. Our scandalous conclusion – bigamy."

As the operation concludes, I begin to regain my sound mind and apologise for telling this very personal story. I would never have related it if it were told to me in confidence. I'm dismissed with a date for the other eye and current instructions. Apply cold compresses every two hours for twenty minutes. And do not drive tomorrow, but of course I have no option with Dave at work.

I ride two horses on day two and all seems fine. As I have make-up over the bruises around the eye and am wearing large dark glasses, no one is any the wiser. I'm instructed to sleep on my back for two nights, which I hate as this position always gives me nightmares. On the second night they wake me up and I lie, uncomfortably, in the still of the countryside of Central Massachusetts.

Then way in the distance I hear the late train going to New York. I love listening to the steady monotone of the wheels coursing along the rails, of the toots at all the level crossings, and crystal-clear images flash in to my mind. I'm back on a steam train in New Zealand.

Six of us Taranaki girls are on our way home from Wellington. We're clad in the green uniform of Samuel Marsden Collegiate School for Girls and at last the term holidays have arrived. For a year now my high school education has continued at Marsden after I was expelled from New Plymouth Girls' High School.

During the many years Mother has now been away fighting for

her life I had run pretty wild, and my obsession with horses far exceeded even a mild interest in academics or any form of obedience and sophistication. I became an incorrigible student and broke many school rules. The headmistress concluded there was but one hope left for me. Boarding school. The slammer. Reformatory.

Ostensibly I was to be taught behaviour modification, to become well educated and to become a lady of refinement.

The train to New Plymouth pulls out of Wellington's railway station with the familiar toots and steam hissing around the great shafts driving the wheels. And, against the rules, we all throw off our regulation green hats complete with the school badges.

After three hours the train slows down towards the Palmerston North railway station and all the passengers will shortly alight and rush to buy food and drink in the cafeteria on the edge of the platform. The tea is always half-cold and is poured into teacups with rims the thickness of full-grown worms. Sandwiches are of white bread, with massive crusts, and the choice runs to fillings of spaghetti or baked beans, ham or Marmite, and there are always meat pies. The cake and biscuit selection equals the best of all the unhealthy foodstuffs one can buy in New Zealand.

Suddenly I have this brilliant idea and to heck with the cafeteria. Two of us will run across the street and buy a load of yummy fish and chips. Let's hope the small shop will be empty of customers, as we will have exactly ten minutes from start to finish.

Before the carriage has come to a complete stop, Margaret and I bounce down the steps and fly across the road. "Quick," I gasp at the attendant, "please hurry. We want fish and chips for six." The old woman throws chips into the metal basket and plunges it into the sizzling hot fat, dips fillets of snapper in thick batter and rushes the fish into another deep container of fiery oil. I whip out a ten-shilling note and keep glancing and glancing at my watch. Five minutes, four minutes, three minutes, two minutes. The worn-out old lady still has to salt the food, wrap the lot in waxed paper and finish folding it into yesterday's *Manawatu Standard*.

One minute.

"All aboard," is sounded over the station's loudspeaker.

"Oh please hurry, lady."

Thirty seconds, ten seconds and the poor old dame begins to figure out the change of my note. "Forget it!" I cry and Margaret and I tear outside. There's no level crossing, and we must wait for a short line of cars to carry on their purposeful way down the street. With a long drawn-out hoot, the train pulls out of the station. We would have made it if only the street had been clear.

By now our carriage has moved away from the end of the platform and our friends are frantically waving and shouting.

"Stop the train!" I shriek back.

"What?" they scream.

I look at Margaret and we don't know whether to laugh or cry. We can hear the train gathering speed as we watch the guard's van disappear.

We stand there, with nothing but a hefty packet of fish and chips and look blankly at each other. New Plymouth is still one hundred and fifty miles away.

"Now what?" Margaret says.

"We'll have to hitch-hike. But let's eat first." Suddenly we hear the screech of the train's brakes. The wheels are skidding on the rails and the stationmaster comes glowering towards us.

"You bloody stupid girls! Now get running down the track. The train has stopped for you. Your bloody friends pulled the emergency handle."

I've never run so fast, holding on to the fish and chips and trying to keep my balance over the rough stones and the edges of the sleepers holding up the lines. As we pass carriage after carriage, passengers lean from their windows and either curse our irresponsibility or cheer us on.

It all ends with a very long drawn-out blast from the engine and away we go towards New Plymouth once more. The fish and chips are superb. We forgot the napkins, but who cares.

Then comes the guard, wearing his uniform with an air of power. What a great important moment as he bawls out Margaret and me, takes our names and of course knows from our uniforms what school we attend.

An hour later the train has a second steam engine attached so we can make it uphill through the long Turakina tunnel. As we grind closer to the tunnel the guard comes through and closes all the windows. He glares at me and smirks. Usually we quietly open all our windows the minute the guard passes through the door. As the train enters the long tunnel, thick black smoke and smuts fill the carriage, the other passengers have a conniption and we put our faces close to the floor to breathe any fresh air we can find. This time we vote to leave the windows closed.

I tell my friends the story of my father going on a train to a Sunday school picnic at the beach. The children, all dressed in shorts and white shirts, were in open-air carriages and were thrilled when the train entered a tunnel. The one locomotive had speeded up before the entrance so the black smoke was minimal. At the beach they collected masses and masses of very long-stemmed toi toi grasses and decorated the sides of every open carriage. On their return trip, the single locomotive's smoke was nothing … the toi tois swept the tunnel. At the end of the day the parents, waiting on the platform for the children's return, had trouble singling out their pitch-black offspring.

The guard misses our next move. All six of us hurry to the open area between carriages where one is attached to another with jangling couplings. We roll up the wax paper and newspaper from our fish and chips and drop it into the Wanganui River way below.

When we've had our fill at the cafeteria in Hawera's railway station and the train starts rolling towards Normanby, I roll into another true story. "Okay," I start. "You won't believe what happened right here. My sister Jill and I had just competed our ponies in the great Hawera A and P Show and had ridden to the railway yard siding. The train was waiting there and our horse carriage was next to the loading dock. We led our ponies on as fast as we could as it was pouring with rain. Hawera is too darn close to the mountain."

"That A and P show *is* huge," Margaret interrupts as an additional audience of strangers listen in. "Did you win anything?"

"As a matter of fact I did." I pause. "A first in a jumping class on a borrowed pony as Mischief didn't, couldn't or wouldn't jump anything – no matter how hard I tried to convince him to at least *try*. But I rode him in the flat class for the best girl rider under fourteen and was second." I think I'm stretching it a bit as I can't remember exactly if those were the ribbons I won at that particular show. "Twice we'd taken the ponies by train," I go on, "and the last time I competed at Hawera my pony had travelled with a neighbour on the back of her truck. The war had now been over for two or three years and petrol was more widely available. After that *I was abandoned at Marsden.*"

"So what happened on the train?" they ask. "Anything more to this story?"

"Just wait. Jill and I, we're freezing and wet. Dad had taken our raingear home in the car. Rain hadn't been forecast. I'm sure it was snowing on the summit of Egmont even though it was November," I continue, relishing all the attention I'm getting for the second time this trip. "When the ponies were safely in their compartments and the ramp lifted back up and locked, Jill and I climbed into the little attendants' area. Soon the engineer came along, checking the train's wheels."

"Why does he do that?" Pam asks.

"He whacks them and from the sound I think he can tell if they're cracked," I report unconvincingly. "Then the engineer spied us two soaking wet girls in the little cubicle. 'Hey kids come on into the locomotive and dry out.' And that was the day I learnt to drive a steam train! We had to be very careful not to be seen or the two men would be in big trouble. I pulled the cord to sound the horn, we were told about all the knobs, and steam fizzed off our wet clothes when the engineer shovelled more and more coal from the tender behind us and into the furnace. I even took turns heaving some coal into the fire.

"Suddenly, our train ground to a stop in the middle of nowhere and the men told us to get out quickly and run back to our compartment. When they'd made sure we'd clambered aboard there was a very long toot and the engineer waved to us as fresh steam poured out of the pistons. We chugged along and didn't stop again until New Plymouth. It was still raining, but Dad was at the station with coats. We rode back to Tupare in the pitch-dark. "

"Wow, Liz. Is all this *really* true?"

"Absolutely, or die before I'm seventeen."

Two weeks after the fish and chips excitement, Dad receives a letter from our very chaste, monastic headmistress, recently imported from Britain. She's clearly wrought-up as she condemns my irresponsibility and how I've let down the reputation and the outstanding character of the school. She finishes by writing, "Please, Mr Matthews, will you punish Elizabeth appropriately."

Dad thinks the whole incident hilarious. "But if I were you I wouldn't try it again, Liz."

Two weeks later I have the second eye appointment and decide to take only half of the tranquiliser pill. I'm determined not to talk out of control. But the doctor and nurse want to hear the end of the bigamy story. It's not really my business, and being under vocal control this time, I short-change them.

"Well, at this point, I'm afraid all I can say is she's looking for a lawyer to file for divorce, and her husband is yet again in Warsaw. He knows she's suing for the divorce, and the rat says he's going to fight for everything they own."

Chapter Eight

In Search of Glamour

"Liz, you look just like a forty-year-old," grins the sag surgeon after removing the second lot of stitches.

As soon as I'm home I hurry to my magnifying mirror. There's no sag but I can't see any change in my peripheral vision. I put it down to my cataracts. The operation for their replacement looms. A friend tells me that, when it's all over, the 'new' me won't be able to stop looking at her lustrous green eyes. Actually, I prefer to call them hazel, as they're a light golden or brownish-green colour. And hazel doesn't denote jealousy.

The friend goes on to warn me I'll also experience the picture of Dorian Gray. "I hate to tell you, but you'll look at your whole face in the mirror, and you'll have instantly aged twenty years. All the wrinkles, accumulating and multiplying since you were fifty, will come into sharp focus. And they don't lie."

Of course, my life doesn't come close to paralleling the life of Dorian Gray who wanted to sell his soul to ensure that the *portrait* of him would age rather than Dorian himself. Then he would stay looking young until the end of time and could forever enjoy his chosen life of debauchery. But each of his sins is displayed with the aging of the portrait. I wonder how many of *my* life's sins will show up on *my* face …

Except for the family, I don't bother to tell anyone about the sag operation. I'm with a friend and, out of the blue, she says, "Gosh, your eyes look exquisite." Mind you, Kay is very prone to exaggeration. And she can't have noticed the soft red hue around my eyes – a fading sunset. With new lenses I'll see myself as a dear little old soul in a nursing home. Then I wonder if perhaps the red is from too much sun.

The cure? I spread layers of sunscreen around the whole of the eye sockets and after a few days the result is impressive. Still, it's odd that the red-eyed elderly in nursing homes are seldom in direct sunlight.

It has to be from mingling with the glamour of the Santo Domingo wedding that my old ego is on an exceptional roll. With my eyes looking a bit more acceptable, I find myself focusing on the area just above them. I have untamed gorse hedges growing – two rows of them, and above the nose are more scattered bushes. To complete the picture there are yellow flowers dotted here and there. On closer inspection I find they're really some of the hairs losing their pigment. Are they dying, I wonder? I doubt it as these particular ones keep on growing longer and longer.

I don't think this SC is overdoing things if she struggles for a little more allure, but the words of an old New Zealand friend ring in my ears. "Gosh, you're becoming so Americanised." I forget what she was referring to, but I guess she was right.

It's also high time I leave hairdresser John. The drive into the city is over an hour and I'm still irked by stupidly giving him the unwarranted tip. He will be upset losing his steady audience, *me*, along with my unstinting tips. I will miss his delusions of grandeur. I make an appointment with a new hairdresser, Jan, and she will also shape my eyebrows.

In no time my gorse hedge has turned into a formal privet hedge. And just like the different ways one can shear this attractive evergreen hedge, my eyebrows have been shaped to suit my fancy. Massachusetts has a new law that hairdressers can't colour your eyebrows with your hair formula ... it might drip mistakenly into your eyes. So I blacken out the flowers by using an applicator with the exalted name, *Brow Expert*.

I tell Jan that I have a double crown and please would she leave my hair longer at the back. "You've got a what?" she exclaims.

"A double crown. If you cut that area too short my hair will stick straight up in the air." It turns out it's called a double cowlick in America, which sounds more barnyard to me than regal. Even after living for nearly fifty years in America, I am caught out by the language about once a year. For instance, I was once asked how long was the bed in my truck?

"What?" It is the tray of the truck. I will never forget praising someone's newly appointed living room with the comment. "Wow! This room is so homely." I can still feel the shocked silence. Homely in American is an insult, (meaning lacking in physical attractiveness or it is very plain), and the praise-worthy equivalent of our homely is a word we don't use … homey. (Comfortable and cosy.)

Feeling quite attractive tonight, I decide to cook Dave a fancy meal from scratch. Of course everything that's not good for you tastes delicious. I'm thinking of going on a diet but keep putting it off because the discipline of dieting keeps getting in the way. I'm not overweight, but my waist has started to sport a larger and larger hillock and it is driving me nuts. My doctor says it's because I've shrunk more than two and a half inches and the distance between all my thirty-three vertebrae is closing. What's left around my middle is now being moved out of place and has nowhere to go but *way out*. If I lose three or four pounds, I'm confident the mound will flatten out.

Ah well. But I do hate these Senior Citizen tangible changes.

I go to the fridge. Oh no! Everything feels warm. The fridge has broken down and there's a heap of food crushed into the freezer. I bought it all today.

It has to be a Saturday night, ten minutes to seven and the appliance shop is about to close. No way can they service or deliver a new refrigerator. But they will sell us a small freezer and will grudgingly stay open if we can get there within twenty minutes. We run into the store and two men are waiting for us. They think the situation is so funny as beer fumes waft around them, but we have a freezer, which the men load on to the tray of Dave's pick-up truck.

Once home the combined effort of two SCs can't budge this tiny appliance. "Damn it," I swear. "Please, more effort, Dave."

"Forget it," he pants.

Worse things happen at sea, darling.

We back the truck into the garage and the freezer's cord is too short to reach the electric outlet. I run to the stable and drag out the hundred-foot cable that attaches to the blower. We plug it in and hear the blessed hum of a motor. Now we lumber up on to the truck's tray as we carry out thawing food, then down again, and up and down ... And I wonder how on earth the *tray* of a truck got to be called a *bed* in America.

There's still foodstuff in the broken fridge's main compartment. I drag out several empty horse buckets and Dave runs out and buys bags and bags of ice. "Must be some party yer having," says the man in the liquor store.

A serviceman arrives on Monday morning to repair the refrigerator. "It's had it, Mrs Benney."

"What? It's only eleven years old."

"You're so lucky. These days they're only made to last ten years."

"Come off it. My mother gave her 1935 fridge to a New Zealand friend in the early 1990s and it is *still* working. She replaced it only because it has no defrosting mechanism."

On Monday I'm back at the appliance store to choose a new refrigerator. The man who helped us with the freezer purchase leaves a customer standing and rushes forward when he sees me. An assured sale. He flutters around as I try to decide. "This one looks so easy to clean," I say. "And I hate cleaning."

This inane remark releases something in the man I now know as Chris. "Oh you know, my fiancée is a cleaning nut. She has just chosen this particular refrigerator and all she does is clean and clean and clean anything and everything. Over and over. She won't even hold my hand until she knows I've washed it thoroughly."

I laugh sympathetically. "Lucky she doesn't live on a farm."

"And you know," Chris continues, "I have to scrub my face then brush my teeth for two minutes before she'll even let me kiss her."

"Oh my goodness. Anyway, when can you deliver the fridge?"

"Within the hour, Mrs Benney."

Chapter Nine

Dealing with Cancer

Dave is away for a week in Hong Kong. He enjoys these trips immensely, advising his host university about mathematics and teaching advanced calculus to the graduate students. I'm looking forward to a quiet day, riding, reading, eating a TV dinner – and the phone goes. "Mrs Benney, this is the Post Office and we've just received a colossal order of trees. We'll gladly deliver them for you, but please be home and show us where they should go."

Forty-one trees! Each is two feet in height and they've come all the way from South Carolina. They're conifers, Thujia Green Giants, and Dave ordered them weeks ago. He has this great idea of growing a shelter belt where we plan on selling a few more acres of the farm. Of course someone will want to build a grand house on the gently rolling acres and we don't want to see any part of it. The Green Giants, as their name implies, are a new variety and grow thickly and to a height of fifty feet. They are resistant to deer, extreme cold, extreme heat and extreme dryness. We hope.

I drag Sue, my great employee, away from the stable and we start our tree work sitting in the field with a cup of coffee. "I'm ripping mad," she tells me. "I've just had a friend hack into the computer of that rotten husband of mine. You know how I hate doing anything dishonest, but I just have to know what's going on. We found a receipt for a $1,400 diamond ring. We also found a Polish dictionary and I managed to sort of translate a letter from Warsaw, mainly about documents necessary for a marriage."

I'm almost lost for words. "Oh Sue, get the divorce as soon as you can. Go for the house, go for everything. You can't lose."

I let Sue open all the boxes and she really rips everything apart. "I'm pretending they're Karl," she laughs. "This is what I'll do to that rat when I next see him. Limb by limb."

We read the instructions.

All the trees must be watered and acclimated for three days, per instructions.

After trees are thoroughly watered, please note that all trees must spend their first night indoors.

Honestly.

On the second night please place all trees in an area that is half inside and half outside.

"Tomorrow, we'll lug all forty-one of them to one of the three-sided horse shelters," I tell Sue.

The trees are to spend their third night outside.

More hauling and a howling wind is predicted.

I phone Dave in Hong Kong and he advises that the trees must be planted six feet out from the white PVC fence and six feet apart.

I send an SOS to our two odd-job Brazilian men. The following morning they set to work digging forty-one holes through numberless stones. Dave insists that he personally do the planting.

The Brazilians do their best, but they're not very competent at measuring. I pay them anyway. If I'd insisted they correct the distances I bet they would have quit. It makes me mad when anything goes wrong. I sweat and swear under my breath even as Mother's words ring in my ears.

Keep everything in proportion, Elizabeth.

And my grandmother's words ring in my ears. *Elizabeth, only horses sweat, women glow and men perspire!*

A thought goes through my head that all these trees have taken us back to *creativity* … more farm work. Forty-one trees will need watering, weeding, pruning and fertilising. Last week when I was complaining about the farm's workload, Dave asked me if I'd ever thought about moving to a condominium in the city. "Dave, that is the dumbest question you have ever asked me. No! And of course, you're joking." Still, the thought of coping with a large farm flits through my head as I figure out what's left of our lives. I still want to be carried off this farm dead, when I'm aged one hundred.

I ring Marylon and say nothing about the problems on the farm. She says, "Liz, the doctors want to do something experimental with some new drugs. But who knows? I'm losing weight and the chemo has done in my hair. You should see the wigs I've bought. I can change my image from a Marilyn Monroe look-alike to Elizabeth Taylor."

"Do you think you can ride soon?" I ask.

"To be honest with you, I don't feel like it. Tucker is being well looked after, and Ken, you know, the stable owner – is planning on showing him. Have you competed lately?"

"Well, yes," I laugh. "I took Minty to a dressage show and forgot two movements in one test and was way out of the ribbons. I thought we were terrific in the second test and she loved Minty, but the judge criticised my position over and over. 'Rider should sit back more. Rider should put her shoulders back more. Rider is slouching.' In a way it's funny. I felt like going up to her and telling her I *am* seventy-three so what do you expect?"

"The problem is you don't *look* your age."

"Thanks. But to be honest with you, Minty was so obedient and he had a fun day showing off."

"I think I'd better lie down and rest now, Liz. Thanks so much for being my friend."

"Just a second more … when do you think it best for me to visit?"

"Let me finish the chemo first. Soon I may be forced into stopping for a while as the white cell count is sliding down. Bye."

Hours later I can't get the picture of Marylon out of my mind. I'm stiff and sore from dealing with forty-one trees, but I can't begin to imagine what it must be like dealing with cancer.

I've just got in the bath when I get a ring from the downstairs tenant in our old farmhouse. "Liz, I have no water. I'm about to go out for the evening and I *must* have a shower and clean my teeth." Ha ha, I think to myself. *My* teeth are now so lily-white from the Opalescence they could pass for a day or two without a clean.

Does she think I can divine instant H2O?

Assuming the pump has gone, I phone the well company and leave an urgent message with the answering service. "Someone will call you right back," she says in a chirpy voice.

I pull my clothes back on, sit and wait, and wait. A ring at last, but it's our tenant again and she's melting down. Another hour goes by before the company calls me 'right back'.

"I can be there in one hour," a man tells me, "but let me make one thing very clear. There's a charge of $240 an hour, added to which is my driving time from Connecticut." A short pause. "How are you going to pay?"

"Look," I say, very aware of the contempt in my voice, "you guys have dug three wells for us and have maintained them and fixed them on more occasions than I would like to add up. We have *never* hung you for money and will pay by Visa, of course, but *when* the water is flowing again."

It's after eleven and freezing when we meet outside the farmhouse's basement. I grope for the length of thin string hanging from the ancient switch near one of the burners. No lights. The serviceman rummages for a torch in his truck and I guide him around the dark, spooky, ratty cellar. He looks for light switches and examines the electric panel. "Hell," he says. "Oops, sorry ma'am, never swear in front of a lady. But there's no power here or there or anywhere, even in the panel with the circuit breakers. Hmmm," he keeps on muttering, "where are the meters?" He follows me outside and I point to them against the side of the house. Conclusion. One of them has been turned off and it's the one that controls the power in the upstairs apartment, the basement, and the well or bore as we say in New Zealand.

It all becomes apparent to me. Our upstairs tenant, a vet, moved out two days ago and had the power turned off in her apartment. She never told the electric company to just read the meter and put the service in our name.

By now the man feels a bit sorry for me. I've been pretty cooperative, it is very cold, and freezing rain is falling. "You know, I'll just charge you the $240 and we'll forget about my travel time. I would recommend you call the electric company immediately."

Back at the house it's after midnight, but the electric company has twenty-four-hour service. I explain what has happened and oh they're very sympathetic, "But, ma'am," the woman continues and how I hate that word 'ma'am,' "we only turn meters on and off on Mondays through Fridays."

"I have a tenant with *no* water. Today is Friday; well it has just become Saturday. There is *no* way she can wait until Monday." Then I add something that often works. "And she has *animals*."

This woman could not care less about animals. "Ma'am, the earliest we can be there is Wednesday afternoon of next week."

At this point, since the animal appeal doesn't work, I try tears. They don't work either. Wednesday afternoon remains the appointed day.

"Ma'am, in what name do we now put the service?"

Ah ha, I think. My very last chance. Dave *never, ever*, refers to himself as Dr or Professor Benney. It's always Mr Benney and I do respect his modesty, but it's my last chance. At least he's not home to react. "Dr David Benney, please."

"Hmmm," she says, and then in a new and very respectful voice, "I see there's a cancellation for the first thing on Monday morning. The company will turn on the meter at 8am."

I return to bed, thankful I have a strong heart, and thinking about our recent resolution that there'll be no more creativity on Tahuri Farm and only *maintenance* from now on. Now *maintenance* is going to drive us nuts, and tenants are already driving me nuts, and add the service industry and the weather ... There's no way I can sleep when I'm restless, so I ring Jill in New Zealand. She's probably preparing dinner, but I'll take a chance. We talk for more than an hour and she tells me about an article she has just read. It's in the *New Zealand Herald* and is all about the atom bomb that was set off on Bikini Island in the Pacific in 1946. According to the piece, a lot of radiation apparently drifted at that time to New Zealand's shores. The places affected the most were in a line from Greymouth and Nelson in the South Island and up the West Coast to Taranaki. *Our province.* "Now listen to this," Jill continues, "The most affected places were around New Plymouth."

"What? I don't believe it." And we grew up at Tupare, four miles outside New Plymouth. "Jill, honestly, you can't always believe what you read in the newspapers." What else could I say?

Maybe the radiation caused my poor younger brother's debilitating Parkinson's disease. But no, Richard was born in 1947 when Mother was in tubercular remission. Whenever I forget something, I can now rationalise that radiation is the reason. As my mind spins in senseless directions, our golden retriever, Rocky, asks to go outside, so I slip from bed, don slippers and a sweater and go out. The freezing rain has produced a slippery crust and I slip and slide heavily on to my back. I manage to stand up, wriggle and writhe and nothing is broken, but my nightgown is sopping. I change and manage a smile ... if I had broken something and lain helplessly in the bitter cold until someone found me in the morning, I'd have become a 'dearly departed'.

Chapter Ten

Paintings Falling off Walls

Saturday morning and of course our tenant is still without water and Dave's still not home. I'm thankful the renter is out when I leave a message on her machine. "So sorry about the water problem, Judy. I had to twist the company's arm to get the power turned on early Monday. Let me know if I can help you in any other way."

I flop into a chair. Why is there so much drama in my life? I always believed that if one were healthy, one's aged years would be plain sailing.

Tenants. I have to admit I was once a tenant, many years before Dave and I became landlords. Did I cause havoc as some of our renters have done?

Yes! But our antics weren't too bad when compared with some of the renters in our farmhouse. The wife of the couple living upstairs, when we bought the farm, was great and so was her husband Archie – when sober. But his drinking increased and Archie started terrorising the children in the other apartment. Eviction.

Another evicted tenant was a 'man of the cloth,' between jobs. We found him to be a very decent person going through a messy divorce. A month after he signed the renter's agreement, his flighty, reckless unmarried daughter and her child joined him. He was trying to turn his daughter's life around. But her drug use was serious, and involved the police breaking down the door into *our* farmhouse, when she failed to pick up her four-year-old from play-school. The police found her out cold on heroin. Then the steady line of bully boyfriends, and a second pregnancy that prevented her working as a strip-tease performer, gave us no option but to give the entire lot the boot.

I too was evicted in my early twenties. Twice.

The first removal is from a stunning old house in Christchurch. I'm a bit of an undisciplined student at Canterbury University College and after living with rules for two years in Connon Hall, the university hostel for women students, I find the perfect flat. I can't believe the convenience of our residence, the comfort, the artistic garden, the affordable price and no rules. What a great deal, but it is not for long. We are three roommates in the airy upstairs flat, with our widowed landlady living directly below us. Connie, a medical student doing her residency, has joined me and there is Doreen who has just graduated in home science from Dunedin and is working in a nearby hospital. We're the old lady's first-ever tenants as she has just converted her large family house.

In no time streams of our university friends are popping in. A visitors' book greets everyone and we always take a piece of each first-time caller's hair to paste into the book. The amount of hair varies from a wisp to a chunk, and it usually depends on our first impression. The amount becomes a secret and subtle barometer. Our constant parties also become legend, and grow noisier, more crowded and somewhat out of control.

We are warned.

Not once but three times our landlady demands that we cut out the noise, and for a while a measure of self-control tempers our get-togethers. But the number of visiting friends and the volume of noise once again slowly increases. One night someone suggests we perform some Maori war dances, and everyone heavily stomps up and down in the classic menacing way of the haka, accompanied by the wild arm actions, rolling eyes and protruding tongues.

Ka mate! Ka mate! Ka ora! Ka ora!
Ka mate! Ka mate! Ka ora! Ka ora!
Tenei te tangata puhuru huru
Nana nei i tiki mai

Whakawhiti te ra
A upa ... ne! ka upa ... ne!
A upane kaupane whiti te ra!

Our landlady starts pounding on our open front door. Words fly up the stairs. "God damn you all and damn you all to hell! My priceless paintings are falling off the walls!" Connie, Doreen and I are to get out by the end of the month.

My second eviction is from the top floor flat of an old Victorian brick house in London. Located on the wrong side of the street from posh St Johns Woods, we are to be a maximum of three tenants. Our flat is minute with two pint-sized bedrooms, a surprisingly large but inadequate rotting bathroom, room for one person in a makeshift kitchen and a rounded Victorian turret for a tiny living room. It both juts into the sky and into the corner of two streets, and threatens to detach every time a bus rolls by.

All the walls are yellow from years of cigarette smoke. The bath is khaki-stained after years of casual tenants. To fill it with hot water one has to collect a handful of pennies to feed into the gas works. Then it becomes a balance of maximum flame and minimum water so the water comes out hot enough. Turning the tap on too much produces lukewarm water. Of course by the time the ideal heat of the dribbling water is three inches deep, it has cooled to an insufferable temperature.

To make the flat more affordable, we add a friend. Then another one and another one until we're six crowded Kiwis. For a short while I reduce the crowding by flying, via Iceland in an old DC4, to America to visit Dave, then a graduate student at MIT. What a time we have after it turns into an unscheduled three-some. A great ex-boyfriend of mine, doing a post-graduate engineering degree at Stanford, has rung Dave and said he is arriving on the East Coast the very day I'm arriving from London. Dave keeps my arrival a secret. Steve's shock at seeing me is right out of Hollywood.

So for ten days the three of us travel up and down the East Coast. Our transport? Dave's very old Buick. It has a three-inch hole in the front floor, through which Dave's pipe drops while we're driving on the busy New York Thruway. A steady supply of exhaust constantly funnels back through the hole and stinks the car's interior. I sleep on the back seat, Dave on the front seat and Steve spends each night outside on the grass, in his sleeping bag. It is 1958.

On my return to London the plane once again stops in Reykjavik. An Icelandic girl sits beside me. She says hello and tells me her name is Anna Hanksdottir. She has nowhere to stay in London so of course I invite her to come and live in our flat. Only a week later the sneaky landlord arrives without warning, counts heads, equates them with the number of beds and mattresses on the floor and shouts, "Out! All of you."

I try to convince him with a stream of words. "We're just very poor colonials, trying to save money to pay for our boat tickets home. Since you insist on evicting us, you know, Mr Cholmondley, I must add that every time it rains my bed gets soaked from that single window over there. It won't shut properly and we *never* complained to you."

"You could have moved the bed away from the window, if there were just three legal tenants."

"Well, I'm just explaining why we had to get more people in here to share in your high rent. You know it will be a hard flat for you to fill again at your price and with all the negatives of this place. Sooner or later the tower will detach and think of how many tenants will be killed. Not just in this flat, but the three below us. And think of the innocent people on the footpath."

He stomps through the fragile front door before I can complain about the bathroom. "*Out!*" he repeats. At least we *have* a bathroom with water just off the chill. I'm teaching English in a rough East End high school and most of my students are very ripe by the time they visit the public baths on a Friday night.

We're all a bit stunned by our eviction and squeeze into the little living room. Where to now? We look blankly at each other.

Now I wish I'd impressed Mr Cholmondley with an account of how two days previously I was briefly a *refined hoity-toity* debutante. New Zealand House had selected me to be presented at Buckingham Palace and we debs had been instructed over and over on how to curtsy correctly before the Queen and the Duke.

My aunt Elinor's very proper ex-husband, and a lord if you please, escorted me in his chauffeured Rolls Royce. Later he squired me around the garden party on the Palace lawns. Was I nervous? Yep.

Especially as I'd had a hard time refining the curtsy, and how I hoped I wouldn't make an unsophisticated colonial blunder.

I was let off in a Palace courtyard and joined a line of girls from all the British colonies. To my horror a Canadian – judging by her accent – and only three girls in front of me, was wearing the exact same Bond Street dress as mine! Elinor had fittingly outfitted me, right down to lending me one of her hats, her gloves and some jewellery.

Ah well. I could hear a live string quartet as the line crept forward. We reached a gorgeous room and there, on a raised platform, sat the Duke on what looked like a throne, with the Queen elegant beside him.

The girl exactly ahead of me was rip-roaring stunning. She did this faultless curtsy in front of the Duke and I watched his eyes enlarge with admiration. She moved to curtsey in front of Her Majesty and the Duke's eyes followed this dazzling girl and did not stop as she made her way towards the door that opened out to the garden party.

Now it was my turn to perform my clumsy curtsey in front of the Duke.

He never saw me. His eyes were still elsewhere.

My flat-mates decide to hurry out and find a newspaper with its endless flat advertisements. We have no rental agreement but the following day Mr Cholmondley lets us know that we can stay until the end of the month.

According to the rental agreements with our current tenants, Dave and I have always given a month's notice. Archie stretches his departure to two months and the minister-between-jobs is out in no time.

It's high time to sell the old farmhouse.

Chapter Eleven

Multiple Downfalls

Marylon can ride a little again, and the chemotherapy has been stopped while she builds up her white cell count. Her hair has finished falling out. "There's no more to drop out," she laughs. "Liz, I've decided I don't like the Marilyn Monroe look-alike wig after all and I've chosen one that makes me appear quite regal. Even Doug loves it. It's extraordinary how I can change my personality. By the way, is Dave back from Hong Kong?"

"Tomorrow, thank goodness," and I tell her how we're so sick of tenants and all about the farmhouse water crisis.

"On a better subject, have you jumped Minty yet?" she asks.

"No. I keep putting off the day." I opt out of telling Marylon that I still lack the discipline to ride without my stirrups or to start flexing my ankles on the stairs or to run up and down the farm's hills. I'm facing the truth that my body is butting out of tough exercise, but it all sounds so insignificant beside my friend's problems. Marylon's changing body is affecting her life in many more serious ways.

In no way am I a born athlete and my reasonable riding skills come only from years and years of riding, from determination, great trainers, super horses and repetition.

From the age of six months, I'm practically living on horseback. Mother rides everywhere while holding me in front of the saddle. It's early 1934 and the effects of the great Depression are still apparent. Dad is often away on business and we have one car. When Mother is alone and wants to go into town she has no choice but to take me with her on horseback.

We're living in a tiny corrugated iron, two-room shack at Tupare. Dad is breaking in the land, overgrown with gorse and blackberry. He has started building the house on weekends, and it takes him and another man twelve years to finish, and he plans his huge garden. (Mother's friends tell me years later that they were absolutely appalled at the sight of her galloping on the side of the roads while holding on to baby me!) But Mother's an exceptional athlete and has many awards for riding, swimming and tennis. I have turned into a clone of Dad, small with my skinny bandy legs, tons of energy and hopeless at athletics.

Mother is confident that ballet lessons will help me develop better coordination and poise. I am nine years old and enrolled in classes taught by Miss Hare or maybe it is Miss Hair. Morning, noon and night the poor soul's head is stuck to one side of her neck. The more she criticises my ballet efforts the less I try and the more disruptive I become in the class. All of us students are dressed in white bunny suits with pink ears and pink tails and our class is forced to practise and practise for an upcoming performance. I barely survive three months of these tiresome lessons when, to my relief, the week before the show is scheduled, I'm expelled. "Elizabeth's attitude and her lack of ability will ruin the performance," Miss Hair tells Mother, who is deeply disappointed. Dad thinks it's hysterically funny.

Dad has different priorities for me, although he does tell Mother, since she sets the very best example of poise and grace, that I will automatically copy her in time. Dad longs for me to share his passions and they're far removed from ballet. Engineering is uppermost in his mind ... my learning to use tools and machinery is much more fruitful. And how about learning to build a bridge? All the finite details he gives me when I'm shown one that he's constructing. (Of course the first child, me, was meant to be a boy.) Learning how to design and build a beautiful house and garden will also serve me well. As the years go by Dad even bribes me with the promise of ten pounds if I learn the Latin names of all the many trees that now grow at Tupare. Me!

Bottom of my high school Latin class. I have zero interest in anything botanical. The money's tempting and I do try for a while – Cedar Cedrus Atlantica Glaucus is the only one that has stuck in my head.

I'm not just a failure at ballet. As the years go by I'm also thrown off the swim team at New Plymouth Girls' High School. After I'm removed to Marsden I'm thrown off the field hockey team and not long after comes my exit from the basketball team. I nearly break my neck in gymnastics. I suspect part of my team dismissals is from a bad attitude. But I do win one prize at Marsden. I'm third in the shot put at the school's annual sports day.

Looking back, maybe I should have taken up golf. Several years later I might have really impressed Dave with how I could play, instead of wrecking our second date. I'm still a student in Christchurch and Dave is teaching at the university and he takes me to Hagley Park to start me in a future of golf. We have but one club and one ball between us and after a few practice swings Dave checks my grip and says with enthusiasm, "Go for it, Liz!" I swing with all my might and wallop the ball. It sails way up into the air, is almost out of sight and then arcs downward to splash right into the middle of the Avon River. It was as impressive as a hole-in-one.

Of course the dates of the three best A and P shows, Hawera, Stratford and New Plymouth, all fall during Marsden's term times and here I am, a bitterly resentful, restless captive in this Wellington boarding school. "Just wait until I can run my own life," I tell myself. "I'll ride and ride and I'll win every jumping competition at every show in New Zealand."

By now my horse obsession excludes everything else in my life. Even when each Christmas comes I pray for horse gifts, *only*. No soap or talcum powder please, or non-horsey books or, worse still, lacy handkerchiefs. My horsey ambition has started with a vengeance as I reach my teenage years. It takes no time for Dad to witness my equine ambition and he panics. He has seen too many girls of so-called good breeding (ugh) become horsey. He equates them with coarse language, drinking beer straight out of a bottle, men's clothing hanging from their limbs … Dad must have formed this attitude from the racetrack. His father was a big-time racehorse owner and Dad had been exposed to the rougher elements behind the scenes.

He tries to turn me away from horses. There's to be no riding on Sundays and whenever Mother is away in the hospital for months at a time, I'm to wear my fanciest dress and become a hostess to Dad's constant visitors. Which means preparing ever more food – and how I loathe cooking. I'm to pick flowers for the house and show at least a modicum of interest in gardening. I am to become a 'little lady'. Thank goodness Jill is my confirmed ally. And at least Dad doesn't make us go to church (he's a confirmed atheist) and he doesn't bother to supervise my correspondence Sunday School that Mother so painstakingly organises for us during her long absences.

But I will show him how I can be successful in other ways … with horses, albeit with my limited inborn skills.

Miraculously I finally make it to university and of course I know better than to join an athletic club, but I do have wonderful weekends riding and hunting the horses of my psychology professor's wife. And I love skiing – oh the speed and the beauty of the mountains. I make the women's ski team as number four, but only because there is no one else to fill the slot. The other three are superb skiers, and I finish the competition with the equivalent of the *drop score*. Then my psychology professor fails me in Psychology II. (Deliberately, I fathom.) "Someone who goes skiing every weekend if she's not riding horses," he glowers at me in his pep talk, "has a bad academic attitude." I know he expects me to repeat his class, but who needs a second predetermined failure? I'm not going to give up riding his wife's horses and I'm not going to give up skiing. And I'm certainly not planning on becoming a professor. I change to a year of Botany II. Dad is delighted. But I choose it because it is an easy course to pass.

I wonder if the old professor knows that I am also running. There's a famous four-mile harrier race called The Bath Mat and there are way over a hundred entrants. I don't like running one bit, and I don't like running any sort of distance and I hate running cross-country even more; but there's this stunning guy, Dan, on the fringe of my life and I dearly want to impress him. I train and train, pushing myself beyond my endurance.

And I win!

But it barely impresses this man who interests me. I try to dazzle him once more in a university diving competition. Of course I am ill equipped to dive off the higher board that rises about ten feet above the water, but very occasionally I can do a decent dive from this height. Today, making a big impression is my big goal. Well, I certainly make *the impression* of the day, right in front of Dan and all of the many students packing the stands. I execute the perfect belly flop. Not only does it sting like mad, but my swimsuit splits right down the front ... from the very top to the bottom.

To my delight and astonishment Dan finally begins to find me appealing ... even though it becomes a somewhat off and on attraction. Here I am, crazy about a man who is jolly hard to get, and I like getting my own way. Dan likes to be the centre of attention and like me he has tons of energy and he has even failed some classes. I too have a very independent mind and I'm willing to share it. But I can hardly call our relationship a successful romance. It weaves back and forth. One minute I'm full of optimism and then I crash when Dan's off doing things that *could* have included me. After a year comes the finale. We're alone on the deck of the ferry travelling all night between the two islands. "You and I together," he pauses. "It will never work." I am baffled, I'm devastated and I'm furious to the point of becoming rabid. Other things are said and I end up slapping him on the face, something I have never done before.

Looking back I am mortified by my assault and I have never again struck someone's face. I can still see Dan leaning back against the rail of the ferry, and golly – I could have knocked him overboard and would now be serving life! It took a long introspective time for me to interpret his reasoning ... and I thought I was a darned good catch.

Lucky for me all the knocks in my life did give me resilience and fortitude. I was slowing maturing into a better person at last. Or so I hoped. I had to accept I could not get everything I wanted in life. And damn it, I would find a much better man. (And I did! Dave. And he still thinks I'm a darned good catch!) For now I would struggle in my studies to get my university degree and I would succeed in the horse world, of course finally accepting I would never come close to competing a horse at the highest level of jumping.

Today as an SC my sole focus has been on just one sport, the horse trials. But that focus is changing. Deep inside I know that serious jumping is out. On the surface I believe I will give it one more shot. But for now I would also like to make an effort to refine my dressage.

For years my long-time trainer, Bill, taught Minty and me during my eventing days. Dressage was just a bit of a nuisance class before the thrill of riding cross-country and then jumping a stadium course, both of which Minty adored. Now Bill has moved further away and is very busy with his extensive judging, teaching and training business. Of course he will help me become what is popularly and somewhat sarcastically called a DQ (Dressage Queen) but he's too busy to give me consistent lessons. And I really have no desire to be a DQ, strutting around with a millstone of medals around my neck. I would just like to be a few notches higher in my dressage education. It takes years to become a Grand Prix rider and long before I ever achieve such a status I'll probably be killing time in a wheelchair.

Kathy comes into my life, and what a trainer. She's taking her time to understand the quirks of Minty, Catch and me, and will help us master many of the dressage movements.

Thank goodness Dave will be back from Hong Kong in a few hours and I can announce my latest plan. "Dave – I can't wait to get rid of the farmhouse and *tenants*. Plus it will lessen your mowing, my weeding, our raking of leaves …" Those do turn out to be almost my very first words, much to Dave's weary astonishment. I small-mindedly forget he has just flown through twelve time zones. With Christmas coming and the full force of winter, we decide that the selling had better wait until the downstairs' tenant leaves after finishing her vet degree in May. We'll keep the upstairs apartment vacant. We could get tenants for a two or three months' stay but we'd be in trouble if they refused to leave after such a short time.

Thanksgiving Day has come and gone and we had a good time at Richard's home with the whole gang and dogs galore. Laurie, Richard's wife, cooks a great traditional meal and our two delightful grandchildren, Luke and Jonathan, appear to be thankfully going the straight and narrow teenage route. "Skipping a generation," Richard quips.

Meanwhile I ride both Minty and Catch four or five times a week and enjoy productive dressage lessons with Kathy. She's widowed, in her mid-fifties and very attractive. With little time to meet any men, she laughingly tells me she has joined an Internet dating service and already has a date. She describes some of the men who have currently been matched to her and each one sounds like the consummate partner, one's dream man … on paper. How about *in person*? We will soon find out.

Two days later Kathy tells me about her first date and we almost rupture with laughter. He's called Paul and they met last Saturday for dinner. He was okay-looking, had passable manners and was a good conversationalist. But by the end of the evening Paul's future will not be with Kathy. "Can you believe what he said to me as we were saying goodbye outside the restaurant?" I can't wait to hear. "'Well, Kathy, I really, really like you so much. Of course we will get back together soon and often. And from here on I want to have sex with you twice a week.'" Kathy is no stick-in-the-mud but we both agree that Paul is from the wrong side of the track.

Now my trip to New Zealand looms straight after Christmas. And what a great Christmas as I cook and cook and think of the masses of turkeys I've prepared over the years with varying degrees of enthusiasm and success. As usual this day is almost controlled by the presence of seven dogs. We have our Rocky, Richard has two, Paul has one, Tonia has two and a friend brings one. When the evening ends, everyone wishes me a good trip to New Zealand and my mind will now focus on all that I have to pack and the lists I must leave for patient Dave and Sue. And Sue now has the first court date about her divorce, and the bigamist had better not wreck the situation with his good looks, charm and fabrications.

I'm so grateful for the opportunity to fly home every year and much of my appreciation goes, with thanks, to our United Airline's credit card. We use our two cards exclusively and both Dave and I have had many free international trips or at least free upgrades to business class from all the points we have accrued. There is no way my damaged anatomy can survive the twenty-five hours in economy anymore, because currently I have to fly via Australia and double back over the Tasman Sea. After the terrorist attack in New York, 9/11, United stopped all service to New Zealand. They have an alliance with Air New Zealand, but it's almost impossible to get a free seat and they don't allow paying for economy and using the points for the upgrade.

Sadly, Dave's heart is not in New Zealand anymore and he has little interest in visiting his homeland. He has no family left, apart from a cousin, and his old friends left years ago for countries that offered more opportunities.

It's odd, but even though I singularly miss my family and friends neither do I want to live in New Zealand. I love America deeply. Still, as Dorothy says in *The Wizard of Oz,* " There's no place like home."

Chapter Twelve

Dodging the Brig

New Zealand at last. We fly low over Auckland harbour, dotted with sailboats. And there is the Harbour Bridge. It brings back unique memories for me. Sir John Allum was the Mayor of Auckland way back, and he was responsible for getting the bridge built. His daughter, Rose Allum, was my old headmistress at New Plymouth Girls' High and responsible for my expulsion to the closeted boarding school with the imposing name of Samuel Marsden Collegiate School for Girls. Looking back I can see that my behaviour gave her no choice. And once again my wonderful mother was in the sanitorium.

I was out of control.

I was disobedient.

I talked nonstop in class.

I was constantly late for class.

I was caught breaking bounds during class to creep into town to buy old horse equipment for my collection. It was being auctioned at the pig mart, where the post office stands today.

I failed to wear all the items of our navy-blue uniform, such as my sash (lost), or beret with the badge … always blowing off and landing in a gorse hedge as I galloped my pony to school.

And worse still, I was bottom of the class in almost every subject but English.

One of my report cards from New Plymouth Girls' High School. I am in my first year and have just turned thirteen.

Subject	No. In Form	Place in form	%	Comment
English	31	22	52	Elizabeth has much ability but is not working. Her written work is hasty and careless. MSJ
Latin	29	29	47	Weak. Elizabeth's work is disappointing. EKR
French	29	29	31	Fair only and often erratic. MD
Maths	27	26	24	Elizabeth could put much more effort into her work. DK
Science	25	23	31	Weak. Needs to be more careful. KAC
Social Studies	30	29	27	Unsatisfactory. Elizabeth needs to concentrate more and take more care. RM
History	28	28	48	Elizabeth writes in too little detail. Her work is very immature. SS
Physical Ed				Very fair. Elizabeth is inclined to be very distracted and noisy in class. NAF
Singing				Very fair. Drop your jaw and open your mouth. JF
Conduct				Elizabeth is uncooperative. Must learn to control her feelings. DW
General remarks				A disappointing term. Elizabeth finds her work difficult but she does not tackle her difficulties with sufficient energy or determination. Rose Allum

I had no desire and no drive to succeed academically. Who could be bothered? I was becoming a hopeless case as I fell further and further behind.

Dad always drilled us to do our very best. But it was too late for me to do even my limited best in school. To make matters worse, our misguided primary school headmistress had written in my report for the high school that I was, "blessed with intelligence and ambition." Yeah! It landed me in the top stream class, which included Latin and French. It was way too late for me to "do my best". I had sunk out of sight and any chance of rescue was gone.

Once during that first year of high school I did try my best at writing. After reading *The Pony Misty*, I wrote my first book, *Monty the Grey Pony*. I was thirteen years old and sent it off to what was probably the only New Zealand publisher, AH and AW Reed in Wellington.

Rejection!

They did encourage me to keep writing. But to me writing success became just a dream, and *damn* AH and AW Reed! But Dad's words, "Always do your best," kept ringing in my ears. I'll show him. I will become a great rider. Yes!

And one of my final high school offences … One lunch break my friend Maddy and I hatched an intrepid scheme. We had heard that some students were planning to creep illegally into a tapu or sacred Maori cave, located just outside the school grounds … and out of bounds of course. We would get there first and scare the daylights out of them. What is more it was rumoured that the cave was haunted and there were skeletons of tohungas or Maori chiefs at the far end.

Just before the lunch bell rang, both of our teachers excused us. We faked bleeding noses with red geranium petals. So far so good. We met in the orchard and hurried through the bush, scaled a barbed wire fence, scattered sheep and tentatively approached the cave. By now our courage had left us and we were scared. But we pushed ourselves inside and made our way along a narrow ridge above a length of muddy water. Flashing a weak torch we reached the back of the passage and to our immense relief there were no bones.

We were a bit goosey as we waited for the other students to appear and I told Maddy about my other cave experience. My grandfather had owned a farm in Mahoenui, the limestone country north of New

Plymouth. Dad had coerced a group of friends to form a working bee on the farm. He needed to collect limestone outcrops to use in his new fish pond creations. While the men toiled, Jill and I gingerly examined nearby caves and not far through one entrance I discovered the complete skull of a horse. That treasure lived in my bedroom at Tupare for years. Then came the day when I returned home from boarding school … and my skull was *gone!* Dad confessed to having thrown it out. It disturbed some of the visitors he showed through the house.

The girls arrived at the mouth of the cave. We could just make out their silhouettes. They were halfway through the cave when we let out our blood-curdling screams. And how they broke rank, jumping into the dirty water and bolting to the outside with a mixture of cries the likes of which I'd never heard before. Maddy and I watched their scrambling forms against the light at the end of the cave.

I can't imagine how long it must have taken them to recover from that terrifying moment. I bet their parents echoed the words that Dad would have used. "You sooky, you boob, you ninny. Rise above it." Years later I told him about our cave adventure. "Liz, your imagination sure carried you away. I know that cave and it was as innocent as they come. It was man-made by the early settlers to keep their food fresh during the summer months."

Name it, I did it at the high school. *But* Miss Allum once said to me after going through her endless list of complaints, "Elizabeth, I must say that you do always tell the truth."

Eleven years later I forgave her. She extended a gesture of extraordinary faith, or was she taking a gamble? After I returned from teaching for two years in London I'd taught for a term at the Hawera high school when Miss Allum invited me back to teach English and biology to the two top fourth forms at my old school. Those pupils were so bright they probably could have passed without me. Sitting in the staff room, with many of my old teachers who had long ago given up on me, could have been the ultimate lesson in humility but I have to admit that I crowed a bit inside.

What accounted for my bad attitude at the high school and when I played on the various school teams, together with my lack of ability? Why did I rebel in everything except my craving to triumph with horses? Of course I had little adult supervision and housekeepers couldn't stand me. And I couldn't stand them ... Was my rebellion a reaction to Mother's absence? Her tuberculosis had become worse and worse since it was first confirmed early in 1943. There was still no cure except for the regime of rest and fresh air, but it was far from tried and true. The disease had drawn Mother closer and closer to death. In spite of her many months in the Chest Block of the local hospital the bacillus had recently attacked a second lung lobe.

While in a short remission from the disease in 1947 she had given birth to my younger brother, Richard. The doctors warned Mother against another pregnancy, but she was determined to have one more child while the tuberculosis was inactive. Sadly, the baby's birth triggered back the active disease where it progressed even further downhill than it had in the earlier days. How long did she have to live? That was the terrible unspoken question and of course nobody said anything negative to Jill and me. But the atmosphere at Tupare and around Mother's family and friends spoke louder than the false words tossed to us children.

Dying was not something one talked about in those days, not even with close friends. If I had ever queried Dad, an older family member or an acquaintance, what sort of answer would come my way?

She'll be all right.

She'll get better.

Grin and bear it.

Rise above it, Elizabeth.

Pray for her.

These well-meaning people were programmed to comfort us children by denying the truth. I give myself some credit for seeing through them to their own anxiety. Their well-intended, but dishonest, replies exacerbated my own apprehension.

Meanwhile our poor little brother John, born two years before Mother first became ill, was often parked out with various relatives or in homes for unwanted children. Later, most of the time baby Richard was in a local home for illegitimate babies. Dad had no other option. Occasionally Richard did come home for a brief stay and Jill and I had to learn quickly how to look after a baby. To this day, I remember the importance of putting the safety pins into the terry-cloth nappies always parallel to the tummy.

And when John was at home, how I bossed the poor kid around, One day the little fellow broke the eggs from the hen-house and I made him eat some of them scrambled. He told me he would be sick if he swallowed one mouthful. I took no notice and made him eat the whole lot. Well, that's how you brought up little kids. And sick he was ... over the wall on the terrace and into the garden below. He has never eaten scrambled eggs since. Such were our child-rearing and our cooking experiences as we learnt to prepare anything and everything when we were in a spell with no housekeeper. Most nights, an aunt or a cousin of Dad's patiently told us over the phone how to make everything from meat dishes to desserts. But always, as a backdrop to everything, was Mother, sicker than ever.

Was this why I was becoming more and more out of control? Was it an outlet for emotional pain? Was it a need for attention? Looking back from my Senior Citizen perspective, the answer is probably, yes. And yet I think our atypical formative years did help Jill and me in some very positive ways. We became extremely independent and, except for Mother's illness, not much ever bothered us. We certainly learnt, at a fashion and at a very early age, how to run a home and deal with a young child and a baby. And how to cook, and cook, and cook. And how to buy our own clothes and shoes. And how did my drive to succeed with horses tie in to this? Was I mad at Dad with all of his distractions and his somewhat removed attention from us? Was I mad at his anxiety over my horse obsession? Or was my drive to succeed also to please Mother, who loved riding, but lay in her hospital bed for months on end, worrying about her children and existing a long way from a mother's normal life?

I certainly don't remember that being such a brat was in any way satisfying. I simply *was* a brat. Nor do I remember experiencing any guilt or remorse. It was just the way life was. But my behaviour certainly got the attention of my friends – admiring attention and to heck with the negative reactions of adults, and especially my teachers. The more I think about it, Dad was too absorbed in Mother's deterioration and in his work and trying to keep his household together to worry much about the downward path his elder daughter was taking ... with the exception of her horse obsession. And he certainly kept all bad news from Mother.

Now I arrive in New Zealand and my brother Richard and his long-time partner Seng meet me at the Auckland airport and say I look just the same after my visit a year ago. Well, my hair colour is a bit better! Yes, I had finally found my hairdresser Jan and she's gifted, but does chew gum all the time. If there's something that gets on my nerves after seeing someone smoke, it's someone chewing gum. I should say that Jan *did* chew gum until the day she offered me a stick. "Well, thanks, Jan," I answered, "but to tell you the truth, my mother forbade me ever to chew gum in public and I've never tolerated the habit." Never again does she chomp in front of me.

It's amazing how I can make somewhat embarrassing but honest comments after reaching the age of seventy. Still, one has to be careful. I'll never forget the story of my Aunt Bertha. She and her girl friends started an informal club in Napier. One day they decided that they must *always* tell the truth to each other and nothing but the truth, no matter how painful. Not even a white lie was acceptable. The club lasted about a week. The friction lasted much longer.

I'm fourteen and a half years Richard's senior, but we are uncannily alike. We have identical senses of humour, identical approaches to issues of right and wrong and we both love to write. We hardly ever saw each other as kids, except during the holidays. Starting two years after Richard was born I was grounded at boarding school. I was then away at university and doing my O E in England. Way back when Dave and I were first dating, Mother felt it was proper for us to take Richard when we set off on a small trip. So our seven-year-old chaperone came with us to sightsee north of Auckland. To be honest, I didn't take much notice of the little nuisance.

Whenever I'm with Richard and Seng our days are full of laughter. "Never stop," I tell the men. "I heard on the news that the more you laugh the longer you'll live." But there's also pain with each meeting. It is easy to see the Parkinson's progression and how the disease is debilitating Richard, more and more. He's not quite sixty years old and the prognosis is grim.

There's medicine for the disease in the form of three different drugs that are given in sequence after each one loses its effectiveness. This can happen from between three to seven years for each drug. Richard is now well into the third drug. It slows the shaking, but as yet there's no cure for Parkinson's. If only President Bush had seen the light and approved promising stem cell research. There's also a remarkable operation where electrodes are placed on either side of the brain and attached to two battery-powered stimulators in the chest. In most cases the results are outstanding but my poor brother is not a candidate, says his neurosurgeon, considered the best in New Zealand. Richard's hopes were so dashed he forgot to ask why he didn't qualify.

We sit on the verandah on this hot summer's afternoon and cover many catch-up topics. A neighbour comes running up the path and wants to borrow some jumper-cables. "This is Ralph Jensen," Seng introduces me, and my mouth falls open in shock. Of course it's not the Ralph Jensen that I knew many, many years ago, but the same name gives me a jolt.

"Why that odd reaction?" Richard asks while Seng searches for the cables.

"Well," I start to giggle, "it's years since I have thought about the Ralph Jensen I met in the 1950s. He was actually a retired brigadier." And this is the story I tell him – I always try to make Richard laugh. When my friend Flick and I were sailing to England to do our OE, Brig, as we called him behind his back, and his wife were returning from a tour of New Zealand and we all four sat at the same dining room table. Brig was stuffy and very proper and Mrs Jensen was not much better. During the four weeks that the ship rolled across the Pacific, through the Panama Canal and finally to England, Flick and I must have seemed very unsophisticated and unworldly colonials. In spite of it, Brig and his wife invited us to stay with them when we visited Scotland.

And what a great stay we had in their home on the River Spey. Brig even found a well-broken in pony for me to ride over the hills. I quail now when I think how naïve and innocent I was – how in gratitude for borrowing the pony I hugged Brig closely and kissed him warmly on the cheek.

Back in London, Flick and I were working again as supply schoolteachers. One bleak evening, I came back to our slummy flat in Maida Vale and there was a letter for me. It was a *love letter* from Brig. He wrote how he couldn't get me out of his mind and all sorts of exaggerated and flattering lies, like how beautiful I was, how refreshing and what a good rider. Brig went on to say that he was coming to London and please, *please* would I meet him at this certain club. I was to leave the office a message if I couldn't make it. I still gasp when I think how he signed off that letter. 'I can't get you out of my mind, Elizabeth, lovingly yours, Ralph.' Even to this day, I can clearly see him and his impressive bushy moustache – and he always wore spats!

Make it to the *club*? It's the last place in the world I was going to walk inside. Flick and I ceremonially burnt the letter and threw the ashes down the toilet. What on earth did he ever see in the very ordinary me from down-under? I'm not beautiful and he had told me he knew nothing about horses – so why wax on about my being such a good rider?

What is more he had asked if I had a boyfriend and I had told him about Dave, and how he was studying at MIT in Boston.

Another letter soon followed and this time I really freaked out. What did I ever do to turn him on like this? How I wish I'd shown gratitude for my ride with just words and not the spontaneous hug and the kiss. And although I *had* aimed for his cheek, he'd moved in such a way I had actually hit a mixture of scratchy moustache and gooey mouth.

So that letter was also burnt. To my relief, there were no more. And never in my innocence or my wildest moments did I ever think I had led him on.

A year later I was back in New Plymouth, working at the high school so I could pay back all the money I had borrowed to sail home. One afternoon I drove back to Tupare from my teaching job and Dad rushed out the front door. "You won't believe who is here. Your great friends, Brigadier and Mrs Jensen. They're out visiting New Zealand again. They were on a tour of Pukeiti and asked after our family. And there I was, right on the spot. So of course I drove them back here."

I tell Richard, and Seng who's rejoined him, that I felt like passing out on the cold front-door brick steps. But I took a deep breath and walked into the living room. There he was on the sofa with Mrs Jensen beside him. I can still see her large diamond and sapphire ring. Mother was sitting beside the sofa on a chair and Dad was rushing around filling whisky glasses.

Don't ever forget your good manners, Elizabeth.

Of course I played the part and Brig never once looked at me. I'm sure no one noticed my unease. And it certainly wasn't a time in my generation when I would ever have told Dad and Mother how an old man misinterpreted their naïve daughter's actions.

Then Dad had to ask me to show them all around the garden. We'd gone as far as the Waiwakaiho riverbank before Brig opened his mouth for the first time and asked about my horses. Back at the house, Dad said, "Liz, you *must* take your charming friends on a tour of New Plymouth." It was awful. Mrs Jensen sat beside me and Brig was in the back seat, right behind me. The whole time he was leaning on his arms as they stretched along the back of my seat. And he wouldn't stop *breathing* down my neck. And he insisted, over and over, that I go with them to dinner, but I managed to make a polite excuse. I had too many English assignments to mark.

Now I tell my audience, "So that's how I met the other Ralph Jensen. Of course now that I'm a Senior Citizen I'd have the guts to tell the old man to sit right back on the seat. Better still, I'd swerve the car violently and let him crash onto the floor. 'Sorry, sorry, thought there was a possum on the road.'"

Richard and Seng agree that there are some good things about my becoming an SC. We click our glasses together.

Chapter Thirteen

Family Stories

I'm on a quick flight from Auckland to New Plymouth to stay in nearby Omata with my brother John and his wife Lynda. John has a stunning collection of pop art in his home and has been a force in bringing the kinetic sculptural art works of New Zealander Len Lye to the public back home.

Now for non-stop talk, visiting friends and Tupare. It's a tribute to Dad's landscaping artistry and horticultural endeavours that after he died the Queen Elizabeth II National Trust accepted our old home. They found it too complicated and expensive to manage, however, so the Taranaki Regional Council took it over with great expertise. Tupare is now open and free to the public every day. The trees, shrubs and especially the rhododendrons are endless. There's not much that won't grow well and rapidly in Taranaki's rich volcanic soil and mild climate.

Lynda is at the airport and we set off for town. The mountain is gleaming and its striking symmetry still has late winter snows shrinking up the deep valleys. "You know, Lynda, this was the perfect province for us kids to grow up in. We had so much to challenge us. Egmont to climb and ski on, the bush to explore, the rich pastures for our horses and the black iron beaches all along the coastline where we could swim our horses and gallop for miles."

As we turn on to the main road leading into town, I have another of the sudden flashbacks that have increased with my expanding senior years. "The original New Plymouth airport was right across that hedge," and I tell her how the town was rightly proud of its tiny airfield with a type of Quonset-hut beside a large pasture with a lone wind-sock at one end. Two or three DC3s each week could land and take off only after the grazing sheep were driven out of the way. During the war there was a fighter airplane prominently displayed beside the hut. The Japanese were escalating the war and everyone was worried they would soon be landing on the beach. Someone thought the invaders might somehow reconnoitre the area and think twice about coming ashore if there were a nearby combat plane, all ready to take off and bomb them. It turned out to be a fake wooden decoy.

I continue about how the old airport was still in use when practically everyone I knew came to see me off for my 1959 wedding in the USA. I was decked out in a suit, hat, white gloves and high heels, in spite of my rotten bunions. And how those fancy shoes pinched my feet as I climbed up the sloping aisle of the old DC3. "In those days," I carry on, "all domestic and overseas flights left Auckland from an old terminal building in Whenuapai, with sparrows flitting around the rafters and hopping around the floor looking for crumbs. After the flight from New Plymouth, I looked in a mirror and my face was smudged with different coloured lipsticks from the farewells.

"I had hardly time to clean up before we took off in a DC4. I was thrilled about my upcoming marriage, but I cried until the last of New Zealand disappeared. The flight took us to Fiji where we changed planes and I had my first trip in a 707 jet. It's hard to believe today that those planes had to land in Samoa or Tahiti and then Honolulu before reaching the USA. There was a sextant in the cockpit and we flew by the stars from Samoa to Honolulu." I pause for breath. "Sorry, Lynda. Tell me to shut-up!"

"No, no. This is great. Hey, my husband grew up here too."

We drive past the old A and P showgrounds. Years ago my brother John bought the site and the annual show moved to the racecourse. Gone is the great arena, the horses' loose boxes, the sheds harbouring the sheep, the cows and the bulls. Now it's a huge engineering complex. "You know, Lynda," I say, "I lived for this horse show. It was always in early February and my first time competing was in 1944. I didn't win a single ribbon. My pony stopped three times at the first jump and I was so pissed that Mother gave me a dressing down about sportsmanship. She even made me go and congratulate the winners of my classes. *'Elizabeth, don't you ever forget to be a good and gracious loser.'"*

"I can just hear her saying it," Lynda laughs.

I describe how Jill and I would wander around the rides and displays during the two days of the show. We would pay to see the fattest woman on earth, ride the ferris wheel and eat candy floss and hot dogs attached to a stick and covered in a thick batter. An important competition was the Highland dancing with a man playing the bagpipes. Whenever I was naughty, Mother, being half-Scottish, would threaten me with lessons in Scottish dancing.

How I missed this show the three years that I was locked away at Marsden.

We approach the Waiwakaiho River bridge and I point up Queens Road. "You can't imagine the riding lessons we had with our middle-aged Irish instructor, Mrs Marfurt. What a tough old bird, but everything she did and told us was always for our benefit. Once at the end of a rally I was just sitting on my pony while everyone else was helping to put away the jumps. She rocketed over to me, slapped my leg and shrieked so she could be heard on the main road, 'Who do you think you are, Elizabeth Matthews? The King of England? Get off that pony and help!'

I'm in a confessional mode and tell Lynda – just in case she hasn't yet realised it – that I was quite the teenage brat. Apart from my banishment from New Plymouth Girls' High School, I left a trail of transgressions around Taranaki. The land being so productive and full of Jersey cows there were no trails, so we enjoyed most of our riding either at Tupare, at pony club rallies at the racecourse, or, with total abandonment, on the beaches.

A friend and I were the very first members of the new North Taranaki Pony Club, I explain. Apart from improving our riding skills and the care of our ponies, we were taught responsibility and cooperation. But I had two very diverse equine personalities. After one big dressing-down at a rally I became a responsible member in good standing, but only at the rallies.

Lynda asks what I had done. I'd complained to Mrs Marfurt that the jumps were too low for my new pony and how I was jumping four-foot hurdles at home. I didn't add that this irresponsibility was also behind Mother's back. Mrs Marfurt freaked out and went on and on about how I was ill-equipped to jump even two-foot-high obstacles and how dare I be so reckless and ruin my pony, and what other stupid things was I doing behind her back? I knew she wouldn't understand if I mentioned all the news about the upcoming 1948 London Olympics, news that had caught my imagination. I had to prepare for my future Olympic-jumping debut.

And then – oh dear. I joined a friend who lived nearby and we rode over the sand dunes and on to the busy Fitzroy beach. We walked and trotted through the crowd until we reached the southern end of the beach and the footbridge spanning the Te Henui River. We clopped over the narrow bridge as women grabbed children and yelled insults at us. Many steam trains travelled on a line twenty feet above us, although we never managed to cross at the same time. Thank goodness!

Returning across the bridge we walked along the sands and reached the town's sewer pipe where it crossed the beach and dumped refuse into the Tasman Sea. I picked up a gallop and headed Pollyanna towards the highest three-foot-six-inch section. The mare stopped dead. I tried again and again and yet again before deciding to move down to the three-foot section. I landed and pushed Polly into a flat-out gallop. The tide was out, the sands were hard and the beach-goers were all over the place, but we felt entitled to 'own' the place. Was it a case, I now wonder, of folie à deux?

Back then dogs took up the chase and sand splayed out behind us, mixed with loose manure. We jumped over the driftwood, we splashed through the streams, children ran out of our path, we were heady and young and our ponies were fantastic. Only the dangerous current at the mouth of the Waiwakaiho River halted our thrilling ride.

"Liz, you'd never get away with that today," Lynda now exclaims.

"Oh, we didn't get away with it sixty years ago." And I told her how Dad was reading the Daily News and the rest of us were hanging around him.

"'Well, blow me down,' he had said, 'Listen to this, Mary.' And Dad glanced up at me. 'This item is headlined East End Rodeo,' and he read it out aloud. I still have the original cutting, yellow with age."

'Two young horsewomen momentarily disturbed people at the East End Reserve, New Plymouth, yesterday afternoon. They rode across the small footbridge and down onto the sand beside the river. One rider then attempted to make her mount jump the sewerage main a few yards further down the bend. After a dozen or more attempts her horse scrambled over, much to the relief of the parents whose children were playing nearby. The onlookers were also not pleased with the trail of droppings over the bridge and in the sand.'

"As Father finished," I tell Lynda, "I was out the door. 'That was you, wasn't it, Elizabeth?' he called out. At least the people who reported us apparently didn't see the end of our wild exhibition along the rest of the beach. A fortnight later the Town Council voted unanimously to forbid all horseback riding on Fitzroy Beach. Today the rules have relaxed a bit," I grin. "Horses are forbidden on the beach only from 9am to 6pm daily during daylight saving hours. "

Only two of us in the Pony Club ever knew, with certainty, who had ruined their riding on the great sands. Mrs Marfurt did look at me quizzically at the next rally. She, personally, totally disregarded the new ruling and sedately continued to ride her horse along the sands. No one ever challenged that intimidating elderly woman riding on old Boke. She may have been kidding us, but she told us that Boke was the Irish word for vomit.

We're in the middle of town. "See that old building? I went to a dance there when I was about fifteen. All of us girls wore long evening gowns and sat in a straight line on one side of the hall and the boys would be pretending that we didn't exist, but were all subtly ogling and talking about us from the opposite wall. Then the MC would announce a waltz, or a fox trot or the Gay Gordons or some other old traditional dance. The bold boys would rush across the floor to grab the prettiest girls. The shy boys ended up with the girls who were still sitting and hoping that they wouldn't end up as wallflowers. I was lucky to be snapped up fairly early in the rush, but seldom by the best-looking boys who'd caught my eye. Towards the end of the evening came the blackout dance and all lights except for a tiny dim one were turned off.

"After the dance, Dad was to collect me at midnight. I stood outside, all alone on that footpath for half an hour. The dance organisers never thought that it was necessary for someone to stay with me. As usual, Dad was very late. 'Sorry Liz, sorry. I fell asleep.' He was in his pyjamas."

The sight of the old railway station brings back so many more reminiscences. "When Mother was first ill in 1943, and Dad had no one to look after us, Jill and I were sent to Queen Margaret College in Wellington as boarders, dressed from head to toe in the royal blue uniform. Mother had been a high school boarder there and she knew the old headmistress well. Dad would put us on the train over there, at eight in the morning and would single out an old lady and say, 'Please would you mind keeping an eye on the girls but especially Elizabeth, here. She is quite capable of missing the train when it stops for tea.' No one worried that anything else might happen to us. We would be met in Wellington at ten past six in the evening. I was still nine years old and Jill was seven.

"Earlier I was at Queen Margaret College for two terms in 1939 when I was five because Mother and Dad wanted to take a trip around the world before the start of the impending war. I can't believe that they sent me to boarding school at that age. Jill went to live with one of Dad's sisters and the boys weren't yet born. I must say that Mother, having been a boarder at the school and knowing the headmistress well, probably helped getting this tiny tot accepted. I was the youngest boarder ever in the history of the school and the first-ever daughter of an Old Girl.

"The matron at QMC was Dad's close and loving first cousin and she was very attentive to me. I remember her struggling to cut my fidgety fingernails and forcing a teaspoon of cod liver oil between my sealed lips every morning. So was I homesick? Mother said she felt terrible when I cried in panic as they left me. She felt even worse when they returned for me and I let out piercing screams of fury and fell kicking to the floor because I didn't want to leave the school and return to Tupare.

"So I was pretty used to being tossed around by my second time as a boarder. Actually, I think now, Jill and I were more scared of a Japanese invasion in 1943 than anything else. Every night the searchlights would pierce the skies above the harbour and we'd have scary air raid drills when we had to run outside in the middle of the night, often down the swaying fire escapes to hide in tunnels. There was also a very bad earthquake in the middle of one night. I was in a long corridor going to the basin room. I'd lost a tooth and needed to rinse the blood out of my mouth. The shaking was so severe I was unable to keep walking. I crouched down against the wall of the corridor and watched the swaying of the one hanging weak yellow light bulb at the end of the corridor. I was so scared I screamed non-stop until someone found me."

We drive out of the city towards Omata, and Mt Egmont gazes down on Taranaki. I think my own thoughts. I've been to the top five times, but the memorable climb was with David … not my husband David! This gorgeous guy asked me to go with him on an Open Climb. I couldn't believe that at last he had asked me out. It took us five tough hours to reach the summit and three to clamber back down. Soon afterwards, David left for England to do a postgraduate engineering degree and wrote me stacks of sweet letters. He wrote that he wanted to marry me after he returned, but I wrote back, gently, 'Please wait a bit. I'm not quite ready.'

When he did return, I'd still not made up my mind. I was half way through my degree and university life was more fun than marriage and a life at the kitchen sink. So he dumped me on the spot. A few months later he married someone else and for the first time I experienced that old cliché that he's a really super chap and right now I don't want him, but I'm darned if I want anyone else to have him!

Chapter Fourteen

In Childhood Footsteps

Today's going to be a scorcher and I pull on a short-sleeved blouse. I glance in the full-length mirror and gape. What a sight. I'm not worried that my arms are winter lily-white but all those conspicuous brown mottles ... and how I love mottles on a horse. My upper arms look like the corrugated iron roofs on New Zealand's colonial houses. Of course the crinkles aren't new but since arriving in Auckland I've been seeing too many smooth upper arms on younger sleeveless women. I pull out a shirt that covers everything down to my wrists.

I remember Mother once telling me that she could tell when a person was really past what we now call the 'use by' date because of all the wrinkles around their elbows. *My* wrinkles aren't just confined to the elbows. And where there are no wrinkles there is sag. And where there is no sag there are brazen veins faking modern art.

I put on lipstick and soon it will creep down the growing furrows below my lower lip. My gaze goes to my throat and neck. Oh no, before long I'll have to give up wearing anything with a V-neck. Years of the powerful sun in my youth have played havoc with my skin and in no way can this amount of wreckage be reversed.

I show all the aging evidence to elegant Lynda. "Come on, Liz. It's not bad at all. In fact I like the way you look," she laughs. "I know people much younger than you who look twenty years older than you. Just slap tons of cream on your arms and neck. Maybe you're dehydrated and need to drink more water."

Aw heck.

"And put bio oil on the skin below your lip and then use a pencil liner to trace out the edge of your lower lip. That'll prevent the lipstick from creeping."

"What on earth is bio-oil?"

"I've no idea, but they'll tell you in the chemist shop."

I think back to Santo Domingo. Before that trip I accepted everything negative about myself. But since my return I've spent an exhausting amount of time trying to improve different parts of my body. Today I change my tune. Blow all that glamour. To heck with glamour. And like it or leave it I'm just plain old me ... I'll leave it!

Lynda lends me their spare car and I drive into town along Devon Street and right past Deers' old shoe store. I quail when I think how Jill and I loved to visit this store when we went to town for late night Friday shopping. Between the adult chairs of the store and the children's section at the back stood the X-ray machine. Can anyone believe that in my youth we could have our feet X-rayed to see if the shoes we were trying fitted us? Of course Jill and I were not necessarily buying shoes and the salesman got to know us quite well and tolerated our visits.

We would race to the machine, position our feet in a slot underneath it and take turns pressing our faces against the opening at the top. From there we could gaze and gaze down at the bones of our feet. Wiggle, jiggle – and the skeletons moved on demand. And all that exposure to radiation ... it's not surprising that not so long after its installation, the X-ray machine disappeared and was never seen again. I've often wondered how much exposure we received and how much I received from my numerous chest X-rays, demanded by our doctor. Every six months I was X-rayed by a huge noisy machine and the radiologist searched for the signs of tuberculosis in my lung lobes. I had tested positive to the Mantoux test, indicating I'd been heavily exposed to TB. Our doctor was convinced it was only a matter of time before this skinny 'type A' teenager developed full-blown active tuberculosis.

She didn't. But I still have the scar from the Mantoux test on my left upper arm.

I drive on and soon am passing my old high school. I'm flooded with high and low memories of my teenage years. There are dormitories now where we turned our ponies loose in the school's horse paddock. I could have taken the school bus but it was much more fun to ride. Every day I would fly out of class when the bus bell went, five minutes before the regular bell announced the end of all classes for the day. I'd rush to the horse paddock, throw my saddle and bridle on Pollyanna, pull on my overalls, and with my satchel banging on my back I'd ride away at full speed. The purpose of my mad gallop was to see how far I could ride before the school bus passed. I once made it to the old waterworks and the bus driver gave me the thumbs up and tooted my success. On weekends we often rode to this great basin-shaped abandoned waterworks to catch tadpoles with Mother's kitchen utensils. How did we ever go barefoot in such slimy, mucky, putrid water?

I pass Rimu Street but the tiny store down from the corner is long gone. When Monty and I rode to Fitzroy Beach, we'd stop on the way home for penny ice creams. One for Monty and one for me. It didn't take long for Monty to refuse to go past the corner if I didn't stop for his ice cream. This was quite a problem on Sundays when everything in the town was closed. On one occasion, Monty's stubbornness gave me no choice but to turn around and ride home on the longer main road.

Today I walk down Tupare's winding driveway. There's so much to appreciate as I take in what the Taranaki Regional Council has achieved. Along with the gardeners and volunteers, they've transformed my old home back to how it looked in Dad's finest creative years. Once again I'm enveloped in magnificent landscaping and a tipsy fragrance.

And a commanding thought fills my head. Weeding. In spite of his employees, Dad made us kids weed for an hour every day. "You children must learn to appreciate your home and not take it for granted." We kept yellow timesheets, like the other employees, and were paid sixpence an hour. Dad couldn't stand idleness. If we wanted to sunbathe and get that enviable tan, we had to hide in distant corners or be discovered and lectured. "Stop wasting time. Be productive," he would demand. And we weeded some more and earned yet more sixpences. It's no wonder I detest weeding to this day.

Yes, he could be demanding, but there were occasions when I outwitted him. I wander on to the terrace in front of the house. Every morning when Mother was away in hospital, Dad would sit here and I brought out his coffee, brewed in an aluminium coffeepot. One morning I had forgotten to ride to Parkers' grocery store at the bottom of Mangorei Road to buy the ground coffee. "You're slipping," he tells me with a grin. "Please make sure you have it for me tomorrow."

I forgot again. "Elizabeth," and he never called me that unless he was mad, "you're way too irresponsible. Get your mind off those ponies and please buy my decent coffee."

Day three and the untrustworthy, flighty me had forgotten yet again. No problem. I just put the instant coffee in the aluminium percolator and Dad never noticed the difference.

But the next incident had Dad outwitting me. He asked me to drive into town to pick up the wages for his employees. They were always paid in cash and I put the bundle of pound notes in the car's glove box. And forgot about them. Later in the day Dad called me into his study. "Where's the money, Liz?"

"Oh. It's still in the glove box. I'll get it right now."

"By the way, did you count it?"

"Um. Sort of."

I bring the bills to his study and he makes me count them in front of him. To my horror I'm short by forty pounds. "Well, Liz, you're going to have to make it up with weeding." Panic pours through my entire body. It would take me years! I say nothing. "Well, as it happens, I actually removed the forty pounds to teach you a hard lesson. Always count money from the bank and if in doubt, count it twice." To this day I have never once ignored his advice.

I wander down to the Waiwakaiho River where I always give a special thought to Barbara, the daughter of our country school's headmaster. She drowned in our river's deep pool, in the bend between all the rapids. Barbara with her two brothers and a girl cousin were not to swim until supervision arrived. Instead they played in the rapids above the pool where both girls lost their balance on the slimy rocks and slipped into the rushing water. Mother heard the boys screaming and started down the hill to warn them that they must never cry wolf-wolf. But she soon interpreted their genuine cries for help and broke into a run.

Mother was not allowed to swim as she was still recuperating from one of her sanitorium time-outs. She stripped off her shoes and outer clothes and powered into the middle of the deep pool where she had seen a hand break through the water. It's amazing to think that in spite of the river's strong current she managed to dive under the surface, pull the cousin to the surface and swim back with her to the shore. Sadly she dived in vain for Barbara, our schoolmate. Then Mother used the advanced life-saving movements she had learnt many years before and resuscitated the little cousin.

Today I gaze at the river with its smoothed boulders, racing rapids and the deep pool of water so fresh off the mountain. Above the high floodwater mark, native trees cling to the cliff on the far side. Overgrown with bush is part of a small airplane that had crashed near the mountain. Dad asked if he could have one of the wings, stripped it down and installed the frame on a concrete base. It became our diving tower. The horizontal piping provided us with different daring heights. I never had Mother's guts to dive off the very top metal rail, all of twenty-five feet above the water.

Behind me stretches the beautiful river field, bordered in part by a great bend of the Waiwakaiho. Today there are still sheep grazing on the rich grass, but no horses. The boxthorn hedge that Dad turned into a jump for us has gone and I look at the lines where we had our homemade jump courses – ponga logs placed on boxes, bitumen barrels, gates propped against trees and lines of stacked winter firewood. It was a challenging course that we jumped with questionable skill, over and over again … more than sixty years ago.

Oh Minty, will I ever jump you again?

I drive past the racehorse farm where Jill and I would hang around, every spare minute of every day. We absorbed so much about riding, breaking horses, foals and weaning, and I was taught things like how to use a twitch. We hated it if the gelding of the colts were ever scheduled during school hours. Of course Jill and I were not allowed to watch and whenever the vet came to geld and we were around, we were sent home. But we would hide in bushes behind a fence line and had a great view of each horse lying anaesthetised on the grassy field.

When I was older, I was often entrusted with riding one racehorse and leading a second one to the blacksmith's shop in the middle of town. To this day I can't believe how I was trusted with those valuable thoroughbreds and how they casually accepted the electric tramcars that would clatter past us on the main street. I'm sure my solid old Minty would become upset.

Three more days fly past and Lynda cooks a superb dinner for my last night in my old hometown, and great workaholic John gets home early. There's nothing like a family evening punctuated with laughter and banter, superb wine and the stunning Great Dane, Atlas, lying at our feet.

Chapter Fifteen

Nursing and Waitressing

I'm on a quick flight to Wellington and a day with old friends. As we approach the airport I gaze down at Island Bay where some of us Queen Margaret College boarders were blown away in 1943 by our first-ever taste of Coca-Cola. And there's the Wellington Hospital – I start re-living my time in the capital city.

It's my last year at Marsden and I'm finally caught up with my studies. What else is there to do while sitting for endless compulsory homework hours? I pass School Certificate the second time around and am judged to be academically far enough ahead in my sixth form subjects to take a nursing course at Wellington Public Hospital. It isn't as much the course that excites me as the *freedom*.

Every Tuesday three of us are trusted to catch the tram to the hospital and take in an afternoon of lectures on physiology and anatomy. On Thursdays we spend the afternoon in the hospital wards, performing pleasant and very unpleasant tasks. On the very first day, when we practise taking each other's blood pressure, I'm the patient of a Wellington Girls' College student. She pumps the pressure up so high I pass out cold on the linoleum floor.

There are sixteen of us in the class, and we're from several Wellington schools. Fifteen of us have strong nursing ambitions and one of us just desperately needs to get out past her boarding school's gates. Added to our newfound independence, every week we arrange to meet natty boys from Wellington College, at the nearby Adams Bruce shop. Here we gorge down ice creams and cream wafers and our teen laughter drenches the shop – until one of my friends (and it's never me) looks at her watch and says we'd better scramble on to the next tram and get back to school.

To my utter surprise, I top the final nursing exam and the different teachers all try to grab this high-scoring-nurse-in-the-making. To make matters worse, the main anatomy teacher somehow knows my mother and applies more awkward pressure. In the end I have to tell a little lie. (Yes, Miss Allum, I have betrayed your trust in me.) Basically, I don't really want to be a nurse, partly because of having to empty sputum mugs and bedpans but mainly because of the weekend shifts. They would coincide with my plans to hunt and show my horses, even though I've giving up my ambition to ride in the Olympics … by now I know I'll never be good enough. But I still want to compete with my dream horses in tons of shows. I've missed enough of these occasions while serving out my three-year sentence in the slammer. The lie that I tell the teachers is very vague. I sort of waffle around where I want to do my nurse's training … Wellington, New Plymouth, Auckland. I tell them I will decide after getting home for the holidays.

Mind you, I've already decided on my immediate future. Firstly, in a roundabout sort of way, I'm a tiny bit grateful to Miss Allum for expelling me. I would never have become a high school graduate and life would have been working at Woolworth's forever. Now I have a new, good-looking New Plymouth boyfriend, an engineering student at Canterbury University College. So I'm off to Christchurch and I'll legitimise my presence by doing a bachelor's degree at the same time.

I adored this guy, who turned out to be a kissing cousin – and now is one of my best friends as is his fabulous wife. Nev and I have the same great-grandmother and as teenagers we both lived on the same road. I suppose it's not surprising that another fleeting boyfriend also turned out to be related to me. New Zealand had only one and three-quarters of a million people in the 1950s.

My visit to Wellington is over too quickly. I wonder how many times I've enjoyed Nev's and Ruth-Mary's great welcome and the sad good-bye at the airport. It's now to Nelson and a night with a great horsey friend and her fun teenager daughter, then to familiar Christchurch. The five years that I spent at the university are all recounted in five diaries: an endless inventory of passing and failing, parties, falling in and out of love, being dumped, ski trips, being on the students' association executive, odd jobs, and endless independence …

Our education is free and Dad pays for my student board and transportation to the South Island. It doesn't really dawn on him that I need any more money. Of course whenever I return home I save my allowance by hitchhiking after the all-night ferry crossing from Lyttleton to Wellington. It does become a bit hit or miss that I get to Tupare before dark. I also have baby-sitting jobs and work for a while at the First Four Ships restaurant, but I'm certainly not cut out to be a waitress. There is so much happening in my life that it messes with my ability to remember and deliver orders. Even on my *very* first day my *very* first order ends in an ignominious disaster. "Oyster stew, please, Miss."

I carry it back to the table of five important-looking clean-cut men, in business suits. *Serve on the left, clear on the right.* As I'm about to place the bowl in front of the first gentleman, it slips in my hand and the *whole lot* of oyster stew sloshes onto the man's left shoulder. I can't stop apologising, over and over. The manageress gives me the sack on the spot, but she does help me clean up the jacket. The gentleman doesn't admonish me and tells my boss to let me have another chance, please. She does, hesitantly. After he has eaten, my customer leaves me a shilling tip – the first and the last tip I've ever received. In those days there was no tipping ever in New Zealand, except when drinks were delivered on a fancy silver salver in a fancy hotel.

My last year gets messed up when that psychology professor failed me in Psych II. So now, with only one subject and one whole year ahead to pass for my degree, I take a job as a receptionist to two notable doctors, an internist and a surgeon. The first thing I have to do is answer the phone as instructed: "Good afternoon, this is Dr McLay's and Mr Armand's surgery. May I help you please?" Unless I'm concentrating hard the words come out all wrong. "Good morning, this is Mr McLay's surgery. Oh and Dr Armand's. What do you want?"

It strikes me as dumb that when British doctors become surgeons they drop the title of Dr and are now addressed as *Mr* so and so. Someone told me that way back in the 18th century a surgeon was just a hack, like a worker in a slaughterhouse cutting the limbs off animals. Medical doctors had degrees and looked down on those men of much lower rank. In time, real doctors did additional study to become highly qualified surgeons. They reverted to using Mr in front of their names, like the hacks of old. But now it was to define them as immediately superior to the regular MDs.

My doctor employers are good to me and very good to their patients. Every single day Dr McLay has old Mrs. Watson arrive for a consultation. There's absolutely nothing wrong with her. She talks and talks to the doctor and he's always late for the rest of the morning's patients. And every single day I record Mrs Watson's visit in an official ledger and the government pays for her visit. At the end of every day's appointments, Dr McLay has me go to the liquor store around the corner to buy his small bottle of Scotch.

One day he asks if I would baby-sit his two children. They're in bed when I arrive in their lovely Fendalton home so there's nothing to do; a good opportunity to study, but I prefer to read my book. When Dr and Mrs McLay arrive home, we chat for a moment on the verandah. I don't know how the conversation turns to guns, but he asks me if I can shoot. "Yes. I'm not too bad. My father has a 22 rifle that he uses to shoot possums and any terminally sick animal. He taught us how to shoot old light bulbs as they floated down the current of the Waiwakaiho River." Showing off a bit, I add, "Bet I could shoot out that light bulb on that street's lamp post."

Dr McLay loads his gun and says that he'll cope with the town council's complaint after I smash the light. Oh how hard I try, and miss. "I think your gun needs recalibrating," I tell him and he laughs. Sadly, not long after I leave university, Dr McLay is killed in a car accident.

Across the surgery from my two doctors works another doctor. His efficient receptionist Bess and I become great friends. Bess and her boss relax and tipple a bit every night after the last patient leaves. One day I hurry into the reception room and look through the open door into the examination room. I see quite an embrace reflected in a painting on the wall.

One afternoon they have a break in the appointments and I hear this tremendous racket on the stairs. Bottles, and more bottles are tumbling down each wooden step to the ground floor. "Oh no!" Bess is yelling. I run out of our waiting room. "Liz, there was no more room in the surgery to hide all these blasted bottles and the trash man comes tomorrow. I tripped on the bloody top stair and look at what's happened!" Some of the dozens and dozens of the largest-size beer bottles sold in New Zealand lie scattered along the stairs all the way down to a heap at the bottom. Other employees in the building start appearing and gaping.

After my final exams in Christchurch I work during the Christmas holidays for Birds Eye Frozen Foods. Almost all workers are students doing seasonal work, and the wages are huge. Every payday I take ten pounds from my little brown envelope and bicycle to the P and O Shipping Line's office and make another payment towards my boat passage to England. The Birds Eye hours are long and only every eighth day is a free one. I'm lucky that all the days on which I work fall on triple-paid Christmas Day and New Year's Day and a lot of them on double-paid Sundays and one and a half paid Saturdays.

And what do I do there all day? Along with three others, I'm assigned to a conveyor belt, and hour after hour we four pick out the shells or any foreign material that's mixed in with thousands of shelled peas, all on their way to be boxed and frozen. It's consistent boring work getting all of that 'matter' out before the peas drop into a bin and move unseen to be packaged. Three of us are on the side of the belt and we rotate with the person at the end of the belt where it moves towards you. For those of us doing our sideways turn, whenever we look up the room revolves and our heads turn all giddy.

We much prefer our turn at the end of the belt, but there's also the added responsibility. Peapods are easy to weed out, but the occasional slug is a whole different matter. There's no way that I can touch a slug. My friends will isolate one and watch as the lump of live slime moves steadily towards me. "Look out, Liz." For five seconds I vacillate between my responsibility, my horror at picking up the slug and the picture of some poor little old lady treating herself to frozen peas for Christmas dinner.

Into the bin drops the slug on its journey to be boxed.

Less seriously, I accidentally drop a red throatie onto the conveyor and before I can grab it, the throat lozenge is also on its way to someone's dinner table. For those of us who survive the belts, we're eventually promoted to assembling boxes. Boring, yes, but it puts us within shouting range of the male students handling the filled boxes.

Finally, I'm promoted to sorting strawberries. We're seriously forbidden to eat a single one. It's not long before some workers sport vivid facial rashes. Those employees are gone for good by the end of the day. Two months later I'm also gone – on a boat for my O E in Britain.

Today it's a further flight to Wanaka for a happy stay with Jill and her husband John. Jill puts me to shame in so many ways. She's a superb cook and she *likes* to cook, has a pristine house and garden, never gets caught for speeding, and never loses her temper. Before they retired she and John were top farmers with four thousand idyllic acres and upwards of twenty thousand sheep in the spring. How I loved watching John direct and control his sheep dogs with different pitched whistles as the dogs herded hundreds and hundreds of sheep down from the high ranges.

Chapter Sixteen

Broken Bones

Back to Massachusetts and one very happy husband. He does such a great job when I'm away. Soon after my arrival home and quite out of the blue, Dave says, "While you were away I read about this company that does cremations for only fifteen hundred dollars. It was all written up in the *Boston Globe* and I've noted the phone number of the company in the Rolodex. Of course you know that I want to be cremated."

"Holy smoke," I mumble. "Of course. But why all these details today, like right now?" But he doesn't answer my question and comes out with another statement. "I also read that one in seven of us who are over seventy have the onset of dementia or Alzheimer's."

"Dave, what's got into you? Are you worried?"

"Yes and no."

"You poor old thing. Well, you definitely appear absolutely one hundred percent to me. So do stop worrying." But I think about the last time that Dave saw his mother in Wellington. She was in her eighties and had been moved to a nursing home. Her dementia was now at a stage where she didn't know her own son. It was a grim moment for my poor husband.

Of course it is inevitable something will eventually go wrong. Old age is so hit or miss. And how I hate the way the days are flying by, quicker and quicker. I was talking to a friend about a big event she had won last year. "Oh no," she laughed, "That was *three* years ago."

I admire Dave for being so organised and so open but it's something we have never really addressed before. He *is* close to eighty. And me? I'm closing in on seventy-five and my projected time left on this earth diminishes, faster and faster. Now that it's down to twenty-five years I decide to up the end-of-the-road to *one hundred and five*. Of course we have wills and living wills and the children will know when to pull the plug if I'm insensate before this seasoned age.

I shelve it all way in the back of my mind. But Mother's words keep popping out:

You're born, you die, and it is a principle of nature.

Marylon. All this brings her plight very much into my thoughts. I ring her and ask if she's up to my visit in a couple of weeks' time, even though she's back receiving chemo. I can get a direct flight from Boston to West Palm Beach. "Just for a night. Any longer and I'll leave you exhausted," I joke and pause. "Sorry, Marylon, that was a pathetic wisecrack."

"It's not. But just please do come." I think she's crying and I feel sick to my stomach.

"Marylon, I'll ring our travel agent tomorrow. I'll get a rental so that Doug won't have to come to the airport. I'll let you know my plans as soon as I can."

My arrival at the West Palm Beach airport always has me amazed at all the waiting elderly couples, many leaning on fancy walking sticks, gripping on to walkers or anxiously reclining in wheelchairs. And younger passengers are rushing past me towards a sea of beaming smiles and outstretched arms. It's so apparent how many elderly people have moved south to enjoy Florida's popular retirement living.

It's not for me, I decide on the spot.

I drive to Marylon's and Doug's lovely home. Marylon welcomes me as warmly as ever and immediately wants all my New Zealand and horse news. She looks destroyed by the chemo but she and Doug have great sustaining news. "We're going to be grandparents. Rachael's pregnant and she and Andy are out of their minds, and so are Doug and I."

"That's phenomenal news. When is it due?"

"Can you believe that I forgot to ask? Oh how I hope I'm still alive. You know, they were giving me those new experimental drugs, but they haven't helped. My white blood cell count is now so low that I'm at risk for infection, so they're planning on again stopping the chemo for a bit. I guess there's nothing that can fight this cancer."

"Marylon, you mustn't give up. You know the old saying about mind over matter and to think positive."

"Liz, I know you're trying to help me, but honestly I'm not optimistic. Ovarian cancer has a lousy recovery percentage."

We don't evade any topic and Marylon tries so hard to cook a superb meal in spite of my protests. We visit her horse and he looks great where he's being boarded with Ken in a notable show stable.

I fly home, so glad that I went to Florida. But somehow I don't think that I'll see my remarkable friend again.

My thoughts are constantly darting to Florida. How would I ever cope with a fatal disease? It's remarkable how Marylon can so unselfishly dwell on the lives of others while never complaining about herself. The phone goes and I welcome the distraction. I'm asked to fill in for someone in a nearby dressage clinic this afternoon. My friend's horse has suddenly gone lame. The clinic is being given by an up-and-coming rider and I'm to ride in a semi-private lesson. Minty needs shoeing so off Catch and I go in the trailer. I lead her into the indoor arena and introduce myself to the clinician, Carla. Rudely, she looks me up and down and wrinkles her nose. "Can you canter?" she asks.

I'm so flabbergasted that I stand there with my mouth hanging open. Is it all the wrinkles on my face that trigger such a demeaning question? Does she think I look past the riding retirement date? "Well, yes, I *can* actually canter," stumbles out of my mouth. It's on the tip of my tongue to add that I was jumping cross-country courses at the gallop only three years ago, but I decide to opt on the side of modesty.

"Then let me watch you warm up." She throws a condescending smile at the twenty-odd auditors sitting on plastic chairs and bales of shavings against the edge of the indoor arena. My blood boils over. I've come across this demeanour in young riders before, and so have some of my older riding friends. We're treated like has-beens and we're not capable of doing much any more. Just give us a chance.

I warm up Catch at the walk and the trot. She's faultless and I pat her and murmur, "Good girl." I ride towards the end of the arena and decide I will show this cocky young clinician that I'm not a complete dodo. I ask Catch for the canter, make a diagonal turn and have the mare perform two perfect flying changes as we cross the arena. Dressage riders know that flying changes are a fairly advanced dressage movement. But I have trained these changes-of-lead for years because they're required when jumping in show hunter competitions. They help a horse keep his balance and this also helps the rails to stay up in the stadium round of eventing. I'm not one to show off – well, I have to admit it can depend on the circumstances.

Retribution. But Carla says nothing.

The other rider in my class has warmed up and Carla starts a wasted forty-five minutes for Catch and me. The girl takes little notice of us until at one point she has me walk canter, walk canter, on and on. Catch finally says enough and breaks into yet another canter with a bit of a resistance and a crow hop when I flick her lightly with my crop. "That's why I hate chestnut fillies," says Carla in a sarcastic voice. I take this as a dismissal and voluntarily leave the ring. The auditors clap with enthusiasm and smile at me. They're a pretty savvy lot and know that I've been short-changed. I overhear someone loudly say, "You know Liz bred that gorgeous mare." Carla's standing in front of the auditors and there's no way she misses this kind remark.

The next weekend I'm in an early spring dressage show with Catch. The heat turns out to be fierce for this time of year. I'm on my own and get Catch dusted off, tack her up and paint her feet. We're ready to go. I always mount her from a high mounting block as my old arthritis defies nimbleness. Remember the backbone that looked like that of a seventy-year-old labourer? Well, it's now the backbone of a *genuine* labourer way past seventy.

The show's mounting block is some distance from where I'm all prepared beside my horse trailer, so I drag out my small grooming box. Surely I can mount Catch's small height from a foot off the ground. She stands quietly as I lift my left foot into the stirrup and I find that it's hard to bend my leg. I'm surprised how hard, until I bear in mind that I'm wearing brand-new riding boots.

Brand-new boots at your *age, Liz?*

I've put on a bit of weight since my skinny days and my two pairs of twenty-five-year-old boots have been mended, stretched, mended and stretched. One pair was made when brown boots were also *in* and have been dyed black twice. In no time the stiffness in my new boots will wear off and the leather will become pliable.

Finally my foot is in the stirrup and I start to pull myself up. With the unforgiving leather behind the knee my jolly leg refuses to bend. Inadvertently I jab Catch's sensitive chestnut side and she makes a gigantic leap sideways. All that centrifugal force is the end of me. I land on my back on the parking lot's hard stony ground. I've let go of the reins and Catch is gone.

People rush to pull me up and yell for bandages. My right arm is lacerated and bleeding all over my white breeches. It's so hot the show had announced that riders might compete without their formal jackets. Just as well, as the sleeves of my lovely jacket with the red lining, albeit twenty years old, would have been ripped. Someone has caught and leads confused little Catch to me. I hear a bystander say, "What a brat," and it rips me apart. What sensitive horse wouldn't leap aside when something sharp and unexpected rammed into her sensitive ribs?

My ride time is in ten minutes. Someone wraps a fresh cloth around my bloody arm and I hurry Catch to the standard mounting block. She's very nervous, but a friend holds her head and feeds her a peppermint while I mount. I feel her muscles relax as soon as I'm in the saddle, and just like the day I fell off jumping Minty, adrenaline drenches my body. We warm up quickly and enter the arena for our test. Somehow my right arm doesn't work very well, but we fudge through the movements as blood keeps soaking into the wrap. Sweet Catch tries so hard.

My friends crowd around me as I exit and their support is touching. But just as with that last fall off Minty, the adrenaline rush dries up and my hands start to shake. A friend offers to drive us home. I'm not a quitter, but I've lived enough years to know when to give in.

The following day something is very wrong on the right side of my upper back. I call my doctor and he orders an MRI. Oh no! The last thing in the world won't get me lying in that open coffin and be pushed into a tunnel. But I can go to Boston and be checked by a new system that is less claustrophobic.

The machine is like a huge spaceship and the round disc is lowered within six inches of my body. I'm mildly panicked, but take deep breaths and cope. At least the disc is open all around its rim. Away goes the machine, whirring, clicking, clacking, and after twenty-five minutes I'm back driving home.

Good news. A friend calls to say that we were third in our large class yesterday. The judge gave Catch high marks for all the movements to the right and poorer marks when we worked to the left. *Rider needs more outside right rein*, was the repeated comment. Then my doctor rings and says that the MRI must be repeated. I moved too much. Moved? I tried my very best to keep still under that spaceship. He does laugh when I ask him how anyone can control involuntary spasms.

The next day the repeated MRI is readable. Before the space ship is lowered I put on the eye shields from my long airplane flights and have no panic. I'm next sent to my orthopaedic doctor. "Another fall from a horse?" he laughs.

"Well, yes. Sort of. I was only halfway into the saddle this time. But something's not right and after those rotator cuff injuries I'm pretty sure that this is a different injury."

He sends me for X-rays at the hospital across the road. I wait and wait in a populated room and listen to the entire range of every possible ailment with their ghastly details. The X-rays are taken of the front and the back of me and after another long wait the radiologist calls me into his office.

He's very friendly. "Well, Mrs Benney, I know you!" He remembers me from when we lived eighteen years ago in that yuppie Boston suburb. He still lives there and I pretend to remember him too, but it means that I can't ask him under what circumstances we ever met ... was it a positive or a negative encounter?

He says he's sorry about what he has to tell me. "You've broken your right shoulder blade. The break is four inches long. And I see that you've broken it before. I seldom see shoulder blade breaks. They're most unusual and you've had *two*!"

He grins and I feel a bizarre sense of pride.

"Yes, in 1966," I explain, "when I was competing a horse for someone. The jump was a high hanging picket gate and this horse, called Kerry Doon, caught the top of the gate. The whole jump broke loose and tripped her up, pitching me off as the poor thing fell on her knees and face. I landed on my back on a small hidden flat rock."

Doc continues chatting. "I see that you've also broken four ribs in the past. How did that happen?"

"I was turning out a brood mare, actually the grandmother of the horse that I fell away from on Sunday. Stupidly, I didn't turn her head to me as I unsnapped the lead shank. She was so happy to see the other mares at the end of the field that she gave this whopping buck and a back hoof caught me in the chest. I was lucky that she hit me fair and square on the right breast. The doctor said that the target was well placed to save me from having a punctured lung."

"Well, no riding for six weeks." Pause. "Now go back to your orthopaedic doctor and he'll fit you with a sling. And by the way, I've just noticed your age. Maybe this is the time to give up riding altogether."

As my orthopaedic doctor fits me with a fancy contraption to stabilise my shoulder, I'm told again that I must not ride for six weeks. Did both doctors forget to forbid me to drive? Or maybe they think that it's pointless. I head for the door and a parting shot follows me, "Liz, I really think it's time you *stopped* riding."

While driving home those words are still ringing in my ears. Yes, I'm now a little nervous riding Catch and I honestly wonder how much longer I can enjoy her super talent. At least my old Minty is extremely solid and easygoing. I take heart that most people think I'm ten years younger than the date on my irrefutable birth certificate. Okay, I might look it, but the raw fact is that I am *not* ten years younger and every darned year goes by quicker and quicker and the terminus comes closer and closer. Damn, damn and damn, getting old! And now poor Dave will have to do my share of the farm work as well as his own. I don't know how willing or capable I would be if I had to double up on the day's routine.

I shove the thought out of the way and turn on the radio.

A month has now gone by and my fracture continues to mend. I can lift my arm within forty-five degrees of vertical, have little pain and can sleep at last. The bruising has almost gone and people have stopped making corny jokes and laughing at them when they see the blackened half of my face. I look up scapula fractures on the Internet and I've certainly beaten the odds. As the doctor said, these fractures are rare and they generally occur in men only, and men aged between twenty-five and forty-five. Added to this information is that the breaks almost always occur in high-risk sports like hang-gliding and rock climbing. My shoulder blade break happens in only one per cent of all fractures and I've had *two* of them. Now it makes sense that the doctors were so interested in the details of my accidents.

Sue has been generously working overtime. She has found a good lawyer who says that her case is the most interesting one on which he has ever worked. Sue is now formally filing for divorce and the lawyer thinks that he can get her the house and chattels. As Sue expected, the bigamist wants everything. "Hey, Karl declared I was dead with that faked death certificate," Sue laughs, "so he should automatically get everything." But I notice a twitch on her face. Finding that forged death certificate and reading how she died in a terrible car accident still upsets Sue.

The lawyer sees right through the bigamist. A court appearance is scheduled and it's a preliminary to the division of the spoils. Sue has also discovered that her husband has signed her name and taken out most of the equity in the house. As Sue points out to me, "Of course if I were dead, it wouldn't be necessary for the idiot to sign my name."

One bright spot in my day is that Kathy, my trainer, has another new date tonight. I can't wait to hear about this man with the consummate Internet credentials. He's exceptional looking (from his photo which we assume really is of *him* and at his *present* age) and four years older than Kathy.

She comes the next day and long-lines my horses as I'll be riding again soon. I can tell by her expression that all was not well. "Another short-lived date, Liz. Good looking, yes, a bit heavy on the wine and questionable manners, but not too bad. Now, can you honestly believe what he did when we said goodbye outside the restaurant? Fred said that he would be overjoyed to see me again and he hugged me. Then suddenly he bit me so crudely on the neck I thought that my jugular vein was going to split open. Is this called affection?"

We laugh so loudly there's static on the radio.

Friends visit this weekend to check me out. They bring some of their youngsters and we do the usual horse tour while I talk about their upkeep and their quirks and the children taste the horses' grain – ugh! We sit for cold drinks and I entertain the little ones with some old ditties. I like being useful again and I'm impressed that I can recall some of the old catchy jingles of my youth.

> *'My Bonnie leaned over the gas tank*
> *The height of the contents to see.*
> *She lighted a match to assist her,*
> *Oh send back my Bonnie to me!'*

> *'Mama, what's that upon the line that looks like raspberry jam?'*
> *'Hush, hush my dear, 'Tis just Papa run over by a tram!'*

> *'Algie met a bear.*
> *The bear was bulgy.*
> *The bulge was … Algie!'*

> *'Mary had a little lamb,*
> *Its fleece was black as soot,*
> *And into Mary's pail of milk*
> *His sooty foot he put.'*

Some psychiatrists condemn horror tales for children. These kids just laugh and laugh over these ditties. They're great for their imagination.

Chapter Seventeen

The Ceiling's Falling Down

Why do the seasons fly by faster and faster every year? Spring has come already and Marylon and Doug are grandparents of an exquisite little girl, Isabelle. I'm hoping that this news will help Marylon fight the cancer. But things don't look good and yet I never hear one whimper from my friend. "I don't think I'll ever ride again, Liz," she tells me on the phone today, "but I've had a great innings."

"I would say a spectacular innings," I tell her with easy sincerity, "what with your being twice the circuit champion in the Winter Equestrian Festival series. You have nothing more to prove."

"Thanks. Right now I'm thinking about finding a great retirement home for Tucker," and she pauses. "Sorry, but I must hang up, now. Better lie down for a bit. They're starting the chemo up again tomorrow. It looks like my darned white blood cells refuse to do their thing. Bye."

The farmhouse is empty, the vet has graduated and at last it is time to sell. Dave and I have spent eighteen years restoring and then maintaining this old house. And add our patience when coping with countless tenants. We reflect back to the vet student, Anne, and her animal collection. She had several adopted dogs including one with a leg missing and the one that had heart surgery with a pace-maker implanted which Anne thinks she'll be paying for long after the dog expires of old age. I can't count the number of rescued cats, including one with three legs, and there was a baby pot-belly pig, pet rabbits, birds ... It took days for them all to leave for another state.

I grit my teeth when I think of the couple who had a great time fooling Dave and me with their righteousness, right down to Mass every Sunday. They always paid on time, and when they left on account of a job change, benevolent Dave and me told them not to pay the last month's rent. Instead they could apply the security deposit which we were holding. Never again, and we still steam when we think of the sickening mess that met us when we checked out the apartment. They spring-cleaned all their possessions and left the throwaways in drawers, cupboards, and the fridge. Everything else was in a gigantic pile of junk just outside the back door. All of it should have been taken to the dump. To top it off we found a broken window, cleverly concealed by a half-drawn blind that wouldn't move up or down. Parts of it had been jimmied. I used to feel sorry for the couple.

Another tenant collected injured pigeons and what a carnage when a coyote got into the large outdoor cage. And we've had tenants who needed to bury dogs in special places, or those whose complaints drove us nuts, such as "There's a bent curtain rod in the living room. And the back door rattles when it's windy. What do I do about it?"

Be tolerant, Elizabeth!

We've also had wonderful tenants who in no way ever complained. Cindy and her policeman husband, Bruce, never told us that three elements on their stove had broken a long time ago. And Cindy was cooking for four people every day. We found out when Aussie Jim and Meghan told us.

But the time has come to cut down on the ongoing foibles of renters, not to mention the work and expense of maintaining the farmhouse and garden. It's tough to admit, but, after reaching our seventies, our stocks of energy and patience are going headlong downhill.

Okay, so we've both decided that it's time to sell the old house, but what should go with it? About nine acres, along with the two antique barns, or shall we sell just the old house with three and a half acres? I'm ashamed to say that I'm responsible for a lot of vacillating. Three different times the surveyors mark off three different lot lines because I'm the one who can't decide how much to sell, or, more specifically, need to sell. To complicate it all, we're going to lose our official frontage, and we'll have to build a new driveway down a steep hill to the main road. Some will view it as a mini ski run. Dave and I view it as more *creativity*.

We finally determine that it is best to get rid of the whole nine acres and the buildings all at once, and we locate a real estate agent named Margery. She specialises in horse properties and after *much* debating over the price the property will go on sale in a month. That gives us time to get back to work cleaning up the interior of the house and turning the yard into a showpiece. We make a list.

The septic system must pass inspection.

The fire department must check that there are functional alarms.

We must put a radon detector in the basement to prove that there's none of this cancer-causing gas which occurs naturally and is bad in certain areas where there are ore-bearing rocks in the earth's crust.

We must prove that we owe no taxes on the property.

That there is no lien.

That there is no lead paint anywhere.

We must quickly make many small repairs.

Meanwhile we try not to take any notice of the news. There's more and more talk about the declining housing market and the US's collapsing economy. But we're cocky owners. How could anyone resist this large private lot at the end of a dead-end road, with an updated one hundred-year-old house, two restored barns and one with two brand-new loose boxes and a large fenced-in field for horses?

We hire a really talented craftsman, Mark, but whenever I appear he stops working and talks and talks, then charges us from the moment he arrives until he leaves. Often I can't get away from him without being outright rude with the chance he'll become offended and will walk straight off the job. He really gets on a roll when he's on to his loathsome wife, from whom he is separated. She does arrive at the farm one day and starts one heck of a fight. She clearly inherited the worst of all physical as well as personality genes. Then suddenly Mark disappears. He has two days left to finish. I phone and phone him and finally he answers and says that he has been offered a great permanent job. He never sends me a bill for his last few working days.

Apart from some minor repairs that Mark abandoned, all is ready.

The farmhouse is on the market.

Six frustrating months go by. Only two different couples ever come to view the property and they think it's overpriced. "Well, have them make us an offer," I tell the agent. And hear nothing more. Meanwhile Dave and I plod on keeping the land looking like a corner of Kew Gardens. So much more *maintenance* than we ever planned.

Our contract with Margery runs out and we welcome great-grandmother Marla. In the local paper Dave read about her record sales and we both agree that this will be our gal. She works in an office managed by Ed who, we find, is a man truly fitting the job. Meanwhile, with the darned economy shrinking ever more, the value of our *irresistible* piece of property is going down and down. Quick, Marla, please see what you can do as winter is coming.

For a starter, she recommends that we sell just the house with three and a half acres. It will be easier in the current market. Later we can sell the two old barns with four acres, now referred to on yet another new survey map as Lot 2.

Within the first week, Marla brings two different people to view the old house and all of a sudden we have our very first potential buyer. "I'm madly interested," she tells us. "I love it," she gushes. "It's out of this world," and she waves her hands in the air. A deal is in the making.

By now it's late autumn, and of course the last thing we want to do is maintain the heat in an unsold house, so we're really keeping up our hopes. But one never relaxes about a deal until the money's in the bank. The buyer could be a Dr Jekyl or Mr Hyde or, in this case she, the potential buyer, could drop dead, or lose her job and her money could suddenly go down the tube. Some potential buyers turn out to be just having fun looking at everything for sale. There are many horror stories that Marla relates to us. But I feel heaps of optimism on this fabulous late autumn day.

Temperature: 42 degrees.

Sunshine: Brilliant.

Wind speed: Zero.

Minty and Catch. Noteworthy dressage lessons on both of them today. And I recall the day, years ago, that my horse had gone so well and I joked that I would have a bumper sticker made and it would read, *Happiness is a horse going well.* I had a friend at this boarding stable whose horse was such a pig on most days he refused to leave the stable yard unless he was given a lead. "Liz, just make my sticker, *Happiness is a horse going!*"

The phone breaks into my flashbacks. "Liz, Liz, quick, for goodness sake quick, get down to the farmhouse. The first floor is completely under water and the ceilings are all falling down."

Holy smoke.

I jump into my car and cut two driveway corners by flying over the grass. Marla hasn't exaggerated. *No way.* More than two inches of water cover the downstairs kitchen floor, the living room and the two downstairs' bedroom floors. Everywhere the ceiling is crashing down and the rafters are being exposed as water gushes from dozens of fresh openings.

I rush upstairs and three of the old-fashioned freestanding heating units have become fire hoses. We race to switch off both burners in the basement, but where on earth does one turn off the water? To make matters worse, the potential buyer – P B – arrives. Marla had forgotten that she was coming.

P B shouts that she knows a lot about plumbing and she splashes to the basement door. She hauls it open and the water floods down the basement steps while P B is a descending jellyfish, glancing off each old step. Marla and I cast extremely doubtful looks at each other. P B hits every knob and turns off every faucet that she can find. We tear back upstairs and water's still gushing through the ceilings, but it lessens as we watch. I feel my soaking feet start to freeze. Slowly the deluge becomes a trickle. I drive back to the house and phone the heating company.

And the culprit?

Aging pipes?

Poor maintenance by the heating company?

Sabotage?

We need an answer and quickly.

P B says she must go home.

Dave has been out mowing a field and joins us. The three of us spend *five* hours mopping up and throwing out the remains of the ceilings, which now include great soaking piles of insulation. Added to our dismay are the two fire alarms that refuse to stop beeping. We disconnect them and they still won't shut up. Much of the insulation remains stuck up in the rafters in the master bedroom, which turns out to have this lower false ceiling. "Get me a ladder, Liz," says Marla. In fifteen minutes, this great-grandmother, who is ten years younger than me, is up the rungs, pulling out screeds of dripping material.

A cold weather front is coming through tonight and the temperatures are predicted to go way down below freezing with out-of-control winds compounding the situation. We *must* have heat in the old house.

At last the oil company arrives and after a long frustrating time they manage to find and fix the problem. We're so preoccupied with finishing the mopping that we just hear the men yell the good news up the basement stairs. "Everything's fixed and working," and they're gone before we can catch them outside.

A new problem arises. "I hate to say it," says Marla, "but of course the sale will be off. Who wants a house that has been flooded and winter is coming?" Could it happen again? The house is approaching its century mark and has experienced the wear and tear of many occupants. Now, with the sale at stake, we don't know how to turn the water back on.

Another call to the oil company. "We're not plumbers," I'm told. It's now after business hours and I get a picture of this guy into his third beer before a raging fire.

Surely the P B will know where she turned off the water. I call her and just get her answering machine. Dave runs to feed the animals and I really study every lever and faucet in the basement. It's hit or miss and I worry about creating another crisis. But ten minutes later I move a lever and water flows once more.

The three of us continue drying off walls and floors with all the old towels we can find. We manage to quiet the bleeping fire alarms by yanking out every wire in sight. We lock up the house, and exhausted Marla says she'll phone P B and tell her all is going to be okay.

We hope.

And of course new ceilings must be installed and everything painted.

Just before going to bed I tell Dave that I'd better check that everything's still working. I unlock the front door of the aged house and there's an earsplitting hiss coming from upstairs. I race two at a time up the steep stairs to the second floor. I follow the sound and grope for the lights in one of the bedrooms. I can't see a thing. The air is a thick haze. I reach the well-seasoned radiator and steam is *pouring* from a safety valve.

Home again to phone the oil company. A man arrives within fifteen minutes. It's nice Frank, or is it Fred, one of the men who had been here earlier.

A quick adjustment is made to a leaky valve and instantly there is blessed quiet. We have heat again and everything can finish drying out as the north wind blasts across a black countryside. But back downstairs I check each room – and, oh no! There's a steady drip of water through one of the fire alarms and another one right through one of the kitchen lights. Back to the house and I find two buckets. The drip is noisier now against the bottoms of the metal buckets. It reminds me of the old Chinese drip, drip, drip torture – or is it Japanese?

I stand in the empty house. Do other Senior Citizens have so much drama in their lives? I've aged ten years in ten hours.

Of course the next day we all wonder what went wrong. The two buckets are now half full but the dripping has stopped. The oil company makes another visit to check out everything. At Sunday rates. The man explains what had happened. It turns out that showing great responsibility, the brilliant-professor forgot to turn off a tap that morning! He was doing his responsible part of a monthly maintenance of the old-fashioned steam heating system, always done by tenants in the past. A lever must be turned on to allow water to fill up a glass container. The water must come up to a certain marked level and then off you turn the tap, quickly.

We don't blame Dave at all for forgetting to turn off the water, because he *is* in his high seventies. But because of that simple task being forgotten, tremendous pressure built up. The force of the water that should have been turned off had to go somewhere so it exploded through the three old heating units.

How lucky that Marla arrived soon after the flood began.

And now – has the wreckage wrecked the sale?

We get up on Monday morning with masses of unanswered questions. We need a person to restore the ceilings, someone to paint them, the insurance company to pay up and then increase our rates for three years. "Sorry, Mrs Benney, but this is standard procedure after a claim has been paid." We decide to forget about the insurance claim and pay everything ourselves. Fewer hassles and we can use the flood expenses to offset some of the capital gains taxes on the sale.

Outside our main house and against the old stone wall are nine heavy-duty black leaf bags, each about four feet high and crammed with the sodden remains of the ceilings. They'll never fit into the dumpster for Friday's collection.

Inside the house I hear the drum of our washing machine crashing against the machine's wall in a drunken spin cycle. Oh no. I turn it off. It reminds me of Mother's very first washing machine on spin. If the clothes were not well balanced, the whole machine would sound just the same, jump off the small floor guards, bang into the table, rattle across the floor and crash into the tub before zooming to the back door. When I was a little girl I loved to picture what would happen if the electric cord were longer or had become unplugged. The machine would spin through the washhouse door and roll its way down the steep hill to end up in the rushing rapids of the Waiwakaiho.

What on earth will now go wrong for us? Tentatively we check out the old farmhouse and the heat is working well and we marvel at the original patterned maple floors that look better than ever. To help our mood, a contractor arrives quickly and thinks that the situation is hilarious. But he does come with a good reputation and gives us a fair quote to restore the ceilings, paint everything and make the old house saleable again.

Later in the day P B comes back with her three delightful children and her brand-new boyfriend. He is very quiet but polite and has a big silver stud piercing the middle of his tongue.

They still want the house.

Of course I would like the sale to go through within a week but house sales always take many weeks as the lawyers add up their hours, going back and forth over the Purchase and Sale and other agreements. There is endless checking to be sure a second time that we've paid all of the town taxes on the place, that there are no liens, no contaminants buried on the land and on and on. But there is one piece of good news. The oil company comes up with a great idea. They set up two units with lights that will flash if the inside temperature drops below fifty degrees. Now, before bed, we just glance down at the old house and hopefully see no flashes.

I think about a temperature of fifty degrees. Not long ago we kept our house at sixty-eight degrees in the winter. A year ago, Dave and I agreed we needed it upped to seventy degrees. Now there are days when I turn the thermostat to a nursing home temperature.

When Dave and I lived in our old suburban home and the children were teenagers, we had a wood-burning stove on the lower floor. Apart from the pleasure it gave us we saved a lot of money on oil for the central heating system. One year, in an insane mood, we – well it was actually *I* – decided to see how long we could heat the house with just wood. Oh how that temperature kept on dropping and the children could see their condensing breath when they were in bed. We would all pile on more and more blankets and more clothes during the day. We made it until January 6 when some of the pipes froze.

Today things are more or less back to normal on Tahuri Farm. I email my eventing friend Margaret in New York, and relate our latest dramas, including how our washing machine chose to break down on top of the farmhouse crisis and how the repairman said that it was beyond fixing and yet it's only six years old. "And there are only two of you, Mrs. Benney. But, um, by the way, do you ever wash really heavy things in it?" he asked.

"I'm embarrassed to confess that I do wash all my heavy winter horse blankets."

"That will do it," he guffawed, and slapped his hands on his sides.

I wonder why people find other people's misfortunes so funny.

Of course I don't usually admit to this very unhygienic use of my washing machine. Only horse people understand.

Margaret emails back that she, too, experienced the identical broken washing machine failure last week. She's lucky to have two machines. She also writes: 'I was running back and forth, from the barn's laundry room and to the house dryer. It's so exhausting. It reminds me of the same thing that occurred many years ago when the house machine broke and I had to use the one in the barn. I happened to be so mad at my previous husband that I put his underwear in with my saddle pads. A couple of days later, he said he couldn't imagine how he got this dreadful irritating rash!'

Chapter Eighteen

Saying Goodbye

I'm not into self-analysis but I do wonder why I've been showing more and more signs of irresponsibility. I give the cats dog kibble by mistake and they gobble it down. Two of them throw up an hour later.

I need a coffee from Dunkin Donuts, drive into the parking area and smell burning. My hand brake is still on. What's more, there's a big red sign facing me on the dashboard: *Brake.*

I go to the post office to get my mail and buy a book of stamps and leave them lying on the counter. I'm home before I've smartened up and have to drive back. Nice Gene is still on duty and hands them to me with a grin. "I'm in a scatty mood today," I apologise.

"You're in a what?" Well it turns out that scatty's not a word used in the US.

Then I'm off to the Town's Collection Office to pay the local taxes on our land. "I'm sure the addition is correct," I say to the clerk as she tots up the figures on her calculator.

"Yes, and *good* for you," I'm told with a mighty emphasis on the word *good*. It's clear she's impressed that this old gal got it right. I almost add, "And I didn't use a calculator." Even so, my eyesight is declining and I find myself writing larger words and bigger than normal figures. I'd better think about the replacement of my lenses.

It's two months since the farmhouse flood and the P B hasn't backed out. At last the day arrives for the formal closing and we're in a predictable lawyer's meeting room – leather chairs, a highly polished reproduction antique table, portraits of lawyers long gone, pens advertising the law office and a fake oriental carpet beneath us.

There's no sign of P B. "She suffers from a chronic tardy syndrome," her lawyer tells us as he savours his words. I'm jittery until we hear someone outside our room in a very one-sided argument. P B makes a majestic entrance followed by her Canadian boyfriend. Perhaps now we can drop that P for Prospective Buyer.

The procedure begins.

We have to show identification and I have to prove that I'm a permanent resident as I'm still a New Zealand citizen. We sign and sign and sign in many places with no time to read anything. I ask the buyer's lawyer what *are* we signing away? "It's all routine, Mrs Benney. Don't worry." Our lawyer affirmatively nods his head.

Pens are back on the table. The deal is done and when the deed is registered in the Worcester Courthouse tomorrow, we'll get the cheque. Money in the bank!

No more huge town and insurance taxes to pay.

No more demanding tenants.

No more floods.

No more *maintenance* of the old house.

No more hard work mowing the lawns, raking leaves, weeding and cutting the farmhouse field.

My mind flips to the sixty-seven acres we have left. More lawns to mow, fields to cut, leaves to rake and weeds to tackle. I'm starting to wonder how many more years it can all be held together.

Meanwhile my dressage is progressing quite well. Of course I still plan to jump … my passion for sixty-two years, but I just haven't got around to it. Sometimes I lie in bed and know that I can do it again, and any doubts are pushed aside. The skill has to be there after so many years consolidating it, and I will definitely discipline myself to ride without stirrups. And I will go to a gym for consultation with a trainer and get his help to strengthen my legs. All I need is stability in the saddle.

This morning I was looking at some of my old jumping photos, taken over the past ten years. As time flies by each photo shows that my legs have slipped further and further back from their old tight, correct position close to the girth. Then I sense from certain well-meant innuendoes that some of my friends are anxious about me riding at all. Two days ago I went for my annual check-up and my doctor's first words, with a big grin, were, "Any falls lately?"

I'm quick today. "You mean out of bed, in the bath, down the stairs or over the edge of a carpet?"

Ah well. I believe my flat riding is totally safe, although I'm still nervous getting on little Catch. She's a smart filly and well remembers how my toe burrowed into her side at the show, and the dramatic consequences. Whenever we go off the farm to ride in a clinic or a show I need someone to stand at her head and distract her with a cube of sugar or a peppermint. Once I'm in the saddle she's perfect. Well, perfect in an arena. In the trails she's also faultless unless something unexpected happens, like a deer flying across the path. Her instinct is one of flight and she likes to add crow-hops as she tries to take off. Will she get me off again?

I must say I'm lucky to have great bone density. My doctor orders bone scans every two years and he reports that I have the bone strength of a young person. Nothing is brittle and the breaks have all been stupid accidents. I guess that *nothing* is going to hold up against the driving force of a large mare's back hoof landing on my right breast and breaking so many ribs. And nothing would have saved my scapula after Kerry Doon crashed over a large jump, and a flat rock happened to be in the way of my back. And anyone would break their scapula again if their back landed on a hard-packed parking lot at a dressage competition. Forget about the broken fingers and toes.

Today I ride Minty in the trails and he has such a sensible attitude. We pass a back yard with children screaming and running around, and the dad burning leaves. Minty barely looks their way. I'm sure that Catch would have exploded and who knows where either of us would have ended up. Way in the back of my mind is the nagging thought – how long can I cope with her random antics? Ten years ago none of these thoughts would have entered my head. I drive to get the mail in our post office box and keep mulling over the rotten passage of time. I quail when I think about the constant foreshortening of my future years and everything I want to accomplish.

"Look at this, Dave!" I call after collecting the mail. "MIT's travel department is organising a trip to the Antarctic in late November. Let's go!"

His face gives away his answer before he speaks. "*No way!* And anyway, I have classes to teach. Nothing would persuade me to go. Honestly, you know I'm too old for travel excitement. But you go. You've wanted to visit this area for years. Where does the tour leave from?" I pore through this new information.

"It begins in Miami and we fly to Santiago in Chile. We spend a night there and get in some sightseeing, then fly to Ushuaia at the southern point of Argentina and from where the boat leaves."

I read on. I've got to have a doctor's health certificate, be able to take the cold, be able to clamber over rocks and over ice and snow. I must be able to leap in and out of Zodiacs. They're described as little motorised rubber boats that can boomerang in rough seas.

I can do it.

Yes.

It's a land I've dreamt of seeing, and I've read so many books about Antarctica. My longing started in my university days when the continent was just opening up and I had a couple of friends who visited Scott Base and sent me exotic postcards. Years ago I planned to make the trip on one of the popular non-stop round air flights from New Zealand. At least I could *see* some of the Antarctic even if it were from the air. Then came the tragic accident when the Air New Zealand plane crashed into Mt Erubus in 1979. That marked the end of the tourist flights.

Ten years ago a New Plymouth friend, George, took a Russian boat from Invercargill to the Antarctic. It is still being advertised, but George discouraged me. The ship takes too many days to reach the remote continent, it is very uncomfortable, and has no stabilisers.

Insurance is highly recommended for this current trip. *If* I have to be evacuated, a plane is all that can get me out in a hurry and at a cost of twenty-eight thousand dollars. I run to my study to phone the MIT travel agent. "Mrs Benney, you're in luck. I can give you the very last single cabin. And it's a fancy one on the top deck."

I pause. The extravagance.

"Yes," I tell her.

"So, do you have a booking?" Dave asks when I come downstairs.

"I've got the last cabin for one person."

"Where's it located?"

"Top deck."

"My goodness. How much is it?"

"I've forgotten," and I dash out of the room.

I tack up Minty and go for a long hack in the trails. It is so peaceful and I become quite pensive. I think about how Dave so readily accepts my independence and my propensity for what I suppose one could call melodrama. Way back when we were dating, it astonished me that he really liked this characteristic in me. The culture of the times was more that man certainly loves woman, but expects woman to be moulded to the house and kitchen sink, raise the children and be free of decision-making and anything financial. Dave and I are total opposites and it is just as well as it wouldn't have taken long for our lives to go down a disastrous course. I call him My Rock of Gibraltar as he does put his foot down when my unrealistic and goofy moments reach the limit.

Of course we women were expected to have some sort of career before marriage, and reasonable jobs were generally limited to nursing, school teaching or secretarial work, and then marriage ended one's profession in 'early retirement.' There were, of course, a few exceptions for brilliant people like Mother's high school friend, Marion Steven. Upon graduation, Marion obeyed her medical father and reluctantly became a doctor. Now, having satisfied her dad, the door was open for her to forget about medicine and pursue the love of her life. She went on to obtain first class honours in both Greek and Latin and became a professor at Canterbury University College.

Mother happened to mention to Marion that I was about to go to Canterbury and from our very first meeting a friendship of almost fifty years began. I used to laugh with Marion about our camaraderie … the intellectual and accomplished professor, and the totally contrasting me. Our only common root was that we both came from Taranaki and knew Mother. But on a lighter note we did share a loathing for cooking and all forms of housework. But where, out of a sense of duty, I did my domestic best, Marion never rose to that occasion. Her house was a disaster right down to the roof leaking, wallpaper peeling off the walls and dirty dishes everywhere.

I wonder where Dave's pride in my independence comes from. And I ride on with a great sense of gratitude until thoughts of Marylon's fight with death choke my mind. Why did cancer strike such a stunning friend? Why isn't she responding to chemo? Then, out there in the lonely woods, I have to grin to myself … Marylon loves to cook!

I'm dreaming of Antarctica and the phone goes. "Liz, it's Marylon." I can tell by her voice that things are not okay. "As you know," she continues so softly I can hardly hear her, "Hospice care is coming every day to our house. They're an amazing team and they regulate my morphine and explain things to Doug. They're keeping me comfortable and free of pain. They also want me to ring my best friends to say goodbye. I have about three or four days left to live."

"Marylon. Oh no. It's happening so suddenly. I thought you still had months to fight this thing." I start struggling for words. "You sound so brave. Do you want to talk about it all?"

"Yes."

"Of course I knew things were not looking very optimistic. Are you afraid?"

"No. Not really. I just don't want any pain. I think I have everything in order, but it's so tough on Doug and the boys and their wives. And my sister of course."

"You're amazing. You always think of others first."

Silence.

"I'm sure you're having a church funeral," I say, "and it will be overflowing with all the people who love you."

"Yes, a church funeral. And of course I'm being cremated."

"Marylon, would you like me to give a eulogy at the funeral?"

"Oh Doug!" she calls out in her old normal voice. "Liz is going to give my eulogy. Oh Liz, thank you, thank you. This is the most wonderful news."

"Marylon, I will truly love doing it for you. You're such an inspiration. What a friend you have been and how I will miss you."

We talk a little longer. Then Marylon says so quietly, "I must stop now, Liz. I love you. Goodbye."

"I love you too, Marylon. Goodbye." And the phone clicks at the other end.

I sit, empty, for a very long time.

The church has standing room only. The family gathers in the front pew: Doug, Marylon's two handsome sons Andy and Gill, and their lovely wives Rachel and Marsha, and Marylon's sweet sister Carolyn. I am right behind them. Doug turns around and whispers to me. "Liz, do remember to speak slowly or no one will understand that accent of yours." We both smile and I walk up to the lectern.

"Four days before she died, Marylon called me in Massachusetts. 'I want to say goodbye,' she said in a tired but clear voice. And she told me how all the life supports had now been withdrawn, how Hospice was coming every day, how she was okay, fine, and totally at peace with the whole procedure of dying. There would be no more pain and her dear Doug was going to be with her the whole time.

"We talked very frankly for about five minutes, when suddenly she said she had better stop now. From somewhere a compulsive comment just came out of my mouth 'Do you want me to eulogise you, Marylon?'

"'Doug,' she called out, 'Liz wants to eulogise me. Yes!' So here I am and it's the least I could do for her.

"After hanging up the phone, I was pretty upset, and thought about our last exchange, 'Goodbye.' No, I decided, don't call our last conversation a 'goodbye'. I grew up with two better words. 'So long' we always said in my homeland, New Zealand, and never the finality of 'goodbye'. I want to use those two little words today, Marylon, since there's nothing totally final about your passing. Because for all of us assembled here you will always be in our minds, our thoughts, our recollections and our hearts.

"You are leaving so many of us a wonderful legacy of friendship, camaraderie, and love. And a legacy of how to die with such dignity and nobility. You were a charitable woman, you quickly forgave those who occasionally bugged you, and what a hostess you were and what an incredible competitor, displaying sportsmanship at its very best. You would call me and recount your fabulous horse show successes and your failures too. 'You won't believe it, Liz, but I lent up Tucker's neck and had the worst chip at the last jump. Blew the class. Stupid me.' And she would laugh.

"All of us here today share so much in common with Marylon, whether it is our love of life, our love of family, our love of horses and dogs, our love of books, and so much more. And I bet many of you also share her sense of humour, her artistry – and by the way, didn't Marylon dress beautifully.

However, I doubt very much that there are many here who can equally share with Marylon the words 'courage' and 'grit.' Honestly, throughout this whole ordeal, her bravery was remarkable and unfailing.

"It was two years, almost to this day, that Marylon called me. 'You won't believe it,' she said, 'but I've just had my ovaries out and some of my intestines. I've got cancer.' It was all so sudden. I had stayed with her and Doug a few weeks before and she appeared in terrific form.

"And so the battle started. 'I'm going to fight it,' she told me with the strength of a warrior. There was no lament, no anger and never any outward sign of fear.

"The months went by with the highs and lows, the CA-125 index falling and falling and all of us celebrating this positive number and then the beastly count rising once more, the chemotherapy continuing on and on with its awful side-effects, and the purchase of wigs. With such humour Marylon modeled them for me when we were last together. We talked and emailed often, and I can honestly say I never once heard this remarkable woman complain, not even in a brief whimper.

"Meanwhile and steadfastly Doug was at her side, supporting, loving and always helping. We all thank you for your many, many emails Doug. Your honesty and sincerity were so moving and we have all shared the agony you have been through. 'It's gut-wrenching,' you wrote in one email, 'but we soldier on.'

"When Marylon decided on the Hospice help you wrote: 'She wants to sleep and be free of pain. At first, the entire Hospice idea seemed monstrous, but the sheer relief in Marylon's voice tells me that it's the right choice.'

"Yes.

"Without her children and her sister, and especially without you, Doug, the end would not have been easy for Marylon. Oh the many times that she told me how much she loved you. 'He's a keeper, Liz.' And how I delighted in your email about two weeks ago, saying that the horrible nasal tube was out at last and you could comfortably kiss Marylon again. Passionately, again!

"And how often she talked proudly of her wonderful sons Gill and Andy, her beautiful daughters-in-law Marsha and Rachel, and her brand-new first grandchild, Isabelle, who is doing so well after a shaky start. And of course her very close sister, Carolyn. How we can delight in the memory that you all spent a wonderful Christmas together this past year. And delight in the thrill she had when her horse won a blue, just over three weeks ago. Good job, Ken.

"To see so many of you here is a magnificent tribute to a special friend.

"God bless you, Marylon.

"Godspeed.

"So long."

Marylon is the third of my close friends to die. My university roommate Jenny was killed instantly on Mt Egmont by a falling rock when she was close to the summit. My old friend Nev came up from Wellington and together we attended her funeral. Later, at Jenny's house on the family farm, her mother took me to her bedroom and asked me to select something of Jenny's. I chose my friend's *World Atlas*. "I'm never going to touch this room, ever again," the mother declared. "It will always remain as when Jenny walked out of it for the last time." Years later I questioned that decision and with such sadness.

Elizabeth, leaving things untouched can sometimes help the grieving cope with their loss.

My first best friend in America, Anneta, died of lung cancer and now my old school mate, Inge, is fighting bone cancer in New Zealand. We talk every month, and like Marylon she is stoic and uncomplaining. I reflect on Dave's and my advancing age. Yes, we are in a generation bracket when more and more of our family and friends are reaching life's conclusion. My thoughts fly to my brother, Richard. Will he be next? At the rate that his Parkinson's is progressing he can't live for many more years. How he joked in his healthy days that he would outlive me by years and I would say, "Betcha wrong."

"Hey, Liz, don't forget that I've got a fourteen-and-a-half year head start on you!"

Until recently I've never really thought much about dying ... that is, about *me* dying. I'm not at all afraid, but I do want to live much longer and accomplish much more. Not long ago a relative said to me, "You do know that you will see your wonderful mother again?" I was quite shocked and replied, "Of course I would love to." *But* I very much doubt that I will. As Richard once said to me, "Leave the door-of-doubt open a crack, Liz. You never know!" But neither of us really believes in the wonderful concept of heaven and hell. To me this started eons ago, to control the masses. "You be good and you'll go to heaven. You be bad and it is hell for you." I read about a study of people dying in nursing homes and how those who doubt that there is a heaven and a hell have a much easier time of letting go.

Getting old is a bummer. So many New Zealand friends of our generation have started moving from the land or from their large sprawling family homes to small town houses and condominiums. Most are ending up with limited outside space to maintain, or nothing at all. Some are even talking about assisted living facilities. While our age group is planning ahead, Dave and I are also planning. We want to downsize, too ... well, four more acres are ready to go. That will mean sixty-three acres left!

Sometimes we look at each other and shake our heads. How long will we be able to manage what is left? How long will we be able to afford all the help we will need? People talk about the golden years. What tommy rot. Getting old is a bummer.

Of course we're now ready to advertise Lot 2 with the two historic barns. My mind spins at the thought of another quick sale. We must also start the construction of the new driveway before the ground freezes and snows blot out this two-acre site. The whole hillside is densely covered in impenetrable regenerating New England woods, and with the leaves now dropping it's easier to see in which direction we should go.

Suddenly the pressure is really on as the bureaucratic town fathers have just told us we're to have the driveway finished before we sell Lot 2. So advertising it is maddeningly delayed, and we commission Duane to create our new access.

A few years ago Duane prepared the land for my indoor arena and we were delighted with his work ethic and pricing. He felled huge old trees, got stuck into filling in the wet land, broke down and never complained. Now our first new task is to try to figure out where the driveway should start and finish. The beginning and end contours are dictated by the obvious places, but the blueprint for the in-between section is taxing us both. The whole hillside is not only covered with the dense trees but poison ivy also abounds, the underbrush is thick with shrubs, many with piercing spikes, there are ticks galore, and lurking snakes. Through all of this we must plan the sweep of the driveway. We want gentle artistic curves and somehow a minimising of the steep slope. I tell Duane how I look into the future and see someone losing control on fresh ice or unploughed snow and ending up in the middle of the road below. Or even worse, ending up in the very deep ditch on the far side of the road. And maybe that someone could be me ...

I ponder the clip I saw on TV this morning. A woman of one hundred and three is still driving and driving well. In fact she squires around her younger eighty- and ninety-year-old friends in her huge red 1960s' car. Then my optimism sinks as on the other hand there's a growing movement in Massachusetts to make it mandatory for drivers over the age of seventy-five to re-take their driving test every two years.

I can hear the inspector's words. "Your hand brake has been on for the last half mile."

Duane cranks up his huge front-end loader and we start our repeated hits or misses. The machine breaks through the edge of the woods and comes to a grinding halt. There's a hidden stone wall in our way. Duane gets through a gap and we press on blindly. I'm the ill-equipped designer and I make mistake after mistake. "Sorry, Duane, sorry. This won't work." And he usually agrees and patiently crashes off in yet another direction.

A number of days later we finally have a track half-way down the hill and come across another very old stone wall, with its rocks covered in a stunning patina. The wall calls for a new change of direction after we discover a natural opening. "Duane, picture this wall when it's reconstructed," and we marvel at the effort of the early farmers with their bullocks or horses pulling such great rocks into place, and way over two hundred years ago. Our small town was incorporated in 1735.

Suddenly the weather takes on winter proportions. I have my upcoming trip to the Antarctic and my preparation is way behind so Duane and I decide to halt all work until the spring. The driveway now has a beginning, nothing in the middle and an ending in front of a very deep trench beside the main road. Of course large pipes will have to be installed and enough of them to allow for a sweeping fan-like entrance. I have this horror picture of horse trailers ending up in the soggy depression on either side, and I think some of my horsey friends are minimally experienced to transport their horses. Way in the future, when Dave and I are gone, the driveway must accommodate eighteen-wheelers with loads of hay and twelve-horse vans if many horses live here once more. In the past huge vehicles drove up the old driveway. It's wide enough, yes, but I messed up designing a sharp turn by the farmhouse and the inevitable truck damage to the lawn has needed constant restorative work.

Kathy comes and I ride both horses. I haven't seen her in two weeks and she relates how a *great possibility* from distant Danbury drove for three hours to date her. "A perfect evening, and no pressures. We had such an enjoyable conversation and that indefinable connection was made." So two days later Kathy drove the three hours to Southwestern Connecticut for the second date. Another outstanding evening, but sadly she decides that it's not going to work. "Damn the distance." So Kathy emailed him to say she was truly very sorry, but he just lived too far away. This is what he emailed back to her this morning: 'It's okay Kathy. I've actually found another appropriate woman.'

"Oh Kathy," I laugh, "How blunt can a man be? Your luck just has to change. It's the laws of chance and I want to return from the Antarctic and hear good news."

I'm in my dressage lesson. It's a perfect day with no wind or distracting noises and yet it's like I'm constantly out of earshot. "What?" I find myself yelling.

"A twenty-metre circle, Liz." After five or six times that I've asked her to repeat herself, I can tell by the tone of her voice that she's getting a bit pent-up with me. Help! Am I losing my hearing?

Next I'm told to ride a ten-metre circle. And I ride a twenty-metre half circle! It's not just my hearing, it's also my concentration that's going to pot. And yet on other days I'm hearing as well as a sound, middle-aged woman, and I can follow Kathy's instructions to the letter. Kathy has two other Senior Citizen students, I know, and I must ask them if they're plagued by the same suspicions.

Working through the long list of required Antarctic clothing, I prepare for my trip. There are many new materials that have been developed to fight off the cold and we're all issued red waterproof jackets with hoods and detachable inner jackets. We'll look like a bunch out of boarding school. I work on a long list of instructions for Dave and Sue, and spend time perking up poor Sue. The divorce hearing in front of the judge was a disaster as the bigamist lied and lied after appearing half an hour late. He is late with two mortgage payments and has a four thousand–dollar cell phone bill. Even so, the judge sided with the good-looker and told him to straighten out his finances, get the house on the market and not to travel to Poland. The judge actually said, "Do you have a girl friend over there?" The bigamist didn't respond and the judge didn't push him for an answer. Sue felt so left out of the proceedings.

The next day she comes to work and is really on edge. The bigamist just told her he's off to Florida for a month to see his mother. And not to call him.

Three days later Sue goes to the ATM and there are only seven dollars in the joint account. The several hundred dollars of his last paycheck have been taken out. She looks up their bank account on the Internet and finds that the latest withdrawal was made a day ago. In Warsaw.

Sue's in a fighting mood and good for her. She would like to email the other wife with the truth, but I say leave it to the lawyers to determine what should be done, and your conscience will be clear. Settlement is not yet decided and another hearing is to be held.

Above: Elizabeth (Liz) Matthews at eighteen months with her mother.

Right: Stalwart in the face of separation, Liz, aged five, sets off to boarding school.

Below: Roughing it – the tin shack near New Plymouth in which the author and her parents lived while the grand plans for their home, Tupare, came to fruition.

Tupare today. The house and gardens gifted to the nation by Russell and Mary Matthews attract a steady stream of visitors.

Right: Liz aged twelve on the pony, Mischief, she went off and bought by herself.

Below: The three eldest Matthews children, Liz, Jill and John on Monty in 1945. The youngest, Richard, was born in 1947.

Left: Parents Russell and Mary Matthews after Russell's investiture at Government House.

Above: The author's brother, Richard Matthews, (right) with Seng.

Below: No helmet required then – Liz (right) on Pollyanna at an early pony club meeting.

The original 1912 farmhouse when it was bought by Dave and Liz Benney.

Tahuri's new house built in the 1990s.

Left: Professor (and farmer) Dave Benney.

Below: Liz with horses Fancy, Catch and Minty.

Left: Liz and Minty take honours in the stadium jumping phase of an event.

Below: Liz and Minty on the cross-country phase of eventing.

Right top: Liz competes with Catch in dressage.

Right bottom: Minty in dressage.

Above: Liz helps move lights from the old driveway to the new.

Left: 'Farmer Dave' moves equipment.

Below: The horse dentist, Mark, checks Fancy's back molars for sharp edges. She is tranquilised and there is no pain.

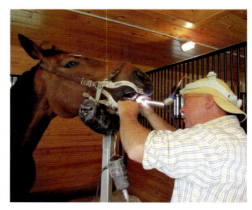

Left: Riders and friends: Liz (left) and Marylon at a West Palm Beach horse show.

Right: Tahuri farm's indoor riding area collapses in Massachusetts' record snow in February 2011.

Triumph at reaching the Antarctic at last.

A greater triumph – Liz 'plunges' into Antarctic waters at one degree Centigrade (33 degrees Fahrenheit).

On one of Liz's visits to China she dances with the minorities in distant Guizhou Province.

Two of the Guizhou dancers with Liz.

Is this Liz's last jump?

Dave's retirement
as professor of
mathematics at MIT
after 51 years is
celebrated as *his* last
jump: Dave and Liz
at the ceremony.

Chapter Nineteen

Antarctic Plunge

Finally my Antarctic departure day arrives. Dave takes me to the airport bus and looks at me as if he'll never see me again.

"Well, goodbye," he mutters and hugs me closely.

"Are you okay?"

"Of course," he grins without any conviction.

"Well, I'm fine. Don't worry about me. I'm a survivor. But for a starter, I've already forgotten my glasses case, my little magnifying mirror and my sunscreen."

This evening I get my first glance of our tour group at the Miami airport. They are singularly *aged*. And guess who's talking?

Dave had assumed that we'd be a bunch of older retired people, since it is still term-time at MIT, but there are also a number of *National Geographic* members on the trip. Quite a few of the women look like long-ago waist-length-grey-haired hippies, wearing elongated earrings down to their shoulders and no make-up. Some of the men look as if they were very lucky to pass the medical requirements. Of course I get the subtle once-over too and would love to read their thoughts.

We have a superb flight on Lan Chile Airlines. I've never heard of them before. Several tour assistants meet us at the Santiago airport and those with American passports pay an entry tax of a hundred dollars. The lone holder of a New Zealand passport pays nothing. We pile into buses and get a running commentary all the way into the city. A member of our tour sits in the front seat and peppers the guide with endless questions. I think he's on his way to being the group's irritating nerd.

We're in the Grand Hyatt Hotel. It is round-shaped and my room faces the snow-covered mountains above this lovely city. Below is an irregularly shaped pool with a circular waterfall, and after a great tour of the city we have a cocktail meeting beside this pool. The group appears to cover an interesting range of dull to gushing.

At first I find everything at the Grand Hyatt is as grand as its name and it is simple to ring Dave on my international cell phone. My mind slips back almost fifty years to when I was living in London. To ring New Zealand, we had to book a toll call and it could take up to *three days* to go through. When I was connected to Tupare, only three minutes' talk was allowed at the cheapest rate, and one that we could barely afford. Inevitably the conversation would go thus:

"Hello, how are you?"

"We're fine. How are you?"

"I'm fine but please, please speak up."

"Can you hear me now?"

"Yes. What's the time in New Zealand?"

"Six o'clock."

"Is that in the evening?"

"No. What is the time with you?"

"Six o'clock in the evening."

I found this extraordinary, as we were very aware of the twelve-hour time difference.

"What's the weather like at Tupare?"

"Raining, of course … what's new? How's your weather?"

"It's raining here too."

The operator butts in. "Time's up."

"Bye."

"Bye. Take care, dear," says Mother, and I would hang up and burst into tears.

Well, yes, the Grand Hyatt is grand, but I write emails on a business room computer and the keyboard refuses to let me use any capitals or commas. And the water from my shower is still in my tub the next morning. It's up at 5am for breakfast before we're whisked in buses to the airport. I ask for a window on the left-hand side of the plane as I want to see all the volcanoes, many of them active, in the great mountainous Andes chain.

We land at Punterenas, a remote airport at the southern tip of Chile, and it makes New Plymouth airport look international. There's cell phone service and I talk to all three children. Unfortunately Dave is out but I leave him a descriptive message. Our last leg is into Ushuaia and it's a wonder our plane is given a clearance to fly. The turbulent flight rivals flying, at its worst, into Wellington airport. At last we're on the landing strip, a tiny length of ground stretching into the sea.

As we go through customs and exit the airport, the tour that has just disembarked from our boat greets us with sways, mock vomiting and the clutching of rails. But we still have a day's sightseeing on this large island. Our guide tells us how it was originally populated with Argentinean convicts. I had read that many of the present population of around sixty thousand are descendants of the prisoners. There were women prisoners as well. I half-jokingly ask our young guide how many generations is she descended from the prisoners. "Oh no, no, no!" Her denial is so vehement, I doubt she's telling the truth.

We drive more miles along the base of the mountains and through great stands of beech trees. Not much grows here with the poor soil and summers in the fifty-degree range. I recall when son Paul and I tramped the Milford Track and our guide pointed out the three species of South Island beech trees. But he couldn't remember the name of the third one. "Son-of-a beech!" shouted out a bright Australian.

It's on to the boat late in the afternoon and I couldn't wish for anything better appointed. The horn blasts and everyone rushes up on deck. As we steam away I miss the old New Zealand boat farewells, how the streamers dropped over the deck rails and connected with family and friends shouting goodbyes from the wharf. And the band played the haunting *Now is the hour, when we must say goodbye,* the last streamer breaking and we were truly off towards the Heads of Wellington's harbour and out into the vast Pacific Ocean.

Now evacuation drill is announced and we're to read the instructions in our cabins. When the alarm pierces the ship, I run into the corridor outside my room. I'm the very last person from our deck to reach the lifeboats. I decide on a much quicker route by running through a door beside my cabin, out on to the stern and then up a steep ladder to the collecting area. Everyone on board is very aware that only two weeks ago a cruise ship, similar to ours, sank in the Antarctic waters. All were saved after a harrowing time afloat. I join up with a new friend called Charlotte. "If we have to evacuate, get on the same boat as my group, Liz. There's only food and water on these lifeboats and I'm going to be sure to grab tons of booze."

We reach the end of the long Beagle Channel from Ushuaia and enter the open waters of the Drake Passage. By the time we're one hundred miles from land and well into the Roaring Forties of this wild stretch of water, we are rolling and pitching. To make matters worse, I'm on a high deck and next to the stern. I'm wearing the seasickness patch and so far so good. Most passengers meet in the lounge for drinks before our first dinner and we're introduced to the members of our team and the leader, Tim, an archetypal Australian.

The second night is the formal welcome-on-board dinner with the captain attending. He just takes this one-time meal at the top table. We're encouraged to *dress* for this dinner. What? I hunt through my suitcase but all I have is thermal clothing and nothing formal. I pull out a pair of earrings. Then out of the blue, an invitation appears on my cabin door. I'm invited to sit at the captain's table with four of the other passengers. Why me? I'm not one of the PhDs on board, or a CEO and I don't stand out in the crowd. Maybe the organiser needs someone to talk-up-a-storm! I try to put on my earrings but it's hopeless. Just like dressing up in the Dominican Republic and without swallowing Advil for my arthritis, my dexterity is shot. I give up and hurry to the dining room. The other invited passengers are already sitting down and first personal pronouns have taken over the conversation. There's a pause and the captain glances at me and sort of nods.

Elizabeth, never focus just on yourself.

"Captain, where do you come from?" I can tell that he likes my query.

"I'm German and I come from the Friesian Islands off the Coast of Denmark. It was a simple life and I didn't even learn to drive a car until my late twenties. I'm still much more comfortable sailing a ship and letting my wife drive."

"Do you have children?"

"Oh yes," he says, his handsome face lighting up. "I have three. Two of them were with women I wasn't married to and the third one is now two years old and I'm actually married to her mother."

The next time the captain talks to me is on the bridge. The same man that fired so many questions at the guide on our bus trip into Santiago is at it once more. I hear him ask the captain what the second flag flying on a mast represents. "And this is my very last question for today," he says in an unconvincing voice.

"It's the flag of Bermuda where the ship is registered." And the captain turns around and whispers to me, "That is his forty-fifth question today."

I love to spend time on the bridge and if the crew have a chance to relax they give us important nautical and Antarctic information. The ship was built in 1962 for deep-sea fishing and the fish were prepared for sale on board and frozen. Later it was refurbished as a tourist boat and is carrying ninety of us today. Most of the staff are from the Philippines and are energetic and well trained. There's only one negative ... time on the computer is charged at $55 an hour. Sometimes it takes twenty minutes of that hour to hook on to a satellite and log in.

This morning we see our first killer whales and our first giant iceberg with deep, brilliant blue fissures. It's way below freezing on the deck and we're now six hundred miles south of South America. Lectures are given daily and they include the bird life of the Antarctic, penguins and their love life, ocean currents, weather, history, geology including a description of the fascinating tectonic plates, global warming ...

In bed tonight we still haven't stopped rocking in a repeating rhythm. I listen to the creaks as the ship hits the end of a huge sideways roll to the right. Then she moves upright and for a brief moment there's an uncanny calm before we continue to roll and creak on to the left-hand side.

Today we arrive at the Shetland Islands and go on shore, ten at a time in the powered Zodiacs. Everyone is wedged together while sitting in two rows on the rounded edges of the rubber boat. It's grip on to a rope for dear life. Getting into the boats is not easy for older folk. The sea churns and the Zodiac rises and falls and crashes against the small suspended loading dock. Two attendants make sure if we lose our balance we fall into the boat and not into the ocean. We are wearing life jackets, of course. We reach the island and must first jump into icy water while a crewmember holds one of our hands. Then a tricky scramble over slippery rocks and we're face to face with a large group of lovable penguins, flirting, building their stone nests or wobbling down to the sea to eat.

Two hours later we're sailing again and the captain stops beside an iceberg that he calculates is one hundred and fifty feet high. There are now bergs of every size and shape around us and the captain ignores questions as he concentrates on navigating, binoculars in his hand. If we need to change course he barks orders to an assistant, who in turn sends the message down to the engine room.

The next day is notable for a first. I am seasick. Very. I can't believe that I am dumb enough to believe I now have my sea legs and can forget about applying the patch behind my ear. And the seas are nowhere near as bad as the crossing that I once made over the Tasman Sea. Only a handful of passengers made it to every meal for those three days and I was one of them. Today, apart from feeling so ill, I get tossed into the wall beside my bunk and then I have to hold on to the outside of the bunk to stop myself being flung onto the floor. I'm living the expression *coming to the end of the line*. I don't care if I expire. I try to find the stamina, the impetus to get up and find a patch. There is no let-up of this hell and I stay pitching on my bunk, concentrating so hard to keep everything *down*. Finally I'm about to lose control and just make it to my little bathroom. Away goes my lunch, but I do find the patch.

After half an hour the patch has worked, even though it makes my mouth very dry. I gingerly inch my way along corridors gone mad and up stairways pitching back and forth.

Don't fall.

Don't break a bone.

Don't think about that twenty-eight thousand-dollar evacuation flight.

I did buy the insurance at Dave's insistence. I bump into the ship's doctor and instantly he knows what has happened. "Dry ginger ale. Drink it slowly. It's great for settling the stomach."

We hear the captain through the intercom and he says he's very sorry about the rotten conditions and he's looking for calmer waters. It is also the day that we're to enjoy our promised swim in a thermal patch of salt water. And I am on.

Feeling better, I walk on to a deck and look at the coastline. Everywhere are mountains feeding glaciers and every sight is an endless pattern of black, grey and white, with the occasional green around the base of the icebergs. Today there's no blue sky to highlight the grandeur of this remote region. Back in America several people had looked aghast when I told them I was sailing to Antarctica. "Are you crazy? What on earth is there to see and do down there?" I've been lucky to see many outstanding sights in the world and nothing comes anywhere close to this distant, dramatic monochromic region.

We change direction and head towards the special thermal area, when the captain comes over the loudspeaker. "Ladies and gentleman, I'm very sorry that we can go no further. The sea's ice is still too thick, so I'm taking you into a caldera and if any of you are willing, we'll wait while you go ashore and swim in the authentic Antarctic Ocean. We will arrive in about an hour's time."

I've never heard of a caldera, but it turns out to be this flooded sunken crater of a volcano that blew her top a mere thirty years ago. I fish out my old, shapeless swimsuit and stare at it. Shall I or shan't I jump into the Antarctic water that the captain announced was thirty-three degrees or one degree Celsius? I'm not crazy about swimming even in warm water.

I change into my suit and don the great thick dressing gown provided by the ship. Somehow I manage to pull my jacket over it and grabbing my woolly hat and a thick towel I head for the Zodiac. All the way to the shore, I decide that I will just sit on the beach and watch the madmen. I'm miserable when I'm well clothed in thirty-three degrees of air, let alone thirty-three degrees of Antarctic water, punctuated with ice flows.

Nineteen stalwart passengers have decided to give it a go. I'm the first to alight from a Zodiac and the doctor is already in attendance with his defibrillator. He greets me and points to the best place to enter the sea. Lumps of ice are floating in the water and the swimming area is almost completely surrounded by a shelf of ice. Doc now points along the beach. Someone has dug a trench, the shape and size of a coffin. But the good news is its bottom is filling with warm thermal water. "Lie in that trench for a moment when you get out. It will help the shock."

It's too late to back out. I ask another swimmer, Jenny, waiting for a friend on the second Zodiac, if she will take my photo or else Dave and my children will never believe what this water-wimp is doing. A man beside me throws off his dressing gown and races to the water's edge, dives in, comes up and screams bloody murder, races out and flops into the coffin.

"Go on, Liz," says Jenny with my camera.

I can't stand people who are chicken. It's now or never …

I cast off my hat, cozy jacket and dressing gown, but keep on my sneakers. I run across the stones and race into the water until it becomes about three and a half feet deep. I sink and touch the ocean floor, spring back up and let out a primordial scream. *I did it.* I splash back to shore, the coffin is empty and I drop into six inches of heavenly thermal water.

The surprising effect of this frigid experience begins as soon as I scramble out of the coffin. Not being under water long enough to shock my old body critically, I find the freezing air bracing. I wrap myself in the thick towel, put on my hat, the dressing gown and then my jacket over my shoulders and suddenly I feel extraordinarily youthful and vibrant. I run and bound around the beach until I'm called back to the Zodiac.

Time is running out and the ship still has many miles to travel. Our captain wants to reach and cross the Antarctic Circle. "That will put you all in true Antarctica," he had told us earlier, "and I hope the sea ice is passable now that summer's arriving."

Summer? The air is way below freezing and I've just been dipping in a 33-degree ocean.

Back at the boat it has been a long time since I felt so energised. I get in the shower for ten minutes and I can't wait to go up to the lounge. The goosey-non-swimmers, required to stay on the ship, ask me to join them for a drink. They ply me with questions and my sky-high energy lasts way into the night. And tomorrow the captain hopes to find a bay with some calm waters. We're all going kayaking.

I wake briefly at 1am and the sun is just setting. Even during the short period between each setting and sunrise, it's never very dark. The curtains don't fit my two windows well enough to cut out the light, and, even if they did, the roll of the ship has them swaying open and shut. From time to time a huge wave drowns the windows and my outside wall shudders.

We're certainly getting plenty of daily exercise and I'm way too lazy to go to the gym. (And start training for my renewed jumping career?) I'm constantly up and down the stairs, hanging on to the rails, up to the lounge, up further to the library and its twenty-four-hour service of coffee, soft drinks, fruit and biscuits, down to the dining-room, up to the bridge, around the decks, back to the cabin, meals, afternoon teas, cocktail hour, lectures and almost every day we go ashore once or twice in the Zodiacs.

Before stepping onto the gangplank leading to these little French-made dinghies with their Japanese outboard motors, I move a small knob. It is labeled with my room number and I push it to the *out* position. When I've clambered back on board, I move my knob back to the *in* position. This way, everyone is accounted for. My imagination really tumbles when I think of being left behind on shore.

As we're about to get into a Zodiac, we don't actually hold the hands of two attendants but hold each other's wrists, which affords a safer grip. Then it's wait for the low point of a wave and the assistants shout *"Jump!"* Someone in the Zodiac catches you – you hope – as he tries to keep his own balance. As we moor against a frozen shoreline, we've been instructed how to swing our legs in a certain direction before *dropping* into the freezing seawater, now often up to two feet deep. Of course there is always an attendant standing in the water to save the less athletic passengers. Salt water sometimes gets into our fancy boots, in spite of the protective waterproof gaiters and over-pants.

The remarkable energy surge has left me by this next morning. I'm once again an old gal hoping for enough power to co-pilot the kayak. Charlotte will be my partner and she tells me that she's a woman on the sluggish side.

We steam into a calm bay surrounded by stunning, high sculptured white mountain peaks and ride the Zodiac to the kayaks that have already been positioned along the shore. Our little boat is wobbly, but Charlotte and I soon get into a rhythm and paddle all over the inlet as we draw on our energy reserves and watch a large group of penguins race sure-footedly over rocks and dive into the ocean. We're warned to stay well away from the open sea, and from icebergs that can topple without warning. There's one with a great cavern gouged deep into its side and a couple paddle dangerously close to it. A staff member yells tough language through a megaphone. As Charlotte and I tire, along comes an official Zodiac and we're offered hot chocolate generously laced with whisky.

Our captain is delighted that we're still able to sail further and further south and that it's possible to visit two research stations. One English location was abandoned many years ago and nothing has changed since the day that the research men left. Two English women and I get a great laugh seeing an old Marmite jar on the shelf, some Bovril and a box of Rinso. On the second of these outings, our guide tells us that this frigid day is classic summer in Antarctica. I'm so cold I wrap my scarf around my whole face and my breath freezes the fabric. Even our modern thermal wear is challenged, but the sweet nesting penguins are oblivious to the cold and wind. We're told never to approach them within fifteen feet, but I'm walking along a path and stop when a little fellow approaches me. He comes within two feet of my boots, stands and squints up at me for several seconds.

Our lecture this evening is given by the Australian, showing us a video of an aborted exit from the Antarctic Peninsula. Winter was approaching and the video shows Tim flying a tiny plane onto a snowfield to take the two research men from the station. But as the plane starts to take off, one of the skis collapses. There's no way the men can now fly out and the three of them have to hunker down for the months and months of winter. At last a rescue is made with the arrival of summer. Tim wore the same clothes for more than a year and when he finally got to wash them they fell apart.

By now I know the life story of some of the passengers. Rona and Marie both had terrible marriages. "I left the bastard years ago," say Marie. "Me too," echoes Rona. Then there is Don who also left his "villain of a wife" years ago. I love the fact he daily wears an enormous *Impeach Bush* button. He likes to show off his erudition and impresses me with Shakespearean quotes and Latin quotes until I can't resist a comment. "Don, I'm sorry, but I can't keep up with you. I did years of Shakespeare and have not retained a lot. I did two years of Latin and failed every exam. And about all that I can remember from Latin is equus for a horse and amo, amas, amat. I love, you love, he loves …"

Two days later we cross the 66.3 south latitude, or the Antarctic Circle. Now we're really in Antarctica and go ashore on the great continent. When we all collect for the evening's lecture, one of the staff asks if anyone present has also been inside the Arctic Circle. Several passengers raise their hands. "Well, folks, I now declare that you are bipolar."

Our ship moves slowly through thick ice that is starting to break up with the approach of summer. But it becomes apparent there are no more open channels of water through which we can sail further south. We hear the captain explain that we have come further south than any boat this season and he's going to ram us into frozen sea-water so that we can all disembark and walk on water, well, frozen water.

Our sail back to Ushuaia begins. I'm called to the bridge and the captain tells me my husband is calling back in ten minutes' time. It's amazing to hear Dave's voice competing with the crackles of distance. I must say our conversation takes a maturer course than prattling on about the time and weather. I exit the small office on to the deck and the captain grins. "Good reception?"

"Great," I respond. "But changing the subject, is there any way I can see the engine room?"

"Another passenger, Chas, has also asked for a quick tour. Check in with the purser."

Only two of us join the chief engineer, Buzz, and start descending. Buzz is very proud of the old boat, gives us earphones and warns us to be very careful as the vast machines are unprotected. As we reach the main noisy engine area the heat is fierce and the whole area is very claustrophobic. So much is crowded into such a minimum space. I'm fascinated by the drive shaft … the heart of the boat, as it extends way out to the propeller. Buzz shouts out his description of everything we see to Chas, *but* he ignores me. Totally. I feel more and more unwelcome and it bugs me. Chas is an engineer and Buzz is so at home in his company.

We climb up ladders to another level and visit the room where repairs are made. There in front of me is an old lathe. "Buzz," I ask, "how old is this lathe?" He can't believe a woman would ask such a question. "Around forty years." He looks at me curiously. "Well, Buzz," I carry on, "one of my sons has an engineering business. They have several contemporary lathes, all controlled by computers and Paul has gone to great pains to explain their workings to me."

Buzz immediately asks a number of questions about Paul's business. I take photos of the lathe and, to impress him more, I tell him how I would love to have been an engineer but when I was a student at university there was no way that a woman would have been admitted to the engineering department. "In fact I would probably have been committed to an institution for evaluation," I joke. We become an easy three-some finishing this memorable tour.

When we reach the Drake Passage, I apply the patch and we see the southern tip of Chile way in the distance to our left. The captain comes over the loudspeaker and reminds us of the many sailing ships and even more modern steam ships that have sunk over the years in this treacherous stretch of water. Our ship's engine stops and the captain calls for a moment of silence.

Then, in respect for the many voyagers who have died in these waters, the ship's horn sounds a long and haunting blast.

Chapter Twenty

The Emergency is about to be Me

"I can't believe you've made it back safely and without a single mishap," are Dave's first words as he greets me.

"Don't sound so flabbergasted, but it's great to be back and still in one piece. What a waste of money buying that insurance!"

It's now the start of winter in Massachusetts and the frigid temperatures are nothing after Antarctica. I look forward to riding both Catch and Minty and catching up with everyone. Sue has great news for me. At the second court hearing, the bigamist husband didn't turn up and the judge granted her everything. Husband will also have to pay some alimony, but good luck collecting it from Poland. I hope Sue can now sell the house and get what is left after the bank takes its share.

Kathy comes to give me a lesson on both horses. She had an interesting date while I was away, a debonair man of sixty, delightful company and very honest and open about himself. The second date went okay as well. But the third date had him producing a large sheet of paper. "On this," he told Kathy, "the last woman in my life wrote all the things about me that she disliked. Then she tells me she really wants to see me again and that she will have a list of further criticisms."

He refuses to show Kathy the second list. We both find this very strange and Kathy decides she can't be bothered with him. "I just can't put my finger on him," she shakes her head. "They're out there!"

Yesterday I honestly started riding without stirrups. My doctor had recommended using Balmex for chafing and it works. I'd never heard of the ointment, but it's used on babies' bottoms for diaper rash! Before long I'll be fit to jump again. Well, perhaps ninety per cent fit. Now that Kathy's improving Minty's and my dressage, I start to sit his trot, and riding without stirrups helps. But Minty's huge powerful gaits and desirable suspension soon begin to play havoc with the old vertebra, L5. And even with the Balmex I've got a rotten irritation of my private parts and I can't for the life of me remember what the inflammation is called.

Recall seems to be a bit of a growing issue. Mother had this dilemma and would pause and say, "Just wait a moment and let me process this." Well, I have found that it helps to go through the alphabet and the word will often come to me when I reach the appropriate letter. I need to find the name of this irritation. I start at A and I don't think it's going to work this time until I reach U. Aha. Urethritis.

Forgetting that word is not all that tests my memory today. I drive to Staples, buy new ink cartridges for my printer, pay for them in a hurry and walk outside without my parcel. The overweight cashier comes huffing to the parking lot to find me.

I drive home and remember that I must irrigate the outdoor arena. I walk towards the outside garage where the switch is located, stop to pull a weed and can't stop pulling, more and more. I never do remember to irrigate the arena and I ride Catch on the dusty footing. Also had some friends drop by for a quick lunch and I forget to serve the home-made cake.

Everyone tells me to stop worrying about such lapses. They too are constantly forgetting things, but *four* incidents in the space of several hours?

"It's because you're so busy, Liz."

Later I have a good laugh and it helps divert my mind from the lapses. The horse chiropractor comes to check out Minty. The old boy needs more and more maintenance and I've felt him moving a little crookedly. Steve finds that Minty's sacroiliac joint on his right side is out. He makes a very good adjustment.

An hour later I too have an appointment with my local chiropractor. I crack up when he finds that *my* sacroiliac joint, on the right side, is also out. Did crooked me cause Minty's joint to be out, or did Minty first mess with mine?

Today we're told out of the blue that we must present our new driveway plans to the Town Planning Board. We need their approval to change our official entrance. And the town adds yet another requirement. The whole farm, except the untouched forest, must be resurveyed and a contour map drawn up. At great cost. "Why?" I ask the secretary.

"Search me," she says with a shrug.

Members of the Planning Board sit like a row of clothes pegs. They're up on the stage of the high school's auditorium where they have the psychological advantage of glaring down on those of us holding on to papers referencing our requests. When Dave's and my situation comes up for discussion, I can't help standing up and arguing politely that a contour map and the surveying of twenty-four acres is overkill.

To no avail.

Dave nudges me and whispers, "Let it be."

"Megalomaniacs," I whisper back a little louder.

Our permit is granted, pending the surveying. It won't present a problem.

For the whole long time we sit beneath the Planning Board, not one member ever smiles.

Later in the week the familiar surveying engineers arrive and I sense that they wonder how many more times they'll be returning when this old gal changes her mind. But the engineers have a new surprise. At one point they set up their transom beside the indoor arena. "You should never *ever* have filled in the wet land on which this structure is built. Such an area should have been left entirely natural." Duane had filled in parts of the area to a depth of six feet. There's nothing the town can now do at this late stage, thank goodness.

They tell us that *if* we had currently filled in the area, there would be satellite photos showing the original pristine unadulterated wet land and later photos showing how we were contaminating the site. "Mrs. Benney, I hate to tell you what the fine would have been."

I don't tell him how I've been telling my friends to build their indoor arenas on wet lands. We never have to water the inside footing to keep down the dust, thanks to the absorption of water from the high water table below.

I lie in bed tonight and for a brief moment wonder what it must be like living in a condominium in downtown Boston, or even in the suburbs. There's no bureaucracy to cope with, and all maintenance is done for you as well as all the mowing and weeding of your pint-sized plot.

No thank you!

The snow goes early this late winter and Duane finishes connecting the two ends of the new driveway and the town sends a man to cut down an enormous tree that's in the entranceway. A police officer is hired to control the traffic and the town pays for everything as the tree is on their land. Duane now puts down an excellent base. So far so good. But this phase and getting the area resurveyed and a contour map drawn up is nothing compared with our new headache – and will it ever end?

The utilities must now be brought in beside the new driveway – telephone, electricity and possibly the TV and Internet cable at a future date. For now we want to retain our present cable that goes under Lot 2. It provides a superior service and we'll have an easement written up when the lot is sold. Just in case it doesn't work out, a new empty conduit will lie in waiting for any future emergency. Let's hope not, as we'd be forced into using an inferior service. When we bought the farm, all the utilities came in from the next-door town in which the farmhouse is located.

Duane digs a very long and deep trench and hits solid rock. More blasting is necessary – and yet again, more expense. The ground trembles as dirt and rocks punctuate the air. Our electrician lines the trench with conduits and it's now time for me to cope with our errant telephone company. We also want to change our phone number as our present one ends in 2220. A combination of those four numbers gets you to a nearby high school, a lawyer's office, a local radio station or a pizza shop. How easy it is for fingers to press 2220 by mistake.

What follows is an hour and a half of raw irritation. I press button after button until I can speak to someone at our phone company, AT&T. And all I have for them is a very simple request. "Please could you install a new phone line from a main road and up to our house? A conduit is already in place."

After I'm sent from one department to another I'm finally told that our long distance carrier AT&T can't install our new line as our *old* line is owned by Verizon, a competing company and the one we use for local calls.

So I ring Verizon.

"Press 1 for English.

"If you want copies of your phone bills for tax purposes, Press 1.

"If you want to make a payment, Press 2.

"If you want to dispute your bill, Press 3."

It goes on and on about account balances, problems with dial tones, problems with static ... Press 4, 5 and 6.

"If you want to discontinue your service, Press 7."

I give this one a go. "If you want to speak to a representative about this change, Press 1 ... You will now be helped in the order in which your call was received."

I hold on for twenty minutes listening to junk music and being constantly reminded to please hold on and that the company values my patronage.

Suddenly, I am *discontinued*. Click click, dial tone.

Melt down. Expletives shoot in every direction.

I start all over. I'm ready to hurl everything within reach through the glass of a window, when finally I get to talk to someone. "I have a simple request," I say, "We would like a new telephone line installed. Please." She asks my name and our present account number and says that I have to be transferred to another department to have it verified.

Wait, wait, wait. Then a man's voice. India answers. "For security reasons, please tell me your mother's maiden name."

I do, and I'm transferred back to the previous woman, and no way can she understand that all we want is a new telephone line with a new number.

"Where is your new house located?"

"We are *not* moving into a new house."

"Then why do you need a new line and a new number?"

"We are selling some of the land over which the present service now travels and we don't want to bother with the complications of an easement."

"With a what?"

"I'm sorry, miss, but damn it, I give up."

"Please don't swear at me."

"I'll swear at whomever I please. And if I don't get out my frustration I'll have a heart attack. I *am* ninety years old."

"You certainly don't sound it." Pause. "Well, let me give you an order number."

Her computer is down. Another long wait, but she does return to me.

"Ma'am, I'm really sorry but I can't help you. I thought that your town was in *Northern New England* and it's in *Southern New England*, so I'm of no use to you. I just deal with installations in the north. I will transfer you."

Wait, wait, wait. Then a message. "So sorry, but I'm out of the office for all of this week. If you have an emergency please ring Mr Thomas, number …"

The emergency is about to be *me*.

Days later Mr Thomas arrives at the farm and we sort out everything. Of course nothing is ever simple. The conduit through which the phone line must be pulled is too long and we have to add something in the middle called a junction box installed by our electrician. It turns out that he's off doing jury duty for days on end. And it is more money here and more money there.

After all this and after many days have passed, we finally have a new phone line and a new number and I'm able, after a long convoluted conversation with someone in India, to obtain AT&T's long-distance service once more.

But – India's not done with me.

"We're so grateful that you are using AT&T. But ma'am, you should have voice mail installed."

"I have an answering machine and that's all I need, thank you."

"But ma'am, if the power goes off in your home you can't get your messages. You can get them with voice mail, from anywhere in the world."

"We have an *automatic generator* that comes on whenever the power goes off and it serves the whole house, so I can *always* get my messages." And I add, "Even from Timbuktu if I need to."

Pause.

"Where is Timbuktu?"

"A hundred and fifty-five miles north-west of nowhere ..."

"*Really!*"

Pause.

"We now have AT&T wireless service. How about a cell phone with AT&T?"

"I have a cell phone thank you, and I love it and I'm not breaking any contract and paying a penalty to register with *you*."

"Do you have a computer?"

"Of course."

"Who is your server?"

"Comcast. And I hate to be rude but three of my horses have just jumped out of the field and are *running wild* all over my garden."

"You have *what* running wild?"

Never lose your temper, Elizabeth.

It's too late.

"Look, I'm hanging up on you. I hate to be rude, but I am an old lady of ninety" – I like the sound of ninety – "and I've had it with this conversation. I want nothing *more* from you or from India."

"Hmmm. Well, thank you very, very much for using AT&T."

Oh give me the old operator telephone that we had way back at Tupare. Even the party line was acceptable except to Dad. When a neighbour was on the line and impatient Dad wanted to use the phone it was, "Excuse me, excuse me, please get off the line. I have an emergency." Of course the neighbours would all listen in with bated breath. It was just my impetuous father and no crisis. Oddly enough, it never became a wolf-wolf situation.

We're now ready to move the driveway lights. Four of them, twelve feet high and with lamps on the top that must be relocated along the new driveway. Duane drives in with his huge backhoe, and another man, Brian, arrives with three assistants and a smaller machine. They start with a question.

"Where do the lights' electric wires go into the house?"

"I swear," I tell the men, "that they go across this west lawn and towards the west side of the house."

A large chunk of our pristine front lawn is dug up and the men call for me. "You're only out by 180 degrees, Liz!"

How lucky Dave is to be at work every day.

Next it's, "We need to turn off the power to the lights."

I can't find the correct meter switch. There are six different meters on the farm and we scan all five with the remaining one in the stable apartment. Our renters are at work and I get our personal key to the apartment and walk in. I consider this to be an emergency. The meter is behind the biggest laundry basket of dirty clothes that I have ever seen. The apartment is one heck of a mess and it relieves my guilt about barging in. I turn off the driveway light switch and realise that the tenants have all been paying for its use since we moved out of the apartment and into our new house, twelve years ago.

Ah well. We seldom use those lights and the renters have a great rental deal after begging us suckers to reduce their monthly rate.

And so the simple task of moving four driveway lights continues. The electrician arrives and two of his men in huge muddy boots tramp into the house and I show them where the wall switches for the lights are located. Of course we would like to use the same switches for the new connections.

A short time later I notice some of the men along the old driveway just standing idly, hands on their hips. They're staring into a hole where they have just removed the second driveway light. I hurry down to see what's happening. I can't believe it. The electrician who installed the lights way back in 1991 actually sealed this particular light's stem to the underground Internet and TV cable and the telephone line in *concrete*. How could anyone be so careless as to concrete over bare wires? No conduits for all the wires were ever installed. So now we have no TV, Internet or email. The old telephone line is also ripped apart, and thank goodness for our brand-new one. I just shake my head and stare at the length of ripped lines so well sealed inside the concrete that is anchored around the stem of the post.

I phone the company. They can't make any repairs for several days. When the technician finally arrives he tells me that his name is Barry. He can't stop talking. "You know I live quite near you and I have just bought this house." Then out comes the story of his recent divorce.

"The witch works as the assessor in this town and maybe you know her."

I don't.

"Well, the very day that I married her I knew it was a *big* mistake, even though we'd been living together for three years. You know what happened at the wedding?"

"No. I can't even guess."

"Well, her father had to be carried home early in the evening as he was drunk as a skunk. Being Daddy's little girl she had a big tizzy in front of everyone. Completely lost it. What a shit. Oh sorry, sorry, never swear in front of a lady. So embarrassing to watch *my wife of thirty minutes* act like a little kid. Then recently I got the divorce and bought this mess of a house, but I'm restoring it and making it a great place for my two boys to visit. I've even got a pond. Amazing how the boys appear to have weathered being around their mad mother." It goes on and on.

After all this, Barry then looks at me and declares that he can't fix the cable after all. He just works with *little wires* and this is a *big* main lead-in cable that needs a specialist with special tools and a three-foot length of new thick cable.

Barry calls a buddy and begs him to come and fix the cable for this 'really nice young lady'. If anything's going to endear me to Barry, this comment helps. On schedule the buddy arrives this afternoon, looks into the hole and shakes his head. "I don't believe this happened. *Concrete* all over the wires. You'll have to pay for my service I'm afraid. Two hundred and fifty dollars."

We finally have TV and Internet service once more. I go to Dunkin Donuts and buy Duane and company iced coffee and donuts and turn on the hose to water my parched garden as our early drought continues. Finally the driveway lights *turn on successfully*.

I get that wonderful feeling that all's well with the world. *Creativity* and *maintenance* are under control. Ha ha. I go to water the horses and the first bucket fills with *orange* water. I forgot to turn off the garden hose and I've let the well run almost dry. We're getting all the natural iron deposits that have sunk to the bottom of the well's deep shaft.

Dave comes home from work and there's no dinner ready. He helps me carry buckets of water from the house to the stable. The house's water tank is big enough to hold enough fresh water for the horses. But now we have to stop drawing any water for several hours, wait for the well to fill up and then open lots of taps to get rid of the orange that's settling in pipes all over the place.

I glance in the mud room mirror. I'm flattered that people are always telling me I look ten years younger than my age but tonight the mirror's image tells the disheartening truth. I'm so glad my old heart's in good shape.

A week later the driveway is surfaced, or hot-topped as they call it here. Now we need to prepare and sow either side in grass, and plant a few trees and shrubs. And I've found an impressive three-man show to restore the great old walls.

There are many crumbling stone walls on the farm. Some of them we pulled down to enlarge the fields and others we have restored. The first one was by a competent man who finished the job just before going to jail for driving while intoxicated, getting into an accident and killing his buddy. So we employed another stone wall artist and soon after finishing the next wall he died of cancer. We tried to locate a third man who had built a beautiful stone wall around an 18th century well near the farmhouse, and found that he too had died. We had actually been a little hesitant about employing him again, as he was often seen strutting around town in a wig and women's clothes, right down to the highest of heels.

I'm inside checking my email and Richard and Seng have sent me the following:

It's that time of the year for our annual Senior Citizen test. Exercise of the brain is as important as exercise of the muscles. As we grow older, it's important to keep mentally alert. If you don't use it, you lose it. Below is a very private way to gauge how your memory is faring. Some may think it is too easy but the ones with memory problems may have difficulty.

Take the test below to determine if you're losing it or not. Cover every line until you get the answer. OK, relax, clear you head and begin.

1.What do you put in a toaster?

Answer: 'bread.' If you said 'toast' give up now and do something else.

2. Say 'silk' five times. Now spell 'silk.' What do cows drink?

Answer: Cows drink water

3. If a red house is made from red bricks and a blue house is made from blue bricks and a pink house is made from pink bricks and a black house is made from black bricks, what is a green house made from?

Answer: Greenhouses are made from glass. Not green bricks.

4. It's twenty years ago, and a plane is flying at twenty thousand feet over Germany. (If you will recall, Germany at the time was politically divided into West Germany and East Germany.) Anyway, during the flight, two engines fail. The pilot, realising that the last remaining engine is also failing, decides on a crash landing. Unfortunately the engine fails before he can do so and the plane crashes smack in the middle of 'no man's land' between E and W Germany … Where would you bury the survivors? East or West Germany? Or in no man's land?

Answer. You don't bury survivors.

5 Without using a calculator … You are driving a bus from London to Milford Haven in Wales. In London, seventeen people get on the bus. In Reading, six people get off the bus and nine get on. In Swindon, two people get off and four get on. In Cardiff, eleven get off and sixteen get on. In Swansea three get off and five get on. In Carmathen, six get off and three get on. Then you arrive at Milford Haven. How old is the bus driver?

Answer. Don't you remember your own age? YOU were driving the bus.

Ninety-five percent of people fail most of the questions.
Hey ho. Make my day. I failed only number five.

Chapter Twenty-One

Hospital Wake-up

This morning I have the agreeable feeling that all's well with the world. I'm riding little Catch most days and am energised by her progress. I can even sit her trot, and unlike when I'm sitting Minty's trot and riding without stirrups, my L5 vertebra can take it. Mind you, after treating the urethritis I'm not sure in what direction I should be pushing myself. But I've entered Catch in a dressage clinic given by a distinguished rider and notable instructor. No one is coming with me, but I'm confident Catch will let me mount her without putting on a frenzied act.

The day arrives and Catch looks stunning, all bathed and shining in her new spring coat. I load her on to the trailer and off we go. It's odd, but ever since I failed to mount her and the ensuing debacle at the competition, she has become a bit of a worrier when travelling in the trailer, and has diarrhoea. I use this nifty New Zealand canvas bag that encloses her tail and keeps it spotless.

We arrive at the farm and I lead Catch around the indoor arena. Soon a rider finishes up her session and Catch and I make our way to the standard-sized mounting block. She stands quietly while I feed her a peppermint and put my left foot in the stirrup.

My next conscious moment is waking up in hospital. I had been vaguely aware when an ambulance attendant became impatient after digging everywhere to find a vein to connect me to an IV. Now, six hours later, I sort of hear Dave's and Tonia's voices. Doctors and nurses keep hovering over me and I listen to snatches about my needing another X-ray and another CAT scan.

Much later I'm a little more with it and overhear someone say, "Doc, that gash on her leg is ready to be stitched." That really wakes me up.

Many people now hover over me. Am I seeing double? I feel nothing but hear a strange snapping noise. It turns out that they have just *stapled* the gash.

Everyone laughs when they hear my first conscious words. "Please someone tell me, is Catch okay?"

"She's fine, Liz," says Dave. "More importantly, are *you* okay?"

"Yes. I'm fine now. Just please get me out of here. I want to go home."

"Not yet, Mrs Benney," someone says in a pleasant voice. It turns out I'm in a very busy trauma room, and Tonia and Dave have plenty of action to watch.

As I become more on the ball, I beg someone to tell me what happened. All I can remember is putting my foot in the stirrup. Dave relates what the nice stable owner told him. I did get as far as dropping on to the saddle and was looking for my right stirrup when someone leading a horse made a noisy entrance through a side door. Catch got a surprise and started quickly backing out of the space beside the mounting block. I lost my balance, grabbed Catch's mouth and somehow she lost *her* balance and fell over backwards, hit the wall and pinned my left leg and thigh underneath her. As she lay partly on top of me, no one knew how to get her off, but she started to struggle on her own. On the way up she trod on my leg, causing the gash right through my new riding boot. She then put all the weight of her other hoof on my right breast. Sweet Catch. I gather she tried so hard not to touch me.

"Where is she now?" I start to cry.

"She's staying the night at the stable where you fell off."

"I *didn't* fall off. I went down with the ship."

I hear several people laugh. Then, "I think she's going to be okay."

I'm released at midnight. Dave drives me home and Tonia follows in her car. Somehow I struggle into the kitchen and with no warning throw up all over the floor. My super daughter cleans up everything. She relates how she heard me tell the nurses around midnight that I truly was fine and to *please, please* discharge me. The nurses laughed and said, "Even though you were out of it you've been saying that since the moment you arrived. But *now,* at last, you can go home."

The next day I'm mad, sore and apprehensive. Two falls off Catch in the space of a few months. What is wrong with me? Sure, I lost my balance and it's obvious my legs don't have much grip anymore. How much strength does one need to keep me in the saddle? Now I must take it easy for a week or two and mend. And the stitches are on the inside of my leg, right where it hits the flap of my saddle. Dave drives me to collect Catch. It's the first time she has ever slept away from Tahuri Farm and she whinnies like mad when she sees me.

It's very moving how everyone is concerned about me. I learn that straight after the ambulance left the farm the kind owner ran to my truck and found my cell phone. From its address site she was able to locate Dave's phone number and those of our three children. She contacted Richard who was at Logan Airport, about to board a flight to Washington DC. When he heard that I was unconscious and on my way to a hospital, this thoughtful son of ours immediately cancelled his flight. He called the hospital and they told him to call his brother who had just phoned the trauma centre and had an updated report.

Catch is fine, but a friend is going to get on her the first time she is ridden again. To think that I didn't get one single dollar's worth of that expensive dressage clinic …

Two days later I empty all my clothes from the hospital bag. The nurses had stripped off everything I was wearing, and thank goodness my new riding boots have zips down the back and didn't need to be cut off. Then, to my astonishment, the same clothes come out of the washing machine all ripped in several strange places. Is our new washing machine packing up? At first it doesn't dawn on me that the hospital had cut off my shirt, cut off my bra, sliced away at my underpants and made a small cut in the waistband of my very best breeches.

A couple of weeks later my head feels sort of back to normal and I drive into Boston for my annual obstetrical-gynaecological physical.

I know that all the Massachusetts hospitals put everything about a patient in the computer. My doctor has seen the report and his first words refuse to leave my head. "Liz, please consider stopping riding. You know, permanent brain damage will set in if you have too many concussions."

I don't tell him that after this fall I couldn't remember the combination of the safe and Dave was away all day. I had to ring the safe company and prove I was the true owner before they told me the numbers. And not long after I had to ring them again. I lost the large key to the safe. It took the technician four hours and mega bucks to break into it. "Might be better if I make it work without a key and with just the combination, Mrs Benney." And he gives me that old-age pity look. The key has never turned up.

Now it's time for the doctor's more personal questions. Years ago when I was first bombarded with them in America, I was astonished and felt uncomfortable. New Zealand's culture was very reserved when I grew up. Today it's everything and anything from how's your sex life to breast examination, discharge and blood spotting questions ... Lastly, the doctor asks me if I have frequency? "Well, I can't go through the night without doddering my way to the bathroom."

"How often do you have to get up?"

"Once. Very occasionally twice. Nothing has changed in fifty years."

"Good girl."

Later, as I start to leave, it's back to the question of my continuing to ride and the potential brain damage. "You're a headstrong one, Liz."

"A neat *double entendre*!" I laugh.

I'm not going to count the first time I was knocked out when I crashed over a jump and got my first broken scapula. That time I was only out of my senses for about twenty minutes. There was an ambulance on the show grounds and I woke up on the way to a nearby hospital. The orthopaedic surgeon was summoned from his golf game and at first it was clear how very unhappy he was about being called to work. And how his tune changed when he studied the X-rays. Now I realise why. He found I had one of those uncommon fractures, one that is typical of young men in high-risk sports.

I must say that the next big riding blow knocked me out for a number of hours and was more serious. About five years ago Meghan was boarding her horse with us and asked me to hop on him for a minute. She was longing to see how his trot and canter work had improved. The stirrups were way too long for me, but what the heck. I was only going to ride him for a few minutes.

He went superbly and I said, "You know, he's ready to learn his flying changes." For fun I rode him diagonally across the ring, asked for and actually got the change – and he bolted. (Kathy told me several years later that she was sure he must have experienced a spasm and it panicked him.) Well, whatever sent him off sent *me* off as well. Meghan later reported that we made at least eighteen galloping revolutions of the arena. There was no way I could stop him. I had thought briefly of steering him into the fence, but I wasn't sure if it would stop him or if he would try to jump it or even crash right through it.

Then my legs gave way.

If only I'd shortened my stirrups I could have managed massive leverage and had a better chance of stopping or turning him in a tight circle.

I hit my head on the top of a fence post and woke up hours later in the local hospital. Nothing broken.

I was well into my SC years for my third concussion and it was certainly *not* my fault or any sort of error by Minty. We were in a cross-country clinic with a famous Olympian from England. On the second day of the clinic I was asked to go first in our group of five.

I remember the required course to this day. A stone wall, a ditch, another huge stone wall with a drop on the landing side and three single close-set rail jumps, then up a bank, two strides across the top of it and a big leap off to the ground below. Now we headed for a small movable V-jump. The open part of the V was pointing away from our approach, so we had to guide our horse to jump accurately over the very tip.

Minty was perfect, *but* the V had been assembled under a tree. My head hit a branch. It knocked me out of the saddle and I crashed headfirst on to the ground. Two whacks to the head in the space of two seconds.

It must have taken a long time for the ambulance to arrive across acres and acres of this beautiful estate. Before he could be caught, I'm told that Minty jumped the entire course again and my reins stayed over his neck and never broke. I woke up a mile from the Beverly Hospital in the north-eastern part of Massachusetts. My legs were powerfully strapped to the gurney. I quickly became alert and felt a rising panic of claustrophobia.

"*Please* undo the straps," I begged the two attendants. "They're so tight they make me feel panicky."

"Well, hi," said one of the attendants. "Good, you're awake. Sure we'll untie your legs, but you must answer some questions first. What's your name?"

"Elizabeth Benney."

"Good girl. What's today's date?"

"Well tomorrow is our son, Paul's birthday and it will be June 2."

"Good. Who is the president of the United States?"

I start to giggle. Of course I knew it was the younger Bush, but I replied, "I know who he is and I can't stand him and I refuse to utter his name."

"Oh, *you're okay, lady!* You are *the* best." And off came the straps.

Two hours later I was discharged from the hospital, still wearing all my riding clothes. But not before the owner of the estate arrived to check on me. Everyone agreed, but not until after the fact, that the V was mistakenly placed under the tree.

I've kept the cross-country helmet that took quite a beating. It strikes me as funny that the company recommends that after the *helmet* has suffered a trauma you never wear this approved headgear again. The blameless branch ripped off the silk cover, in my colours of royal blue and white, and when I hit the ground a stone the size of a chestnut lodged itself into one of the venting ports that allows for maximum air circulation. To this day, helmet and attached stone hang on one of the walls in our mudroom.

Now I wonder if my occasional memory lapses have anything to do with these concussions. Certainly that Senior Citizen quiz on which I got four out of five correct answers is encouraging. And with some relief I rationalise that Mother, to my knowledge, was never knocked out riding or under any other circumstances. And she was prone to the same odd memory lapses as mine. But always with recall … it might take only a minute, but the recollection always showed up by the end of the day.

But there's good news about my hearing and the apprehension I was having over my concentration. My two SC friends tell me that they too have the *same* dilemma and the old saying *there's safety in numbers* comforts me. Actually, my hearing and the forgetful issues are pretty rare these days. Of course the occasional *straying* does fit into the zone of an oldie, but whose mind wouldn't wander when one is very busy or distracted by other things? I convince myself that the really bad day, when I frustrated Kathy, was an aberration.

What is more, the bruises from my recent disastrous crash are fading and my head feels clear at last. I've also removed the metal staples in my leg. Lot 2 is finally on the market and I blot out the uneasy real estate market that is ceaselessly slowing down. Marla has written an excellent advertisement for the land with the two old barns, and Dave has worked endlessly preparing the lot. I try my recovering-best to help him sweep out the old barns, mow the two fields, mow the lawns, and weed and clean up the vines overrunning the striking large outcrop of scalloped granite ledge.

But it's not just the endless *maintenance* and the uncertainty of the real estate market that is bothering me.

Chapter Twenty-Two

'Pass the *Hook,* Nurse'

It's odd, but my weakening eyesight has suddenly gone into a tailspin. I can't see a darned thing, even with my glasses, and I have a ton of books waiting to be read. My appointment with the recommended lenses ophthalmologist is a month off but I manage to persuade someone in the office to give me a cancelled appointment time.

I'm in the waiting room, surrounded by frail Senior Citizens shouting to each other and making trips to the toilets. At last I'm ushered into an examination room and a technician puts drops in both eyes. I wait some more until Doc Henry hurries in. He has already been told that I'm half-blind and asks if I've had any change in medication. "Well, yes," I tell him. "My doctor recently prescribed a second pill to control my blood pressure."

"That can suddenly increase the severity of the cataracts. What has been added?"

"I've been put on ... Sorry I can't remember the huge word. I think it starts with hydrochloro..."

"It may be hydrochlorothiazide."

'That's it. Not a word that I need to add to my lexicon."

"I'm sure that is what hastened the clouding of your lenses," and he studies my eyes through an enormous machine. While he's busy, I recall the structure of the eye and what we did in my high school biology class during my brief teaching career in New Plymouth. To heck with the textbook diagrams of eyes. I went to the abattoirs in Waitara and got a bucket of sheep's eyes for the kids to examine. A collective "*Ugh*" could be heard all over the classroom. But the girls soon got into the dissection. Doc interrupts my flashback. "High time to replace both of your lenses."

I know that Doc Henry's wife and son are very successful riders and he seems to know that I'm also in the horse world. He likes the fact I'm British and tells me how he is a devotee of Winston Churchill. So I astonish him by relating how I once stood fifteen feet from Churchill in St Paul's Cathedral. A friend, Margaret, and I were sightseeing and a verger told us to go down to the crypts of the cathedral where Churchill was unveiling a memorial to a famous deceased general from the days of British India. There were only six people in the room and Margaret and I stood in the doorway while Churchill spoke the dedication. The skin on his face had the texture of a baby's, and he was standing so precariously that someone helped him stay upright.

I drive home very confident in Doc Henry but apprehensive at the thought of someone digging into my eyes – and I will be wide-awake. I listen to the radio and hear a news report on how researchers in Australia have found a simple and effective way to cut the risk of falls in elderly people who wear bifocals or other glasses with multi-focus lenses. These types of glasses impair depth perception, which could affect an older person's balance. Oldies should wear single lens distance glasses when they go outdoors and also when they walk up and down stairs. I picture a pair of glasses on my nose and a pair with single lenses living around my neck. Here and now this SC decides that she'll risk any future falls.

Dave's at work and I feel I need someone to commiserate with me. I ring Richard in New Zealand. "Guess what?" I announce. "My eyes are going to pot. I've got yet another symptom of my beastly old age." We talk for an hour and I'm soon forgetting about my complaints when I hear more about the state of Richard's Parkinson's.

It's now at the point where the poor man is suffering from dyskinesia. Basically this movement disorder diminishes voluntary movements and many movements now become involuntary. For Richard it's a violent uncontrollable flinging around of the arms and shoulders. This embarrassing action is actually a byproduct of the pills he's taking, but without the pills there would be severe limiting of mobility and the constant shaking. The on and off dyskinesia lasts pretty much all day with ups and downs of severity. If Richard needs to go somewhere and be seen in public, he knows when to anticipate the worst of the shaking and can decide on the best time to take one of the thirteen pills that he swallows every day. Or he splits them in half so they're taken more often and this tends to diminish the dyskinesia's moments of high intensity.

He also tells me how the right side of his body now feels like the tyres of a car that have been pumped up too high. The left side feels like two flat tyres. He has been having chiropractic adjustments and massages for ages, but they're no longer giving him much relief. And here I am worried about a small operation on my eyes.

Dave drives me to the eye clinic, miles away in Boston. He's armed with mathematical books and will wait in the car. I check in and find myself one of a dozen others in the waiting room. Everyone is elderly, and walkers and walking sticks abound. Some patients have even arrived on the arms of assistants. I'm out of place here.

'Remember, Liz,' I correct myself, 'you fit exactly into this picture, like the last piece of a jigsaw.' At least my legitimate murky white hair is hidden under light brown chemicals.

I'm called into a small cubicle and a very cheerful nurse takes my blood pressure. It's a whopping 187/100. "Can I still have the operation?" I ask in an anxious voice.

"Yes, but I can't put the special sponge into your eye with all the necessary medication that has been oozed on to it. That would further raise your blood pressure." Instead I sit there and *eleven* different drops are popped on to my left eyeball. They come so quickly they overflow and flood down my cheek. "Don't worry about it," I'm told.

From here I'm escorted to the prep room and a long needle is stuck into one of the prominent veins in my left hand. I feel a mild cold surge fly up my arm. At that moment Doc Henry comes running into the room. He's eating a banana and greets me. "How are the horses, Liz?" He looks stunning in a navy blue jacket and a bright red beret, and his beard is neatly trimmed.

More drops and some glutinous jell is oozed into the left eye. "Keep it closed for two minutes." And I'm led into the operating room and helped on to the operating table.

There's no turning back.

I observe all the equipment as I lie down and take a very deep breath. Next, a nurse with the most gorgeous eyelashes that I've ever seen sticks a shield over my face and cuts out an opening to the left eye. She distracts my apprehension with her stories of many bungy jumps and skydives. So with the effects of the medicine really loosening up the inborn glib in me, I tell her about my recent polar plunge, and then my paraglide jump into space and how we floated down through eighteen hundred feet.

Every year I'm in New Zealand I usually fly into Queenstown to visit Jill and John in Wanaka. When the weather conditions are ideal I've hankered to do the paraglide jump even though Mother warned me years before that the jumpers sometimes were hurt or even killed.

Anyway I decided to check it out thoroughly. I phoned the company and said I didn't want to be rude, but could I possibly jump with their best guy?

"Ma'am, we have three excellent paragliders, but unfortunately only Bob is available. One of the men has a broken leg and another one has disappeared. We haven't seen him for three weeks. I hope we can offer you a suitable time with the available one. He's a very technically trained expert and Bob is an Australian."

Now, as the eye doctor hasn't yet appeared and I'm beginning to think that eye surgery is better than leaping off a cliff, I tell the nurse how Bob joined me at the base of the chair lift. And how at the top we climbed up this incredibly steep side of the mountain for half an hour. Bob was running up like a fit thoroughbred and I was trying my best to appear fit and young. We reached a flat area and I was strapped into a harness and tied to the front of Bob.

The nurse asks if I were scared.

"Oddly enough, I really wasn't worried. Ask me if I'm scared this minute and I'll give you a different answer."

"There's really nothing to worry about. Doc has done hundreds of these operations with superb results. Now tell me about the jump."

So I relate how Bob and I ran towards the cliff's edge and how I closed my eyes and jumped into space. We soared into the sky with an unbelievable feeling. The updraft was superb and we glided out towards Lake Wakatipu before finally flowing down to land. "Bob started to head straight for a row of trees. I knew he was kidding, but of course I reacted. We just missed getting tangled in the top branches and landed with a bit of a bang. I fell back into Bob's arms and let out the same primordial scream that flew from my chest when I dropped under the Antarctic water."

"Don't scream in my presence, Liz." I recognise Doc's laughing voice. "Are you okay?"

"Sure," I lie.

"Okay, here we go."

I can feel a lot of what's going on, but not much pain. At first I can see a shining light, then the murky appearance of what must be tools. I now have quite a bit of discomfort combined with the fact it is always hard for me to lie still. Suddenly someone takes my hand. Then doc gets mad at his assistant. "*No!* Not that one, nurse. I want the *hook*. Pass me the *hook*." That's enough for me to squeeze the lifeblood out of the mystery hand. The light now almost disappears with the defective lens being pulled out. It feels as if Doc is taking it out in three separate pieces.

Next I get the impression that Doc is having trouble pushing the new lens into the 'sack' and I discipline myself to follow his sharp orders: "Keep absolutely still, Elizabeth." I decide to count to one hundred in my head and if I reach it and the operation isn't over, I'll keep going. I peter out before reaching the end of three hundred.

Finally Doc says, "All done, Liz. It went really well."

The female nurse now helps me off the table and a very handsome male nurse takes my arm. "Was that you who held my hand?" I ask.

He grins, "That was me. You did well."

It's into the recovery room and I'm given a mug of coffee, something I seldom touch after eight in the morning but it tastes great with a slice of pound cake. It's *over*. Well, eye number one is done, with just days and days of five drops in the morning and again in the evening. I'm also given a shield to wear over the eye at night. "Why?" I ask.

"Well, we don't want you thrashing around and hitting your eye."

The second eye gets its new lens and again everything goes well, but I'm thankful I wasn't born with three eyes. No riding for a few days and I say to myself, "Well, not on Catch."

Dave drives me home and I run to the mirror. It's true. I'm looking at the picture of Dorian Gray, AKA Elizabeth Benney. Twenty years have just passed by me in the time it took to install two new lenses. I turn off the mirror lights and I look slightly less superannuated. It's also a shock to know that for years people have been looking at the *real furrowed me* through their healthy lenses.

I can ride again, but I'm more nervous than ever when mounting Catch and I can feel her tension. I'm almost at the point where I'm going to quit riding her. I laugh to myself when I think how Mother would never let us use the word *quit*. It wasn't until I was well into my adult years that I realised what she meant. *Quit* was not some sort of naughty swear-like word but it meant giving in to something. I think how giving up riding Catch is giving in … to what?

Fear?

Injury?

Old age?

Muscle weakness?

For the first time in my life I understand when people say they're afraid to ride.

Chapter Twenty-Three

That Old Yearning

Summer arrives with endless grass to mow, endless weeds to pull and endless areas to fertilise and lime. My Lumbar 5 is acting up, but I can control it with Advil. With a mixture of reluctance and hesitation that has lasted days, I've decided to stop riding Catch. She knows I'm scared to mount her and I'm scared of her response when something startles her. I'm at the point where I can't trust her.

It's not her fault that she reacts this way. It is something inherent in her make-up and it goes way back to the days before horses were domesticated ... that instinctive response to fear, and hence the flight. And she knows I'm afraid. Better not chance another blow to my head or broken bones. Catch is so perfect ninety-nine per cent of the time and it makes me crazy that I can't cope with a horse's reaction that would never ever have bothered me a few years ago.

Elizabeth, all good things come to an end.

Yes. It's the end of a very long and privileged chapter of my life. Thank goodness Minty doesn't have the same instinctive-type reactions. I know he'll never hurt or scare me, and after Catch and my demeaning fall from grace, I feel a new determination to redeem myself jumping. I must stop constantly putting off the necessary strengthening groundwork. Quite frankly I'm embarrassed by my continuing procrastination.

Dave's off again to Hong Kong for a week and Marla comes to update me on Lot 2. "I've a great couple interested, but they have to sell their house first, then rent a place before they can buy your land and plan on building. They're crazy about the lot."

"Marla, I'm not filled with confidence, and the housing market's still sinking." And my mood is also sinking fast. Was my decision to stop riding Catch made in haste? If only I'd worked harder to strengthen my legs for jumping, they'd be strong enough to cope with Catch's antics as well. I've already entered the mare in a show, but decide that solid old Minty will go instead.

Sue comes with me and she's in a great frame of mind. Her house looks like it's sold, but she'll have to find somewhere to live with her cat, Henry. There are still bigamist-articles left in the house and Sue looks forward to chucking them out or selling them.

Show day starts off well. Minty is *on* and our warm-up is terrific. My number is called and I ride around the dressage arena until the judge rings the bell. I now have forty-five seconds before I must enter at A.

In we go and halt obediently and squarely at X in the middle of the arena. I track towards the judge and catch a glance of approval on her face. A couple more trot turns and we start our canter circle. It feels so balanced and light, everything a rider wants to experience.

Suddenly, quite out of the blue, my great old Minty collapses on to his knees and off I pitch.

He struggles to his feet, leaving me inert on the sandy footing. Sue hurries over and even the judge appears above me. I try to get up and they insist I lie still and to take my time. At last I'm helped on to my feet and see Minty standing stock still and looking at me with a baffled expression: *What the heck are you doing down there?*

A good question, Minty.

I can't believe I've just had another fall. There's no way I can get back on and I can barely drive home, at which point I can't heave myself out of the truck. Sue thoughtfully does everything, and, with Dave away, I know I'll need some heavy-duty painkiller that hasn't expired. I simply can't believe this has happened to me … and on my trustworthy old Minty? Reluctantly I ring my doctor. As it's a Sunday of course he's off duty. I leave a message with the answering service and shortly the associate doctor rings me back. "I hear you just fell off your horse?" Her voice sounds so critical. "And I see that you're well into your seventies."

What the heck has that got to do with it? "Well," I respond, "I didn't fall off. My horse fell down and I had no option but to hit the deck."

"Why did your horse fall down?"

"I have no idea. Everyone agreed that he never tripped or stumbled but just sort of collapsed."

"Maybe he had a heart attack."

Oh *please.*

"I don't know. I had his heart checked with his spring shots. And I'm alone right now. My husband's in Hong Kong."

"All right. I'll prescribe something strong." And the doctor says she'll call our pharmacy. Sue goes to collect the prescription.

Enough to say that nothing is broken, my head is intact and Sue, my children and friends all rally to help me. But why did Minty drop down without any warning? He's not one ever to stumble or trip and the footing in the ring was perfect. Dave, my loyal blacksmith, comes and checks his shoes. No problem there. Jay, my superb long-time vet, comes and checks for neurological problems. Minty passes everything, one hundred per cent. He does have a heart murmur that we know about, but it's nothing to worry over. Horses can get a form of narcolepsy, but Jay and I doubt this was the cause.

I lie in bed and suddenly I have the possible answer. Minty dropped to his knees the way that I used to drop to my knees so many years ago, after that initial Lumbar 5 injury when Jill and I tried to swap our ponies without touching the ground. In the morning I ring the horse chiropractor, Steve, and he says he'll be here in two days.

Drugged to the gills, I try to function. I must get better as I leave for China in three weeks' time. My Tianjin friends have arranged so much for me, and with all of Dave's and my travels in China I know I'll need plenty of energy.

Our trips began in 1983 when Dave and another professor were invited to China to examine students wanting to study mathematics in the USA. China would select the top elite students from the best universities and Dave would examine them in applied mathematics and the other professor in his field of pure mathematics. For those students who qualified and also passed an English language test, Dave would recommend which United States university each student should apply to. He would then advise the university to accept this or that particular applicant.

I flew to China as well, fulfilling a longtime dream to see this great country. During the four days of the exams I had a chauffeur and an interpreter – and the time of my life. Then we three would be taken on a trip to many corners of the continent. Unfortunately, after Tianamen Square the programme was discontinued but Dave often went as a guest of different universities, and I had become the friend of a Tianjin University family who have begged me to come to their country every year and travel with them to see more unique sights.

Now I simply must get better. We're also still longing to get Lot 2 off our hands. With no break in the housing market's continuing decline, Marla rings me and says it's very doubtful that the family interested in the lot can sell their own house for quite some time. But she has brought another person to view the land. He's a man who is ripe to put down his money, practically on the spot. He's going to turn the North Barn into his house and he has employed an architect to see if it's possible. Thank goodness Dave will be back by the end of the week.

As we all know, nothing is final until the money is in the bank. Then, after all the effort of making plans to convert the old barn, the man suddenly vanishes from the scene and his phone is disconnected.

Steve the chiropractor arrives and goes all over Minty, starting with his hind quarters. I also explain my theory and I like his response. "Oh, I've had the odd patient with a problem just like yours." I stand silently and watch. Steve pauses and then instructs me to lead Minty down to the tack room and put on his saddle.

That turns out to be the culprit. "I can see where it can sometimes pinch up here near his backbone," Steve explains. "When you, Minty and the saddle are in a certain position, the saddle will press on an important pressure point and it affects a nerve running down to the shoulder. The muscle just gives way when that nerve is pinched. Minty had no choice but to go down on his knees involuntarily."

For two months I'd been using Catch's dressage saddle. I thought that it fitted Minty. It certainly fitted me and was easier on my back than my other saddle. "Oh poor Minty." I give him a peppermint and he softly rubs his lips on my face. "And it's odd," I tell Steve, "but for some time now, he sometimes sort of dropped that left shoulder an inch or two while I was riding him. It's almost like something was giving way. I never considered the saddle and just thought it was part of the old boy aging."

"Never use this saddle again," Steve instructs, "and give Minty two weeks off. I'm positive it won't happen again." He checks Minty's regular saddle and it's a perfect fit. I sigh with relief. My biting the dust, yet again, had nothing to do with my weak legs.

It's great that Minty's not ready for retirement and I feel a new determination rising in my head. Intellectually a little voice says that I should forget the whole idea of jumping again, but I just can't get past the yearning. I wish I could glide over this longing just as I sailed over two other passions in the past. I was in my last year at university and was devastated at the thought of graduating and facing a life of boring nine to five grind. How could I ever leave this fantastic independent, unleashed university life? And yet I graduated and never looked back.

The same feeling came over me about skiing. How could I *ever* be too old or frail to ski? It didn't take long to end that desire after skiing in New England's constant bitter cold and down *narrow trails framed by trees* ... I was never good at having to make quick slalom-like turns. How I missed the wide open treeless slopes of Arthurs Pass, Craigieburn, Mt Cheeseman and even the limited skiing on Mt Egmont. Sometimes there were days when we could tear down the mountain slopes in T-shirts.

I'm getting too old to be falling off all the time. These irritating words keep ringing in my ears. Okay, I definitely won't event again. I really will get ready for trainer Paul to help me ride Minty over some little beginner courses. (So infra dig, so beneath my dignity!) And I bet Paul says, "No way, Lizzie."

Maybe I'll take Minty to a hunter show and compete in one of those newly offered classes where the jumps are so low you can hardly see them. But no, I would be ribbon-pinching entering such classes. But I could go HDC (hors de concours) and be judged but not placed. When I first competed in America there were never any classes with obstacles that were under a solid three foot six inches.

Then I will think about retiring from my long-time passion, with no black bruises on any part of my body. I will go out on the crest of a wave, albeit a wave that is pretty low in height.

Elizabeth, stop daydreaming!

Dave is back home, thank goodness. His quick trip was very successful except the long hours sitting in the plane and walking everywhere over the university campus seemed to have bothered his right hip. "I hate to say it, Liz, but my left hip started this same way." It was nine years ago and Dave finally decided to go to the orthopaedic doctor. The joint was bone on bone. The replacement was very successful.

"Oh Dave," I respond, "*Please* don't be stubborn. Please go and have it checked out."

"No way! It'll go away. I just did too much in Hong Kong."

I have to laugh to myself … here again comes the old New Zealand cultural attitude of *Rise above it and never complain … she'll be right.*

I prepare for China and the trip to Guizhou Province. I'm feeling much better about flying around this vast continent than in past years. In the early 1980s there was no way that I could stop Mother's ongoing anxiety the minute Dave and I flew into Beijing. And she really did have every reason to worry. Plane crashes were no surprise. The first plane we ever took was from Beijing to Xian. As we climbed on board I noticed the CAAC letters of the Chinese airlines and underneath the paint I could just make out the words, Zimbabwe Airlines. Once on board I sat down and my armrest fell on to the floor and my seat wouldn't move to the upright position. We finally took off and liquid started pouring down the aisle from the unmanned galley. All the Chinese passengers pumped away at their call-buttons, but there was no hostess.

The next year we flew from Beijing to Inner Mongolia to see the grasslands and sleep in a yurt, and I wanted to ride a Mongolian pony. And ride one I did, but the native man insisted on keeping me on a beginner's leash from his own pony. I kept on telling him, in my very halting Mandarin from lessons I'd been taking, that I could ride, but he spoke only the local dialect. On the flight back from Hohhote we were crowded into a tiny propeller plane. It taxied to the end of a short runway and started to rev one engine and then the other, until they sounded like they were going to detonate. This went on for many minutes as if the pilot couldn't decide whether to go or to stay.

He decided to give it a go.

We had just left the ground when a colossal backfire rocketed the plane, but worse was to come. Smoke started coming out of the wall above the luggage rack in the front of the plane. The Chinese passengers on board spied it too and started jumping out of their seats. They kept on pressing buttons to alert the hostess. Again, there was no hostess! And the pilot or co-pilot made no appearance. I nudged Robert, the other professor sitting beside me, and when he looked at my horrified face he knew that something was seriously wrong. I pointed to the smoke. Robert gasped and then started to laugh. Smoke was now pouring out of more orifices above the passengers. "Liz, it's the air conditioner coming on. It's condensation."

The next year we were flying from Chengdu in Sichuan Province to Shanghai. Dave and I were the only Caucasians on board and soon after take-off the pilot announced that we were flying over the Chang Jiang or Yangtse River. A sea of black heads rushed to the port side of the plane. Only Dave and I were left on the right hand side.

After several hours the plane descended through heavy rain towards the scattered night-lights of Shanghai. All the passengers but Dave and me were now out of their seats, pulling down piles of luggage. Then we touched down. Touched down? *Ground down*. We were sliding along the runway. The plane was shaking, and there was a massive crunching sound below us.

Mercifully we stopped at last and all the passengers were once again back in their seats, rigid and silent. A lone voice rang out from way behind us. *"Holy shit."* We hadn't seen the third Caucasian on board. The plane was unable to move and we all disembarked into the bleak wet night and hiked a long way in the dark to the terminal. After an endless wait our sopping wet bags arrived.

But that was then and this is now. Well, China, here I come again.

Chapter Twenty-Four

Into the Heart of China

It's May now and with the arrival of a mini-bus I begin my trip to China. Dave is still happy with my globetrotting and again confirms that he just can't be bothered with any sort of sightseeing any more. "I love hearing about your adventures," he always says when I try to persuade him to come, "but the old travel bug in me quits." I wonder when I too will reach this stage of my life and can't be bothered with the effort.

The mini-bus moves on to an empty road and immediately our driver becomes non-stop chatty and it's 4.30 in the morning. I ask him what was the longest time he was ever kept waiting for a passenger. "Seventeen minutes. And when I complained, the passenger said, 'And what are you going to do about it? Shoot me?'"

I'm flying via Hong Kong and it's magic descending through fluffy clouds and then the reality of the hundreds and hundreds of wall-to-wall high rises contrasting with the green uninhabited hills behind. Polite officials stroll everywhere in the airport and I have a short walk to the only available hotel, advertised as a five star. Ha ha. Well, there is always something in a Chinese bathroom that doesn't work. It's the shower curtain this time. It's eighteen inches too short and what a flood. Thankfully and without exception, Chinese bathrooms have big, efficient drains in the middle of the floor.

The following morning I enjoy a mixture of a Western and an Eastern breakfast and surprise, surprise. I've never seen them before in China, but there are salt and pepper shakers. *But* the pepper is in the one with the single hole, and salt floods out of the many pepper holes.

Back I walk to the airport and with time to spare wander around the many shops. Hermes covers a lot of space and there are two Hermes saddles, each costing thirty-four thousand Hong Kong dollars. (Divide by seven for US dollars.) "Yes," the sales clerk tells me, "we sell quite a few of these very expensive saddles."

I'm the only woman on the three-hour flight to Tianjin and the turbulence is really bad. For a while I look down at the isolated ranges with tiny villages tucked in here and there. We're served a meal in spite of the jarring impacts and it's meat with rice and seven tiny green peas on the top. The English menu calls it *solonaceae* vegetables.

In Tianjin I fill in the arrival and customs forms and swear on the penalty of jail and a whopping fine that I possess no marijuana. Wang, my host, meets me and we taxi to his incredible new apartment on the eighth floor of a brand new high-rise. I have my own room and my own bathroom. What a change from when I first stayed with the family and there was just a dribble of hot water for two hours three times a week. On the other days Wang would boil a huge pot of water and place it in the tiny toilet area with a very clever assortment of rubber tubing, one connected to the cold water tap. Under a trickle of warm water from above, I would shower until the pot of hot water ran dry. Plastic sheeting covered the toilet bowl and I wore community plastic thongs on my feet.

Tonight his daughter, Ping, prepares a Peking duck dinner, and granddaughter, Yuan Yuan, plays the piano for me. She has just passed the ninth piano grade and is only twelve years old. She plays Chopin's Polonaise from memory and technically it blows me away. Sadly Wang's sister and brother-in-law have decided not to accompany us to Guizhou after all. "They're not feeling in the best of shape," Wang tells me. And they *are* over eighty.

Friday, and Wang and I leave in a university taxi for Beijing. On the super new highway we make a toilet stop and there's still the 'hole in the floor' in a low-walled cubicle with no door. Two little kids watch me, fascinated. "Kan, kan Waigouren xiaobian!" 'Look, look foreigner wee, wees!' We arrive at the airport at 2.30pm and the plane is due to leave at 4pm.

Lucky for me, Wang is a member of the prestigious Chinese Academy of Science and qualifies for all first-class lounges. We find that the plane is delayed, but the cozy lounge also affords us the rare luxury of regular updates. The first update is that the plane from Guiyang, where we're visiting in Guizhou Province in south central China, is *slightly* delayed. As soon as it arrives, it will be serviced and it will depart from Beijing at 4pm.

4.30pm. The plane's arrival is now delayed by storms.

5pm. Our plane is on its way from Guilin of all places, and has yet to arrive in Guiyang, where it will quickly pick up passengers and proceed to Beijing.

5.30pm. The plane is now in Guiyang.

6pm. The plane is stuck in Guiyang because of storms.

I go to the computer serving the lounge and there's not one storm across the whole expanse of China.

6.30pm. The plane has left for Beijing.

7pm. There is a further problem. Plane is delayed once more and no reason is given.

Nothing further is announced. I hold my critical tongue.

I suggest to Wang that he checks in case there are any other flights going to Guiyang, but he's hesitant to ask. At 8pm he finally decides to inquire and finds that there *is* another plane but five other passengers in our fancy lounge have already taken five of the six available seats.

I hold my tongue.

Finally, the attendant tells us there's still just one seat available and, just in case another does become available, we're told to walk for twenty minutes to the departure lounge in the old terminal building.

Again we sit in the first-class lounge awaiting instructions. A further crisis. Wang has lost his identification card. We'd already been told to submit all our documents and a while later they're given back to us and Wang discovers his card is missing. He rushes all over the place and officials help him. After a while, on a whim, I look in my passport – and there it is, the missing card that would have kept us in Beijing for the night and who knows how many of the following nights.

We're now told that the new flight will leave at 9.30pm and now there just *may* be two seats available. We're given a plate of rice porridge and I manage to find some milk and sugar to turn the porridge into Western fare. We're also told that the original flight on which we were booked for Guiyang is now cancelled.

We're *on* at 10.00pm. Wang kindly insists that I take the first-class seat and he sits at the very back of the 737. It seems unfair as he *is* in his eighties, but I doubt I could have survived three hours in that tiny seat, what with the endless days I've had recovering from Minty's involuntary drop.

I sit back and wait for take-off. The interior of the plane looks as if it has been through seven lives. Everywhere there are holes in the walls, and scratches, but it's very clean. Moments before we take off I call Dave on my cell phone – and how today's technology blows me away. It's ten in the morning Boston time and all is well. "Honestly, Dave, who knows if this worn-out plane will make it to Guiyang. Just in case, I must say that I love you all. Make sure my horses get good homes!" We laugh.

At last we're off with a lot of aircraft creaks and squeaks followed by moans. We reach our cruising height in a pitch-black night.

My section of our plane has two charming flight attendants, girls who look about twelve years old and have dyed red and permed hair. They're also wearing double earrings, very high heels and mini-skirts. How China has changed since my first visit so long ago when the entire population dressed in the standard Mao look-alike clothes … everyone, without exception, in a white shirt and dark blue or black pants. I'm starting to recall lots of Mandarin that I learnt years ago when we first started going to China. I chat with the girls and find out they're both twenty-five years old and one of them giggles as she tells me she's married.

A meal at last. Delicious cold cuts, garlic bread and an exotic salad. In the 1980s foreigners were warned never to eat tomatoes, lettuce or watermelon. I remember watching Ping wash the lettuce in warm *soapy* water.

A full moon rises and I can't wait to land and get into bed.

We descend into thick fog and with no warning the undercarriage suddenly takes a beating as we drop on to a dimly lit airstrip. Guiyang at last, at 1.30 in the morning. It's a tiny airport and the ebullient president of Guizhou University is there to meet us. We pile into a car with the windows tinted black like those in stretch limos and it's hard to see anything even in the moonlight as we drive an hour to our hotel. And what a hotel. It is so grand I pinch myself. My room is tops and the bathroom is equipped with everything down to the rows and rows of bottles containing shampoos, all sorts of lotions and scent sprays. There's also a bottle full of bubble bath, but I have no bath. Plus there's a shower cap, dental floss, razors, comb, toothbrush, matches, scales and bottles of fresh water *and* little plastic-enclosed wipes, written in English, 'Sanitary pupos.' And underneath is written 'Lady's rag'.

There's lots of hot water and for once I'm confident that *this* Chinese bathroom will be a hundred percent. It is really no surprise, however, that the drain in the shower is completely blocked and after a couple of minutes the water rises to the edges of the shower compartment and spills over. Thank goodness for the ubiquitous drain in the middle of the floor.

I always check the emergency exits in a hotel, and read the directions under the heading *Security Scattering Sketch.*

Please don't worry if a fire is occuring. We hotel have owned superior scattering facilities to ansure you transmitted safely. (Stairs?) *Please follow the information corridor and there safeguards will take you out to security belts. Red point stand for where you stay now.*

I recall our hotel in Chengdu where a sign on the back of our bedroom door read: *In an emergency please evacuate yourself along the corridors.*

My luxurious double bed has been pulled back and the covers are anchored with a tiny doll in the local minority's costume. She is one and a half inches long and beautifully hand-made. The Miao Minority are famous in Guizhou Province.

Saturday breakfast is in an enormous stunningly decorated room and not another Caucasian in sight. It's hard to recognise any of the copious dishes of food except for hard boiled eggs (no salt or pepper) and some shredded cabbage. I have the delicious Chinese rice porridge that I smother with milk and sugar to the astonishment of nearby Chinese. I also recognise some noodles, and there's a bowl of very fresh strawberries.

A car appears per kind favour of the university president and we're driven to a long trail beside a riverbank. It's only 13 degrees C, which is around 56 degrees F and it's raining. In spite of the conditions, several people are swimming in the chilly river. Then it's off in the car over potholes and open manholes and why did anyone bother to mark pedestrian crossings? Our driver toots at people to get out of our way, but they take absolutely no notice. Pedestrians and cyclists have the right of way on this main road and we swerve around them. I recall someone from Guang Dong telling me how pedestrians reacted when traffic lights were first installed. All the people would saunter across the road when the lights were green and cross flat out when the lights were red! Every hundred yards along the side of the highway, women in bandanas are sweeping the road and the footpaths. We're off to Kaili, two hundred kilometres away.

Guizhou Province is one of the poorest in China. We pass strange hills like toes poking out of a blanket and there's little else but rock, and on all flat surfaces there's a very thin layer of topsoil. In some of the low areas, water buffalo are preparing the rice paddies as they strain in the shafts of a single plough and slosh through a foot of muddy water. We have a toilet stop and it's the same old ubiquitous hole in the ground and no privacy. My balance is challenged as I cope with a host of unfit muscles and a body that's recovering, ever so slowly, from my latest fall. Of course you must always carry your own toilet paper.

Our car doesn't have dark-tinted windows and I'm told the one that collected us last night is used only for VIPs. I am treated as a sort of VIP, always being introduced as 'wife of famous MIT professor' ... and how unpretentious Dave hates these words! The president thought we would like to see more scenery today so we have a normal-windowed vehicle.

We arrive in Kaili at lunchtime and are driven immediately to an enchanting old wooden structure. We climb up an outside stairway and enter a very small room where our Kaili host and others connected with the local university meet us. Of course our driver and guide come with us for a sumptuous banquet. Ten of us sit around a table and tackle twelve dishes. I'm warned that two Miao Minority girls will soon appear in their native costumes and will sing and then offer us a very heavy and potent drink. *If* you touch the horn in which the drink is being presented to your mouth, they make you drink the whole lot.

I have one sip and the burn travels way below my navel and up to the top of my head. The girls sing a native song that's more like a shriek in the higher octaves and a moan in the lower ones. Then one of them picks up chopsticks and first comes to my side. The procedure is that she is to start lunch by feeding me. You would never guess what this beautiful girl picks up in her chopsticks from one of the many plates of food. *A fried locust.* There's no way I can be rude, but, just as the thing is three inches from my mouth, Wang yelps out, "Ta bu yao!' She doesn't want it. The girl is annoyed, picks up a huge type of pancake and deliberately shoves it into my mouth. There are ten of us at the table and everyone but Wang and me and a lovely girl called Qin is smoking.

Qin is now assigned to me. She's a twenty-year-old and teaches English at the Normal School, a type of junior college. Wang's going to the college to give a talk. But first we're taken to our hotel and it's so odd that there's no registration and no viewing of our passports. This is certainly a first in my many visits to China. I'm delighted with my large room. The Grand Dragon Hotel is clean and I have a comfortable bed.

Qin and I tour the town and the Normal School and I bond with this sweet and naïve local girl. And then it's on to another banquet with twelve dishes, including a delicious whole fish, its eyes glaring at me, since I'm still considered the guest of honour. As usual the two drivers eat with us. There are two cars now because we seem to have collected quite a few Kaili university people.

I've lost my glasses case and later in the day Wang and I wander through the town and find a large underground-shopping complex. I buy a solid case for fifty US cents. My bathroom is okay that night but it takes me an age to get the best mix of hot and cold. And my towel is *six feet long* and drags on the floor.

The following day Wang and I eat a 'street breakfast'. It costs thirty US cents each for a dish of rice porridge, (I'm given milk and sugar by the appalled vendor), and two types of tasty pancakes, one very salty and one very sweet. Then our group is collected in two cars and we head for the mountains and the famous minority Miao area.

There are fifty-six different minority groups in China, most with their own language and specific culture. The Miao live in the mountainous area of Guizhou and we drive into their realm via a long steep valley with a rushing river. Beside it, ranges rise to around fifteen hundred feet and every available area is terraced and cultivated. On the lower slopes are the rice paddies, being ploughed by ponderous water buffalo. There are children everywhere, playing right beside the road and often in the middle of the road, regardless of the traffic. As in Guiyang, people on foot have the right of way and I have no idea if they are acting legally. Toot, toot goes our driver and swings around groups of tiny tots and avoids the many dogs, not unlike pitbulls. Pedestrians and playgroups and dogs do come first on these roads. It's as if they're not even aware of an approaching car. It's the same with the farmer who's leading a slow-motion water buffalo down the middle of the road.

Villages cling to the steep hillsides, and are consistently built with black stone. Everywhere are the twisting tracks winding up the cultivated terraces above and called *yang chang shao dao* – sheep's intestines. In every available spot on the edge of the road grow cabbages and corn.

We drive more than two hours until we reach a famous park, thick with strange-looking trees. Except for the ferns, I don't recognise a single species. I give Qin a fun lesson in fern reproduction, and everyone becomes glued to my description about the mature spores on the back of the many fronds.

It's strange but only this morning I found a computer in the hotel that I can use. I log on to the *Taranaki Daily News*, my New Plymouth home newspaper, and sadly read about the death of my old university botany colleague, David Lloyd. We shared a microscope and did study ferns, and from the other half of that microscope he became a world-famous botanist. David went to Harvard and used to visit us in the '60s. Some twenty years ago he went to a conference in the USA and fell in love with an American. Back home his paramour had a fit and was charged with slashing his car tyres and ripping his clothes, and then with trying to poison him with a deadly chemical. There was a famous court case but the charge was not proved. David became blind and paralysed from the poison, and still married the American girl. How he would have loved this forest.

Now we climb and climb way up past the ferns, and for fifteen minutes I think I'm going to collapse with exhaustion. Then my second wind sets in. Everyone wants to turn back, but Qin, another man and I continue way on up to view a splendid waterfall. It takes us more than an hour before we return.

Back we drive down the valley, eventually crossing the river via a covered bridge in the old Chinese classical architecture and drive up a very steep hill for lunch at a small restaurant in a private home. We're in a tiny room with the drivers of the two cars smoking away. Fifteen dishes are served one after the other and I'm presented with a chicken head, in its entirety, floating in broth. Its eyes are open. I glance at Wang and ask in English if I have to eat it.

"No!"

Suddenly two minority sisters come into the room and *scream* out a song about the mountain and how welcome we are. Both are dressed in their spectacular native costume, heavily embroidered in solid silver. Later they tell me that it took their mother two years to make just one of the costumes. After the song they come first to my side and offer me local rice wine. They put the dish that contains the liquid to my lips and I nearly choke. Wang sits next to me and I ask him to identify some of the dishes. He has no idea, or is unable to translate. I stick to what looks like the fish, vegetables and rice.

There's a story about the Miao Minorities that goes way back into the past. Han or the regular Chinese men would come up the valley to have affairs with the beautiful Miao girls. The men would promise the girls they would return, but they always died if they did not return within a year. The girls had secretly given them a poison. If the men returned, the men were given an antidote and didn't die. It seems distinctly far-fetched to me, but I'm given the name of the poison, Yu, and the man who relates this story swears that it is true.

After over-eating, we wander outside and wonder at the views, the strange construction of the wooden buildings and the clear atmosphere. Then a hike up a very steep hill to a small arena where we're entertained with local music produced by four men playing huge whining wooden instruments. This is followed by a dance where you jump over bamboo rods. Eight men, one each at the ends of four poles, click and clack the poles sideways and back again, and the locals jump deftly over them, from one side to the other. The poles are about six inches off the ground.

Visitors are called to try the jump and of course dumb me tries. It looks so easy and I just about break an ankle. Later I'm invited back into a circle to join hands with the many dancers and we do a sort of three-beat step to the bonging of a drum. It feels great once I'm into the rhythm and it helps my lingering stiffness.

Finally it's the long drive back to Guiyang and once at the hotel we're told to be ready to leave in ten minutes. We're driven to a banquet given by the university president who'd met us at the airport. Wang is a famous scientist in China, and oh the red-carpet treatment. And am I treated as just old Liz Benney? Yet again I'm flattered to be ridiculously introduced as 'wife of famous MIT professor,' and heads nod in approval. Wang and Dave have long been close colleagues and I'm amused at the spin-off, which inevitably horrifies Dave.

More food. Again we're in a tiny room seated at a round table. There are twelve of us and everyone smokes but Wang and me. We eat for about two hours and not a single one of the *twenty-one* dishes is finished. Everyone toasts everyone else with the terribly strong grain-based *maotai* and I have a hard time declining. No one will accept my *'No more, thank you.'* It's great fun and although I'm encouraged to eat the frog, the Chinese are now more aware of the things that Westerners can't swallow. I eat a lot of the *jaozi* or dumplings, the noodles, pickles, cucumber soup and fabulous fish. There are four of them tonight all served whole with their eyes looking askance at me. Some of the Chinese love crunching the heads of the fish. I stick to digging my chopsticks into their bellies.

At last I can get to bed and call Dave on my cell phone. The 'famous professor' is well and all goes smoothly on the farm. I relate every detail about today – and again he groans at being so academically acclaimed.

I sleep soundly. I don't think there's another person staying in my enormous hotel wing. I've no idea where Wang's room is located in another distant wing. I should have got his number or phone extension in case of *fire*.

As arranged I meet Wang for breakfast, but this morning the whole cavernous dining room is empty. There are no employees around and there is no food. It turns out that we're the only guests in this huge, magnificent hotel and we should have requested breakfast the night before. However Wang locates a man who eventually brings us a huge plate of chocolate cake. Oddly enough I don't like chocolate cake. I long for some coffee, but all they can serve is powdered coffee and I know it is way too sweet and full of dried milk. Wang begs the man to get us something else and we're each given a boiled egg and some pickles. No salt and pepper.

Wang is off to the university to give a talk to the students. He tells me it's about things that are happening in the current emerging Chinese society. I long to know what it all means but he says it's too difficult to translate. It's funny, but I don't think he wants to explain it. He is so very private. Meanwhile someone has arranged for a car and a grad student to accompany me downtown to do some shopping. Guo turns out to be splendid company even though he speaks no English. He also turns out to be mad on *cats*. Cats in China. An easy topic for my limited Mandarin.

Guo collects strays or unwanted cats and a veterinarian checks them all before Guo tries to find them homes. He has just placed two cats with an American couple and the cats will emigrate with their new owners when they return to the States. I'm surprised to hear you can buy kitty litter that clumps and all sorts of prepared foods for cats, but Guo prefers to order all his cat food on-line as the quality is better.

Our driver takes us downtown to a good shopping area and I find almost all the products are made by the Miao Minority.

Back at the university I'm now introduced to Juliette and we wait for Wang to finish his lecture before going to a 'famous place'. All places in China appear to be categorised as 'famous places'. We have a new driver with the tiniest moustache and we drive through the suburbs and out into the countryside. I am so surprised to see large new Western-style houses, belonging to the 'new rich'.

The famous place involves taking a shuttle bus through a park to a lake, climbing aboard a boat and getting poled through a labyrinth of caves. We're guided all the way by subdued lighting. There are stalactites and stalagmites, many in strange forms.

"See the lobster," we're told.

"See the Buddha."

"See the little boy urinating."

"See the water lily upside down."

Finally we enter a man-made tunnel that connects us to another series of caves and the exterior. This passage is narrow and we're told it's three hundred metres long and facilitates the one-way system through the caves. It is only a few feet deep whereas the natural ones are up to ninety feet deep. We keep on crashing into the sides of this tunnel, and it's hold on tightly.

When we exit, Juliette takes me to a ladies' room and explains that the government of Guizhou is demanding that all such places be upgraded so foreigners can enjoy the Guizhou province. Juliette adds, "If a foreigner has one bad toilet experience it will negate ten wonderful Chinese experiences."

We board a different boat and cruise up a river before climbing up and down more steep valley walls to get back to our car, and it's off to a wonderful venue for a very late lunch. We're virtually in an enormous greenhouse chock-full of exotic plants. There are even natives from New Zealand, including pongas. Of course our driver eats with us and digs out his favourite pieces from each and every one of the seven dishes. He also devours every single black mushroom and chain-smokes.

When I report all this later to Richard's Chinese friend, Seng, I'm heartened to hear that the Chinese *never* actually let the chopsticks touch their mouths. Next time I'll pay closer attention.

Late in the day we're driven far into the countryside to visit a six-hundred-year-old Ming Dynasty village. I love the ancient architecture, but it's so spoilt by cluttered souvenir shops. I don't know how they make a living as almost every shop has the identical junk items. Some of the buildings are well restored and others are very dilapidated. We wander along tiny stone walkways and pass a Catholic church, a Buddhist temple and a Taoist temple. If you believe in Taoism, fairies and all that, you'll enjoy a very good life with many possessions and a good fortune. Today there are not many followers of Taoism as they never seem to get to the point of enjoying a very good life or acquiring many possessions or good fortune.

We're back where we began the walk, and a number of people whom we've already met have driven to this restaurant. They're at an outside table in an ancient courtyard and have ordered twelve dishes. Once again Wang and I are guests of the Guiyang University. We start eating pigs' feet and they're not too bad if you don't dwell on their origin. Our two cups are constantly filled … one with excellent rose tea and the other with superb wine. It's interesting to note that our driver doesn't drink, well just a little nip here and there. He says he's our designated driver.

The following morning Wang and I meet in the lobby at 6.30. We're to proceed to the airport after checking out. A simple procedure? No way.

It's complicated by the fact that I'm paying with my US visa card and not with cash or one of the new Chinese visas. It's further tangled by the fact that Wang suggests I pay for his room so I won't owe him so many yuan at the end of my stay. I sit down and sign this and that and watch stuff being ripped up and the procedure repeated and repeated. Finally I sign two separate bills and trust Wang that they're accurate.

"Why two different bills?"

"Because we stayed two different times." I thought we had already paid for the first stay, but no, those are now cancelled. If there are mistakes, I quail at the thought of my visa company tracing my bill to the heart of China.

I get out of my chair, go to pick up my small suitcase and it is *gone*. All I can think of is my blood pressure medicine. What is more, this is the first time I've ever put it in a suitcase and not in my backpack, but our bags are small so we don't need to check them at the airport.

Several of us look all around and there's nothing in the huge lobby. Then the bellhop races outside and just manages to bring the departing tourist bus to a stop. Out come a dozen almost identical bags, and lastly mine appears. The tour guide, who had been sitting beside me checking everyone out, had got up and just assumed my bag belonged to the tour. Ten seconds later it would have been out of sight.

We arrive at the airport and try to tip our driver. He absolutely refuses to accept the money. "Not necessary, not necessary," he says in Mandarin. So I grab Wang's notes and, along with my own, throw the money through the open passenger window and wave goodbye. We run.

We go to the first-class lounge and I've yet to see another Caucasian in many days. We're brought tea and sweet things to eat and suddenly one heck of a row breaks out. It seems that the airport now charges foreigners a hundred and eighty yuan which is well over twenty US dollars, and a lot of money in China. Wang is furious. Nowhere else in the entire country does an airport lounge charge foreigners, he tells the two women. Not even at the International Beijing Airport. "If you're going to charge," Wang continues, "you should have told us when we entered." This goes on and on. The Chinese love to repeat themselves. More staff keep coming to watch the fun, but Wang wins after fifteen minutes. He won't tell me what his punch line was and I doubt I could have understood it if I *were* able to hear anything through the hullabaloo.

I don't have to pay.

The flight back to Beijing is comfortable and made more interesting as a security man in plain clothes is sitting next to us. I ask Wang how he knows this and he tells me to watch the man. He often gets up and glances around, he's not given any delicious in-flight food, he wanders into the first class (empty) compartment and several times the flight attendants whisper in his ear. As we descend into Beijing I can see the Great Wall below us and the man takes off his jacket. His chest is covered with security badges and patches.

It's 37 boiling centigrade degrees in Beijing and the crowds are so thick I doubt that our driver from Tianjin University will find us. Seconds later he does spy us, gets us to the new underground parking garage, packed with cars, and we're on our way back to Tianjin. When I first arrived in China in 1984, twenty-four years ago, there were just three old Russian-made cars in the whole of the Beijing Airport's tiny parking lot.

Wang has to go back to work and I spend a lot of time with Ping and her husband, Zhou. Two days later I'm back in a university car driving back to Beijing Airport. Such sad goodbyes. I've no idea if and when I'll see my old friends again.

The flight to Hong Kong is great although I still wonder what they mean about the landing announcement of "We're at double zero three." What's more, I'm blown away by the announcements being first made in perfect English, by our captain who is unmistakably a

New Zealander. (I'm later told that Kiwi pilots are being employed by some Chinese airlines as there are so many new flights and not enough Chinese pilots have had sufficient training.) We're on Dragonair, a Chinese airline, and the young flight attendants translate all the public announcement information into Mandarin and Cantonese. We're offered a vile-smelling and vile-tasting brown freeze-dried morsel as we land, and it's into a bus to my hotel in Kowloon.

The next day I take a taxi to tour Hong Kong Island and Sha Tin racetrack where the Olympic horses will soon be housed when Beijing hosts the Olympics Games later this 2008. Because of quarantine problems, and how Hong Kong is so well set up for horses, the equine classes are being held here. Jimmy is my driver and we become great mates. He speaks about as much English as I speak Mandarin and between us we manage well. The racetrack is beautifully laid out with a large park in the centre. There are dozens and dozens of dogs of all breeds, shapes and sizes being exercised. Well, I would really give a broader description of *exercise* as a mixture of flirting, fighting and fleeing, as those dogs off-leash have the time of their lives, and those on leashes struggle to be part of the scene.

Jimmy drives me back to the airport and my flight to New Zealand, only ten and a half hours away. I've never had such a short hop home and I bet I have minimal jetlag. When I had booked for China, why not make it a round trip so that I can visit my ailing brother and Seng in Auckland?

They both meet me at the airport and I am upset at the change in Richard. He's now carrying his head partly to one side, his shoulders are no longer square and I witness the disturbing dyskinesia when the shoulders fly in all directions and out of control. Richard is having more and more trouble with his balance and has twice fallen down the stairs. I watch the tremors, the spasms, his trouble walking, and the difficulty he has feeding himself. Driving is pretty well out and he can't even hold on to the telephone receiver but must wear headphones.

What sort of future does he have? There's only a nothingness. And probably death within five years. He never complains and in spite of his handicap we have a very happy time. But the undercurrent of the future looms.

Time is also running out for my old school friend Inge, in Carterton.

Bone cancer has run its ugly course and Inge is now in a wheel chair and is not responding well to chemotherapy. I ring her and we talk and talk. Like Marylon, she never gripes. "Inge, I will drive up from Wellington to see you when I'm back here this summer," I tell her.

I return to Boston with a feeling of hopelessness, both for Inge and for my brother. There are some positives for Richard, but they're way in the future. Stem cell research will surely resume under another president and there's interesting Parkinson's research being done by a Professor Dewey, a New Zealander. He has had good luck injecting a virus into the brain, but the Food and Drug Administration is drawing out the testing procedure, while advanced Parkinson's patients watch their time run out.

And I know that time is going to run out for Dave's right hip. It has suddenly started deteriorating at an inescapable pace. When he thinks that I'm out of sight, his limping becomes more pronounced. He never grumbles about it and *rises above it!* "Dave, you know that it's not ever going to improve without the replacement operation. Just think how great that surgery helped your other hip."

"Well, if it keeps on bugging me I might consider getting new hardware at the end of the year. After the MIT term has finished, and I'm *retired!*"

That is months away and of course deep down he knows that the hip will keep on sliding downhill. I quail when I think of my obstinate Rock of Gibraltar declining in health. How we have taken the years of our excellent health for granted ... "And *I've* never even been knocked out or broken a single bone, Liz!" he points out with a chuckle.

Chapter Twenty-Five

Her Royal Highness

I've been back on the farm for almost two weeks and Minty couldn't be going better. We have an awesome partnership and I *must* stop putting off the elbow grease to become fitter. But I have to wonder if my procrastination is psychological – that deep down, after my recent crashes, I know I shouldn't jump again.

Ah well. We will see.

Minty has shown no more signs of the pinched-nerve problem and I've made time to ride him as often as possible. But I'm still catching up with mail and bills and phone calls and emails. And I'm trying to sleep, while fighting the stubborn jetlag. Is it an old age problem that I now take many days longer to get my inner clock re-set?

In my early travels to New Zealand the flights were much slower and took so much longer and my jetlag lasted a mere four days. What is more, many times I was travelling with three spirited children on the old 707 plane. Without the range of today's flights, we had many stopovers. In some ways those were fun flying days. I could turn my youngsters loose in the aisle and tolerant passengers would entertain them. They were often invited into the cockpit and were always given certificates and pins for crossing the International Dateline and the Equator. When they were ready for sleep I'd lie them on a blanket on the floor with pillows under their heads and curl myself up on the empty seats above. Seat belts were only for the take-off and the landing.

For several years we used to change from the 707 jet in Fiji and finish our journey on an Electra or a DC4. I was on the second jet ever to fly into New Zealand, and it looked as if half the country was at the airport to witness our arrival. The terminal building was overflowing with people staring, drinking tea and eating scones, sandwiches and sponge cake topped with rich whipped cream.

I had two little boys still in diapers on one particular trip. On our return to Boston, by the time we'd reached San Francisco I was lugging a heavy bag of wet terry-cloth nappies. (Disposable diapers were just hitting the market, but they were made only for tiny tots.) We checked in for Boston and my luggage had become overweight. The officious man behind the desk announced that I would have to pay an additional fee. "I have no money," I blurted out. "And that overweight plastic bag is full of wet diapers. Obviously this has increased my weight above the allowance. Everything was fine when I left New Zealand." I let my voice quaver a little.

"Well, give me a cheque," he demanded. I had no cheques, nor any traveller's cheques left. And in those days there was no such thing as a credit card.

Stalemate.

I forced some tears. Paul, at fifteen months old, joined in. It worked. The man couldn't deal with two people staging a scene, and told us to go straight to the departure gate.

It appears I learnt the power of tears at a very early age. I found this out as I read my brother Richard's memoirs. He's been writing them for more than a year and has given me a rough copy to correct. My word he can write, in spite of his failing School Certificate three times. This has to be a New Zealand record, but after reading his autobiography I'm presenting him with an Honorary School Certificate. In one of the chapters, this is how he describes his big sister – *me!*

'Elizabeth, my elder sister by over fourteen years, is a typical Matthews and a clone of our father. When she arrives in a room it's a bit like having a brass band show up. Small in stature and with a compulsive talking disorder, she also has a song and dance act that can be most amusing. Liberal in her views, both selfish and generous, she is fun to be with and one can be carried away by her exuberance.

'She has lived in America for almost fifty years where she has acquired some interesting habits such as clicking her fingers at waitresses, and calling out 'Miss! Miss!', and eating in the street when in a hurry and having a cardigan knitted out of her pet golden retriever's hair.

'She's very loyal to the family and her friends and has a great attachment to New Zealand, which she still considers 'home'. She has crossed the Pacific Ocean more than a hundred times on journeys back and forth from Boston to New Zealand and to China. She hates cooking, and, stocking up on prepared foods, she would happily live out of the microwave. She loves horses. When Mother would announce a letter from Liz, Dad would retort, "More about bloody horses, I suppose."

'Elizabeth can be the absolute master of manipulation and will even burst into tears for maximum effect during a guilt trip. I recollect an occasion at Tupare when she responded to Mother's request to me. I was to refrain from running off all the hot water when I was showering, because of the limited supply. Hearing the water still running some minutes later, Elizabeth burst into the bathroom and tried to turn off the taps, although only one was now on, for the cold setting. I pushed her away and she landed heavily against the wall. I could see in her face the opportunity to make a drama of the situation and sure enough, with great acting skills, she howled loudly and slowly slid down the wall to the floor. Of course I got into trouble!'

Richard has summed me up remarkably well.

Tonight, as I lie restlessly jet-lagged in bed, my mind keeps twisting in numerous directions. Getting more and more aged and at such a fast pace is nothing short of disturbing. On the other hand I think gratefully about all the fabulous opportunities that life is still giving this aging SC.

But as the weeks fly by, Dave's having trouble pulling himself on to his beloved tractor. And that is only half the battle. Once he has flopped on to the metal seat, which badly needs replacing, he finds that accelerating and braking the machine exacerbate his hip pain. At least his current distress will be relieved with the hip replacement – when he obstinately stops *rising above it*.

I sometimes wonder at what point I will begin falling to pieces.

Every year the probability grows and grows.

We have a further anxiety. Interest in Lot 2 is dead and after all the expense of getting an architect to analyse the North Barn, that potential buyer still hasn't reappeared. And forget about the family who can't sell their house. I ride Minty in the trails, and a man on a Western horse catches up with me. "I believe you have some land. Anything for sale?"

"Yes, as a matter of fact we do have four acres and two old barns go with it, one with stalls. There's also a fenced-in field." By the time we part I swear that I've sold Lot 2. I should be a real estate agent.

I never see him again. Nor do I hear from him, and the economy keeps sliding further downhill. Marla tells us there's absolutely nothing moving in our town, or in all the communities surrounding us.

Our stable apartment has also been empty for several months. But we have a new tenant at last. I'll call her Fay and she's very pretty and slim and is doing some sort of local internship. She arrives with her quality horse and three mixed-breed dogs. Three days later, a man with whom Fay connected on the Internet arrives to take her out. Within twenty-four hours he has moved in.

It takes just one more day for things to go awry. The smallest dog seriously bites me on my bare right thigh. I'm wearing shorts and it happens as I'm leaning down to pat him. And what do I get for my warm greeting? A deep gash with blood flowing everywhere. Fay shrugs her shoulders, picks up the dog and cuddles him while throwing me a cold remark. "You're lucky that he doesn't have all of his teeth." I ask her if the dogs have had their rabies shots. "Of course." I wonder if I should have her show me their vaccination certificates but decide that it's better to look like the trusting landlord.

It doesn't take long before we're made aware of the fact that Fay's father is a lawyer and that he is loaded with money, and it's easy to see that he inordinately indulges his only child. Then I overhear Fay on the phone reprehensibly castigating her mother and it makes me sick. The poor mum is obviously having trouble finding some horse equipment that Fay needs. Urgently. Although I hurry away from this private conversation, I hear enough rudeness, sharp demands and demeaning comments to sicken me.

The tone is set.

I check my wound and it doesn't appear that the little dog has *any* teeth missing. I make a cup of tea and think about Fay's poor mother. Then I recall an incident when I too was an insolent little brat. New Zealand was in the middle of World War II and we were all scared that, any day now, the Japanese would invade our two islands. My loving maternal grandmother was looking after us while Mother was having one of her long spells in the sanitorium. I was the ever-expanding little horror and had just finished a fight with Jill. "You're nothing but a little Jap," said my distressed grandmother.

"I'm your relative and if I'm a Jap, so are *you!*" I yelled. I'm still full of remorse over that, and to this day I wish I had apologised. But it was nothing when compared with Fay's cruel remarks. Unexpectedly the girl's conversation gave me another perspective on my old response, way back in the washhouse at Tupare. My grandmother had a wonderful sense of humour and when I had spoken so rudely she had surprisingly turned away without a word. I now wonder if she thought this ten-year-old was trying to be witty, and was my grandmother hiding a smile?

A couple of weeks after I was bitten, our electrician also gets bitten by one of the larger dogs. Dennis tries to be cavalier about it but the skin on his ankle is broken. I beg Fay to keep all three dogs on a leash. But she's innately inconsiderate and within a few weeks one of the dogs is running loose again and the man servicing our tractor is bitten.

"That damn thing just came at me from out of nowhere."

This time we *demand* that Fay and her boyfriend always control the dogs. They never appear to be under any sort of duress, but will literally have a go at anyone they spy. Fay tells me that I need to regain the confidence of the dogs. "Regain what confidence?" I ask. "I've never had it in the first place."

What is more, I tell her how the dogs are always jumping up and scratching the windowsills and barking their heads off. Even the little one is constantly up on Fay's bed where she can reach the sill with her nails. "I'll pay for any damage," Fay tells me.

Things roll along until I employ Megan to work on Sue's days off. Sue needs more work and has just completed a course in assisted living and has been employed by a nearby nursing home. Megan is great with my horses and is also a dog trainer. It doesn't take long for Fay, to whom I now refer as HRH, (Her Royal Highness), to tell Megan that she will pay her to walk all three dogs every day.

Megan knows what she's doing, but the smallest dog bites her. Twice. Her skin is broken and Megan works hard to get what trust the dogs are capable of giving. We go for a while without any more blood or teeth imprints. And Megan faithfully walks all three leashed dogs together on my galloping track. One morning they're out hiking and without warning a hunter, carrying a bow and arrow, appears around a corner. Even though we hate to give permission to hunters, the deer population has to be culled or there'll be a severe shortage of their winter food.

The three dogs spy the innocent hunter and charge. Megan is pulled off her feet, and, gripping the leashes, she gets dragged along the track – on her stomach. After his initial shock the hunter gives out a murderous yell and flails his bow and arrow. The dogs stop and Megan, still holding on to the leashes, picks herself up, returns to the stable and says to me, "Those rotten dogs. I quit."

It's now a month later and things have been quiet around here. But we can't believe that the dogs are *still* taken outside without leashes when HRH and her boyfriend, whom I now refer to as IQ 80, think that we're not expected to be out of the house. And what do Dave and I do? Wait until the darn dogs are back in the apartment. Or we throw caustic darts at both HRH and IQ 80. I hate it when someone brings out the worst in me but we're becoming prisoners in our own home. Why do we tolerate the dogs and for *so* long? We can't believe Fay won't show some sort of responsibility. We also sense some very unpleasant consequences if we report the dogs to the animal control officer of our town.

There's growing tension in the air. And Dave is off again to Hong Kong. He's worried about leaving me but he does enjoy these quick academic trips. I picture the banquet in his honour and everyone telling mathematical jokes …

I'm tacking up Minty and chatting with Kathy about Internet dating and all the baggage carried by the men she has been seeing. Something flashes past the grooming stall window. We both think it's a coyote. These days they're becoming bold enough to travel close to residences. But it's no coyote. It's one of HRH's crazed dogs and he bombs into the stable. I grab my dressage whip and flail the air in front of him. I yell at Kathy to grab the lunge whip and I run to the house to phone Fay. The beast chases me. I've never been afraid of dogs before Fay's arrival. She answers her cell phone and I tell her to please get back home immediately and put the dog in the apartment. "I'm too scared to try putting him back myself," I tell her. She says nothing and hangs up. Or were we disconnected? I dial again.

HRH seems totally unconcerned and mumbles that she'll come home shortly.

I hurry back outside and it turns out that all three dogs are loose. Fay had never locked the door to the deck of the apartment and the dogs have learnt how to slide it open and rip through the mesh on the screen door. The largest of the dogs is charging me. He leaps in the air towards my face. Thank goodness I'm still holding on to my dressage whip and I cream him across his chest with all my might. He slinks away and I have an awful pang of guilt. I've never thrashed an animal in my life. He cowers, but the little one now appears and keeps growling his head off as he targets and targets me. He's smart enough to stay just out of the range of my whip.

Holy smoke. I *am* an SC. Doesn't Fay have *any* consideration?

Kathy's now leading Minty towards the indoor and my large attacker starts leaping at my horse's back legs. And the little monster quickly joins the assault while the third dog looks on. Good old Minty keeps on kicking out but misses his targets. At last we shut ourselves in the arena.

Five minutes later HRH drives in and starts *cuddling* her dogs.

By now I'm seeing scarlet and yell out of a crack in the arena door. "Fay, your irresponsibility is getting me down! I've a good mind to report these dangerous dogs to the animal control officer."

It's hard for us to believe Fay's effrontery. Then IQ 80 drives in, and, after some whispering between them, they take all three dogs into the apartment.

Minutes later the man doing some work for us comes into the arena. "Liz, I saw all those dogs trying to kill you. You know, one came after me when you were in the house and got me in the calf."

"Are you okay?"

"Yes," he says hesitantly.

"I'm so sorry. I'm sick of how these dogs are ruling our lives. They've got to go."

Later I find a note in the stable's grain room. 'Liz, I am sorry about the disturbance … my boyfriend forgot to lock the door on to the deck. Report the dogs if you must and my attorney will be in touch with you. Remember that my Dad sits on the Supreme Court of … State as a judge.

Well that's big news to me. A *supreme court judge*?

I write Fay a reply. 'You call what happened yesterday a *disturbance*? I would call it an attack. Fay, your boyfriend leaves for work long before you ever leave the farm. It is your responsibility to check the two doors when you leave the apartment.'

We serve notice. HRH and IQ 80 are to be gone by the end of the month. We have no idea if they'll comply. A few days later I ask Fay when they are moving and rudely she says that she has no idea as she's trying to buy a house.

Next I hear from Ed in the real estate office. She hasn't bought a house, for goodness sake. She's only in Massachusetts for six more months. She has rented a small house in a nearby town and is definitely going to be gone from our apartment by the end of the month.

Her horse moves out, ostensibly to one of the top stables in our state. Another lie. We hear that the mare has gone back to Fay's parents' home. A U-haul appears and over the next three days the apartment is emptied. I ask IQ 80 for their address. "It's none of your business."

"It is our business if you want me to return some of the security deposit."

Ed then reports that the Supreme Court judge, SCJ, demands instant refunding of the security deposit. He denies the dogs did any damage and a cheque is to be mailed *immediately* to his daughter.

I report everything to Dave when he rings me from Hong Kong, "Those dogs have done so much damage to the apartment. I'm talking to our handyman to get a quote for the repairs. You know the dogs even busted through the screen door the other day." I can't believe that a father has to dictate everything for his *twenty-six-year-old* daughter. I'm busy all day and try to put the demand out of my mind.

That evening our phone goes and I see from the caller ID that someone is ringing from the SCJ's State. I don't answer. The SCJ leaves a threatening message. We're to pay his daughter the full security deposit of twelve hundred dollars *immediately*, and to ring him back at this certain number.

No way. I wish Dave were here.

It's now after 10pm and the phone goes again. The SCJ. I don't answer and there's no message.

By now I'm frenzied and report everything in an email to our own splendid lawyer. And how do I cope with the father's threats?

The reply comes soon.

> Hi Liz,
>
> You should take pictures of the damage and get the written estimates as soon as possible. And if there's a balance you must refund it within thirty days. If there's no balance, you should still send her an itemised list of the damage and the cost. You truly are lucky that she is gone.
>
> Please keep in mind, if you do not know already, that Massachusetts has some really onerous requirements for landlords like holding security deposits in separate interest-bearing accounts, notice of this to tenants etc. A knowledgable lawyer can make life miserable for a landlord who doesn't follow all the rules.
>
> Also in many states, like NY, the Supreme Court is the lowest court (like our district court here in Massachusetts.) If your former tenant wants to be represented in Massachusetts she'll need to be represented by a member of the Massachusetts bar. It's unlikely that her father has that credential.
>
> I'm more concerned about the dog bites. I hope you're okay and that the dogs don't have rabies.
>
> Let me know if I can help further, any time.
>
> Marvin.

I'm chewing over the letter when Dave rings me from Hong Kong. "Hi there. All okay?"

"Yes, sort of," I laugh. "HRH and IQ 80 finally moved out this afternoon and the SCJ is really bugging me for the security deposit. Of course I don't have all the damage quotes yet."

My thoughtful husband tells me not to worry. He'll take care of the so-called Supreme Court Judge. Right now Dave's at the Hong Kong airport. He went to check in and they asked if he could possibly leave for Boston on another flight. The original flight via Denver was over-booked in business class. I can imagine the big United Airlines panic in progress. Dave has opted to fly direct to Chicago and they're giving him three seats to himself in economy, plus two hundred dollars, a free upgrade to use to anywhere at any time and credit for the 'miles' that he used for the original free upgrade.

So to Chicago. Dave rings and tells me how he was bombarded with people wanting to use one of his three seats from Hong Kong. He explained that he had bought two of the seats and moved to the aisle seat. Finally he had to clarify his situation to the flight attendant and was at last left alone for the thirteen and a half-hour flight. He was given a business class blanket and pillow. It turned out that he was too long to lie down on the three seats and there was very little room between his knees and the seats in front of him. Now his flight is leaving for Boston on time.

The flight is then delayed because of a missing *bolt*. Time passes and the passengers are told that they're going on a different plane and to please proceed to gate so and so. Complaints all around. Half an hour later the passengers are told yet again to move to another gate. And again to a *fourth* gate. They become a migrating herd.

I'm monitoring all the delays on the United Airlines Internet site.

Dave rings me again. They've reached the fourth gate and a passenger can't stand it anymore. He starts shouting, "What the f... is wrong with this airline? Why the f... can't they find a jolly *bolt* if you please? I'm f... sick of United Airlines." He doesn't stop, his voice rising and rising until security arrive and say that he'll be arrested if he doesn't shut up. Immediately.

Finally the plane takes off for Boston and I alert the limousine service of the number of the new flight on which Dave is now flying.

9pm. I learn from CNN that a plane has gone off the runway at Denver International Airport and has caught fire. All flights out of Denver are now delayed. Dave's original flight would have been one of them.

9.15pm. I check United's Internet site and Dave's flight has landed in Boston. I figure that he'll be home by 10.45 at the latest.

11pm. Still nothing.

12pm. I check the traffic alert for the turnpike ... no crashes or tie-ups are being reported.

And I wait and wait. Soon after midnight I call the limousine service and ask if he has been picked up, or have they even found him? "Yes, we have just collected him and he'll be home in about an hour. He will tell you what happened."

1.30am. Dave finally makes it home. "The plane taxied into the gate," he recounts, "and the exit tunnel door wouldn't open." He goes on to tell me how there was much struggling and banging the door but it was stuck. The man who had the meltdown in Chicago was sitting opposite Dave and was desperately trying to keep his mouth shut. At last the plane was towed to another distant gate and all the passengers moved to the carousels, only to find that the conveyor belt and the floor were littered with bags and nothing was moving. Finally, as the minute hand kept sweeping over the clock, the belt started and Dave's was the first bag out.

We stay up another hour as I relate the SCJ's and HRH's tales. We decide that I should fax the SCJ and hope it ends there.

> Dear Attorney ...
>
> It is with regret that we find we are not in accord with your account of the damage that your daughter's dogs have done to our apartment.
>
> From day one, whenever anyone was outside, the dogs would leap up at the windows and frantically scratch the sills. The little one was even getting up on the bed in order to reach the window. Not long after Fay moved in I asked her if she could possibly control them and she replied, "Don't worry, I will pay for any damage."
>
> Now the damage story has changed and Fay says that it was all done before she moved in. Of course there was no damage at that time, and, if there were, she should have drawn it to our attention. Like when one hires a rental car, it is smart to check if there are any dents, scratches etc.
>
> My husband and I are really upset that you dispute the aggression of two of the dogs and that all three never contributed to the

damage in our apartment. Your disagreement certainly makes us feel that you are questioning our integrity. I can send you the names and phone numbers of a lot of people, including some from MIT who have known us for almost fifty years, and they will all vouch for Dr Benney's and my principles and probity.

I am very happy to hear you say that the dogs have never shown any aggression in the past. However I have many witnesses to the problems that we here have endured. If you need the names and phone numbers of all those people whom the dogs bit we will gladly supply them to you. And I will have the list notarised.

Fay wrote us a note saying that we could go ahead and report the dogs to the Animal Control Officer in our town, but we would then hear from her attorney. She also reminded us, as she has done on several occasions, that you are a judge on the … State's Supreme Court.

We were advised to report the dogs several times, but were reluctant to upset your daughter and have the animals subsequently quarantined. How we implored Fay and her boyfriend to keep the animals on a leash at all times – wishful thinking. We never knew when one of the dogs would be loose outside. We have many people who can attest to the fact that we were becoming prisoners in our own home.

The bite that the smallest dog gave me last July was so bad that I had to email my doctor for advice. I have that letter in my sent box.

Regarding the boy friend, he moved into the apartment within four days of Fay's arrival. We should have had him checked and put on the contract. I guess 'trust' is our downfall.

Of course we will return the balance of the security deposit after we have got all the repair estimates.

Elizabeth and David Benney.

We hear nothing more. I write out an accurate cheque for six hundred and seventeen dollars and Ed gives me the address of Fay's new rented house. From the Internet, I print out a very recent photo of the Supreme Court Judges of the state in question. There is no SCJ listed. I wrap the photo around the cheque and post it.

Case closed.

Chapter Twenty-Six

'Rise Above It and Never Complain'

We're once again looking for new tenants. "Just a year or two now, Dave," I moan, "and we'll find someone to live in the apartment who can *work* for us – all over the farm and in the house too. And just think of the free time you will have when you retire!"

A mother comes to look at the apartment, tagging along her unemployed twenty-something-year-old son. Her first words give us the long list of her son's allergies. She likes the fact that the apartment has electric heat as the guy can't live in an oil-heated environment. However from there on it's downhill. The fact that we use the tractor around the fields is a no-no. The fumes will be disastrous for the poor boy. Of course horses are a no-no, and dogs and cats, even though our four cats can't go outside anymore because of the killer coyotes and fisher cats.

Recently the fisher cats have been migrating further and further south from Canada, and like the coyotes they are ferocious predators. But unlike the coyote they can climb trees with great agility – and it's too late for any poor escaping cat. The fishers are furry animals, around fifteen pounds in weight and they seldom eat fish in spite of their name. Their claws are huge and their cry sounds just like a child or a woman in trouble. That's enough for the mother and her allergic son. They drive out and we hear nothing more.

Than a middle-aged couple come and let us know that they're *only* renting because they've sold their expensive home and are looking to buy a new one. It's odd, but in my gut I don't believe their story. Thank goodness we always have our agent do a credit and a police check on potential tenants. It turns out that this latest couple are both unemployed and they skipped three months' payment in their last rental. They were evicted, of course. As a departing shot they tell Ed that they never seriously considered our apartment, as there isn't enough storage for all their valuable antique furniture.

Sue has finally sold the bigamist's possessions and sold her house. Now she's thinking of moving into a small rental, advertised by a man around Sue's age. She will share it with this guy – but he's a complete stranger. Maybe I'm old-fashioned, but I'm uncomfortable for her and have put a police check on the guy. Dave and I are lucky to have a police officer as a friend. He soon reports that there's nothing wrong with the man, who works as a security guard and surely needed a clean clearance for such employment. His name is Brian and he had planned on becoming a priest and did some years in a seminary before deciding that women needed to feature more intimately in his life.

Sue moves in.

Kathy comes and gives me a great dressage lesson on Minty. He's going so well, and to my relief, has never had any repeat of the pinched nerve problem in his back. Kathy relates the saga of Gary with whom she has now had two dates. "Nothing changed on our second date. He still could hardly open his mouth," she tells me. "I can't stand the thought of seeing the bore again."

I was the one who begged Kathy to give Gary one more try after the first dull date. "Kathy, he was possibly intimidated by your attractiveness."

Next Kathy relates what has just taken place on her way to the farm. "My cell phone rang and I saw by the caller ID that it was Gary. 'Hi Gary,' I answered. You won't believe what he said. 'Hi Barbara!' I hung up on him, oh so quickly." Kathy's and my shrieks reach every boundary of the farm.

After three months we're really worried about filling the apartment. The economy is still going downhill and Ed says that there are many rentals available. But it doesn't make sense to me as people are losing their homes and there is a growing need for apartments.

We lower the rent. And wait.

Lot 2 is also nagging at us more and more. How we long for our old age to be relatively worry-free, with less and less work. The lot has now been on the market for many months. Another couple loved everything dearly, but just as with the first couple, the bank denied them a loan until their own house is sold. And Marla says it can't be sold until there's a new septic system installed. They can't afford it.

Personally, we'd love to see a horsey family buy the lot. When we moved here one of the two old barns had about a year left before it collapsed. There were many stanchions for holding the cows in place during the long winter months, and several layers for loose hay storage. The floor was so rotten we couldn't walk inside or we'd land up in the basement, full of water and water snakes. We filled it in, snakes and all, with rubbish and many pieces of discarded cars, farm equipment and plumbing supplies from the surrounding neglected fields. Now well restored the barn is ready to house horses.

I'm sure that the man who wanted to turn the barn into his living quarters will never reappear. It was not hard to imagine him walking in the dark through his new abode and colliding with all the heavy support poles. Every twelve feet they tower from the floor to the ceiling.

We get a ring from Ed saying that he has a great chap to rent the stable apartment. "But there is one small problem," he tells us. "Well I guess it's a big problem … the man has a gigantic dog that *occasionally* bites."

Occasionally is too often for Dave and me. We say we're not interested.

Out of the blue we get an email from our lawyer, Marvin. Essentially he writes that there's no denying that we're both aging and reaching the point where we must review our wills, our financial situation with retirement not far off, our living wills, who we delegate to control our assets *if* or *when* we become incapacitated …

"Aw hell, Dave."

"Liz, you have to face this fact."

"I *am* facing it. Every day that I look in a mirror I see a face more jaded and faded. I laugh when I think of my grandmother saying to Mother, 'Mary dear, you must get your photo taken before you start to fade.'" Too late for that photo for me.

So we make an appointment with nice Marvin to review our 'end of life' decisions, and with Vic, who is recommended as our financial advisor. Those two words sound way too grand to describe our life style, but we do need advice. Very soon Dave is retiring and his MIT salary will stop and he will turn an inconceivable eighty years of age. He has decided that this should be the time to end his fifty-three years of employment at this one university.

I think of brother Richard and wonder if he has tied up all the loose ends in his life. I would hate to have something like Parkinson's disease dictating my demise. It's 4pm (New Zealand time 8am tomorrow) and I phone him and Seng. As usual, I hear Richard endlessly fumbling with the headphones.

"Hi Liz!" He sounds ecstatic for so early in the morning. "I was just going to ring you. You won't believe the terrific news," he tells me. "My neurologist says that I'm ready for the electrode implant operation – well, if I qualify." He tells me he has to be examined by a shrink with another examination by a psychologist. The doctor wants CAT scans and MRIs, and Seng is to make a video of the worst and the best moments of Richard's day. He must have his eligibility approved by seven different New Zealand doctors, but his neurological doc is the head of the group. He's pretty confident they'll all agree. And the government will pay. Richard and Seng will go to Brisbane in Australia as this type of operation is not yet performed in New Zealand.

"Richard. I'm stunned. This is such incredible news. Oh my goodness – congratulations! But I thought your neurologist told you a year or two ago that you weren't a candidate for this procedure?"

"Seng and I thought so, too, but we both misinterpreted his words. Doc meant that I was not ready for the operation *at that time*. Still, I've first got to pass a lot to qualify. And I haven't talked to you since I broke four bones in my hand. I just sort of collapsed in a heap the other day."

"Oh no. Are you in a cast?"

"Yes. And when Doc saw me yesterday he was shocked that I was at this stage of the Parkinson's. He berated me for always saying I was doing okay. You know, like Mother was always telling us *to rise above it and never complain*."

"I know exactly what you mean. I still have a hard time calling my doctor. I mainly see one when I have no choice, like crashing off my horse and getting knocked out or breaking something," I laugh.

"Well, nothing is decided of course and first we're to get the video made."

We talk again a few days later. "John sent up his video camera and it took us three days to figure out how to use it. Anyway, we've sent Doc the tape and you bet we posted it as registered mail."

A week later Richard rings me. "You won't believe it, but Doc rang me last night at 8pm and on a Sunday too! He wanted to congratulate us on the value of the video tape. I'm seeing the psychologist next week."

"Why do you need one?"

"I asked the same question. But there's an associated disease called Lewy Body Disease that often afflicts Parkinson's patients with Alzheimer-like dementia, and they won't operate if you show any signs of losing your marbles." He hesitates, "Liz, in any way do I seem to show these symptoms?"

"No way. And don't you dare ask me the same question!"

Another week goes by and our whole large family bursts with renewed optimism for Richard's new chance at a longer and better quality of life. My wonderful sister Jill tells Richard that she's praying for him every day. "Do you believe in prayer, Richard?"

"I will, Jilly, if I get better!"

The psychological exam goes very well. It takes one and a half-hours. At one point the psychologist asks Richard to take seven away from a hundred. "Please don't be too hard on me," begs my brother. "You know, I failed School Certificate three times." He passes the psychological test with honours and the psychologist tells Doc that he has never enjoyed working with a patient as much as he did with Richard.

The psychiatric examination also goes very well, plus the required scans. Doc now tells Richard that it may take weeks for all the doctors to come to their decision. "But, Richard, I'm the boss. And as far as I'm concerned you're going to qualify."

Chapter Twenty-Seven

Facing Facts

Our meeting with Vic, the financial advisor, goes really well. "So you have a horse farm?" he says on our arrival.

"Yes," I tell him, "but I've retired from boarding horses."

"You know," says Vic, "I have a niece who is also my goddaughter and she's a great rider." Blow me down, but it's Alexandra whose old horse Jax came to us to live until he died, and what a great retirement he enjoyed. Eleven years of extra life until we had to put the old horse down last year. He was perfect until the day he couldn't walk, probably from a stroke ... but he could still eat ravenously. And it turns out that Vic also attended Alexandra's celebrated wedding in the Dominican Republic. "In fact, Liz," Vic continues, "I remember now ... you were one of those guests dancing on the table."

"*Liz!*" Dave erupts.

Vic quickly interjects and congratulates Dave on how he and MIT have managed his portfolio.

Next we have our meeting with Marvin. There's so much to update and he's eager to meet the children, but, more importantly, he highly recommends that I become an American citizen. As I am a foreigner, even though I have a green immigration card, if Dave dies before me the government will tax our estate much higher than if I were a citizen. I ask why.

"Because you could avoid paying death taxes, take every penny you have and hive straight back to New Zealand."

I tell Marvin I will start the procedure. And finally I will get to vote for the first time in my life. When I was eligible to vote in New Zealand I was either overseas, or had not been living in the country for the six months prior to election day.

For a long time I've felt that I should become a citizen. I love America and I don't want to live anywhere but in Massachusetts. *But* my heart is in New Zealand and it will always be 'home' to me. I'm a Kiwi through and through. I grew up in the North Island and all my ancestors arrived in the early immigration waves during the mid-1800s. And what a tough, adventuresome and admirable lot. They wanted to embrace new challenging experiences and were not escaping any sort of religious persecution or difficult times. They were just plain old middle-of-the-road citizens in overcrowded towns when New Zealand was advertising for settlers. Who couldn't be excited by the allure of a new life in the open spaces of two very beautiful islands? Mind you, to turn that excitement into reality took extraordinary grit.

Letters to their families back in Great Britain showed the new arrivals' ingenuity, their capacity to work hard, to play hard and to cope with adversity. They were made of dauntless stuff. My paternal great-great-grandparents' 1851 voyage to New Zealand, with five children on board, was disastrous. (We've no idea why they left behind their six–year-old daughter and a fifteen-year-old son.) They embarked on the sailing ship *Gwalior* and the voyage lasted more than six months with water and food running short by the time they reached the Horn of Africa. There was a mutiny on board and the captain kept suffering from delirium tremens and eventually committed suicide. My great-great-grandmother, Grace Hirst, courageously nursed the captain through his bouts of delirium. The ship was leaking and badly trimmed but it was very well insured. It turns out that the owners were after the insurance money and never intended the boat to reach New Zealand.

Fortunately the ship put in to Cape Town for food and water and an able first mate joined the crew. His superb seamanship finally got everyone safely to New Zealand. Some years later, Grace and her husband Thomas returned to England for a visit and on their voyage back to New Zealand their sailing ship the *William Brown* caught fire three hundred miles from Madeira and sank. The couple spent a dreadful night in an open boat and were lucky to be picked up the following day by a passing ship. It let them off in Madeira.

There were continuing signs of unrest among the Maori and the settlers were very afraid of more violent outbreaks. Grace and Thomas were now living in New Plymouth when Maori attacked and defeated a patrol of imperial and colonial forces nearby. Ultimately the rebellion was put down, to the huge relief of the immigrants, but it must have been hard to overlook the fact that Maori culture included a past history of cannibalism.

At parties, Dad, the gifted raconteur, would sometimes recount how he and one of his brothers pushed an empty water tank off the top of a steep hill. It made a marvellous sound as it barreled downward before crashing into a pa below. Out came a gigantic Maori who chased them home, screaming, "I'm going to eat you. I'm going to eat both of you. I like the flesh of little boys." It took the youngsters years to believe that he was just kidding.

Dad recalled peering around a door, as a five-year-old, and seeing his great-grandmother, Grace, who was now nicknamed Aged, having all her top teeth pulled out by the doctor. It was 1901 and there were no painkillers or antibiotics in those days. The doctor said he would be back the next morning to do the lower jaw, and Aged said, "No, go ahead and take the rest of them out now, please." I wonder if she possibly was given opium. Dad had no idea. She died later that year, aged ninety-six. With no teeth she ended her days eating rice pudding.

How I loved my paternal grandmother, born in 1857. She was a hard working second generation New Zealander and bore ten children. Granny loved to recreate the old traditions of England that were handed down from her grandparents, such as paying close attention to the home, to one's appearance and to family manners, and even the traditional afternoon teas. As a little girl I was sometimes invited to these very formal occasions and had to swear on my honour to behave. It was tough showing self-control when a maid pushed in the laden trolley. If I had ever over-eaten the tiny thin cucumber sandwiches, the pikelets or the sponge cake covered in thick Jersey cream and strawberries, I wouldn't have been invited again. Tea was poured from a solid silver teapot into dainty thin-lipped cups, and hot water was in an ornate silver kettle kept warm by a tiny methylated spirits flame. The seven or eight ladies would make a fuss over me for two minutes and then turn to gossip and much laughter, making sure that the little eight-year old wasn't corrupted in any way.

I would go home still hungry.

One afternoon, as the guests were departing and the trolley with still a lot of uneaten food had been taken away, this *well brought up little girl* sneaked unseen into the kitchen, and wow! Mind you, when Grandpa, the Bank of New Zealand manager, had good luck with his racehorses, everyone enjoyed his excessive generosity. There was no maid when times were tough. Of course in my youth Grandpa had long been retired. In fact he boasted about getting more years living on retirement than the years he had worked in the bank.

Granny was very tall with great deportment, always wearing long black dresses with starched white collars, and around her neck was a black or dark blue velvet ribbon with a cameo attached to the front. She had a beautiful nature and her hobbies were doing crossword puzzles and playing bridge. When Grandpa complained that she would talk about nothing but these two passions, she would respond, "And you talk about nothing but horses, horses, horses." (There's no doubt that I have his genes.) He trained his own horse, Star Rose, to win the New Zealand Cup in 1906, but from there on the horse never won another race and became a grocer's hack, being ridden from door to door with the rider taking orders. Another of his horses, Ouida, was so little known to the public that no one bet on her first race. Only twenty-six pounds' worth of tickets were sold, all of them being held by her owner – Grandpa. When she won dramatically, the totalisator didn't have sufficient money to pay him his huge windfall until later in the day.

Grandpa was also a staunch right-winger with a vigorous hatred of the Labour Party. In the 1940s it produced a daily newspaper, the *Southern Cross,* and on one occasion a copy mysteriously appeared on Grandpa's reading table. He absolutely refused to have his hands tainted by such trash, and using his walking stick he nudged it on to the floor. The prankster was his daughter-in-law, my mother.

When Grandpa was dying, one of his sons took him to the New Plymouth Hospital and said, "Father, I'm taking you for a little holiday."

To which Grandpa replied, "Some call it a holiday, some call it a holy day, but I call it a hell of a day." He died forty-eight hours later.

I start the process of citizenship, thinking about my ancestors. How easy it was for me to begin a new life in a new country. How predictable everything was. How easy it has been to make trips back home in under twenty-hours instead of many months in a frail sailing vessel. How did those ancestors of mine prepare for the unknown, and with children in tow? Dad's grandmother, Alice Matthews, sailed from England to New Zealand in a three-mast sailing ship. It was 1842 and she travelled with her eighteen-month-old child and another one who was not quite three years old. Her husband Richard, a doctor and my great-grandfather, had already arrived in the very young country. Alice falsely called herself Mrs Matthews on the boat as the two children were born before she and Richard were married. Tying the knot was forbidden while Richard was in his medical training years.

Now I gather up the required documents for my new citizenship – birth certificate, marriage certificate, green card and the required list of all the times and dates that I have left the United States. For me it's made easier because I've kept a record ever since I started taking the children back home in 1961. I'm told that it won't be long before the initial hearing date. The fee has gone up to seven hundred and fifty dollars and the cost along with the collapsing USA economy is turning off a lot of applicants.

Next I'm summoned to appear in a Department of Immigration room in Boston. I must answer ten pretty general questions about my present whereabouts, country of origin, age and occupation, and have my fingerprints taken. I was warned on the summons that I'd better keep the appointment or there'd be a long wait for the next opportunity. I sit with forty-three other applicants and all forty-three of them don't appear to speak English as a first language.

As three or four applicants at a time get moved into the fingerprinting room, we play something like musical chairs and shift our behinds further up the three lines of seats. I feel rather sorry for a woman hidden in a burqa as she tries to contain a two-year-old, and with every move she struggles to gather up her child and swaddling clothes.

Finally I'm in the room with the digital fingerprinting machines. There are five of them and it's a much better technique than when my fingers were pressed on to an inkpad in 1962 and I was applying for my green card. Oh the questions they had asked, and when I answered honestly that, yes, I had had parking and speeding fines, the man said, "We know all about them. But it's okay!" Today I am ushered to one of the modern stations and have a fun time refreshing my Mandarin with a young Chinese immigrant. "I like talking with you," he murmurs, "so I will take my time."

Meanwhile the stable apartment remains empty. And Lot 2 remains unsold, but we have further interest from a charming man with a delightful wife and two children. "These are the ones, Marla," I tell her and she just grins. I doubt that anyone knows the business inside out as well as Marla, or works as hard.

Then trouble.

The prospective buyer, John, rings Marla and says that he hates to complain, but Marge, the lady who bought our old farmhouse, had just intercepted him on the driveway and blasted out the following:

"The Lot 2 boundary line is wrong and 30 more feet are really in my favour." (Apart from the fact that when she bought the house, she insisted that we have that lot line resurveyed and pegged.)

"If you let anyone use the two old barns, for any use at all, like storage, I'll report you. Lot 2 is not zoned commercially.

"And let me tell you that the driveway is like a highway, with no privacy around here." (Ridiculous, as we now have our own private and very new, albeit steep driveway.)

"I'm building a huge barn right next to your lot-line.

"And I'm warning you that I have wild noisy parties throughout the summer months."

Poor John is rightly upset. This interference actually happened once before with the couple who wanted the land so badly, but couldn't get a mortgage.

Dave and I decide that Marge has gone too far this time and we report it all to Robert, our good friend and real estate lawyer.

And what a letter he writes to Marge. It's full of legalese like Cease & Desist, The Unfair and Deceptive Acts and Practices … and all about Marge's false claims and emotional ranting to our prospective buyers.

She even wanted Lot 2 for herself and she had already offered us twenty-five thousand dollars with thirty years to pay off the balance. Her current boyfriend was going to give her the money. (The man with the shining stud in his tongue is now long gone.) Of course we refused to even consider the offer after which she immediately dropped the new boyfriend. He was too fat was the reason she gave me. Dave guffawed and said he would be long gone before the thirty years were up.

"An excellent letter, Robert," I tell him on the phone. "And thanks so much. Honestly if I ever received a letter like that I would become a member of your church so that I could go to confession every day for a month."

The next time Marge sees John, she falls all over him.

John is still interested in Lot 2. We have already had the land tested and found a suitable spot for a septic system, but it is on the site where John would like to build a house. Of course we said that he could employ the engineers to try to perc in another area.

I sigh. Here we go again. Are we alone, or do others in their seventies have so much ongoing theatre in their lives?

Chapter Twenty-Eight

Becoming an American

Now for some decisive news. Richard has the approval of all seven doctors for the Parkinson's operation, but no date is set. This is by far the best news of the year.

And at last we have tenants in the stable apartment, a young couple with a delightful two-year-old boy, a baby on the way, two cats and the wife who has never learnt to drive a car.

Sue and her flat-mate Brian are falling in love.

I was glad to see Mark, the equine dentist, this morning. The teeth of horses develop sharp points which must be floated or filed down and I like my horses to be checked every six months. Because Fancy and Catch have small refined jaws, sometimes Mark needs to use a power tool to reach their back molars. Today he tranquilised Fancy, held her mouth open with a clamp and steadied her jaw on the padded curved arm of a stand. The procedure looks appalling but it doesn't hurt and the mare can once more comfortably chew her food.

Had my annual mammogram last week. The next day I got a phone message from the mammography centre saying I needed my right breast X-rayed again. I will have an ultra-sound as well.

Now it's three days of waiting for the appointment and alternately feeling convinced I have cancer and convincing myself it's nothing. It feels as if it is six days and not three when I enter the X-ray room. The technician shows me the prior film of my right breast. "See this," she says pointing to the suspicious round spot. It certainly doesn't look like any other part of the film. She positions me in front of the great machine. "I'm sorry but this will really hurt. The radiologist wants a magnified X-ray of this spot." My poor old breast suffers another big blow when it's crushed into a pancake. "So sorry," the technician says, "but this picture is too grainy. Don't move. I need to take another one."

Whew.

Lucky for me it turns out to be a benign overlap of normal breast structures. There's no need for the ultra sound. A nurse reports all this from the radiologist. I ask her if the overlap could be from the kick of a horse I had to that breast and which resulted in four broken ribs. And I add that the area had another trauma when Catch stepped on this same breast after she fell on me and was struggling to her feet.

This really catches the nurse's attention! "Wow!" she says. "I'll definitely include all this information in my report."

Another year retrieved.

Now for some indecisive news: John, the potential buyer of Lot 2, is told that the only place where the land might perc would involve wrecking the historic 18th century well, And, for some obscure reason, the cost of a septic system anywhere else on Lot 2 would be prohibitive.

Dave and I discuss giving John our present leaching field as it's bordering Lot 2 and John could then pay for us to have a new system installed. Ninety per cent of the cost is in the leaching field. We know where our land would be suitable for a new system. We'll sleep on this idea.

I haven't jumped Minty yet. What's wrong with my *discipline*? I really must work without stirrups today and *every day*. Well, almost every day.

Dave is now convinced his hip will need replacing … "I suppose I'd better go to the doctor and see if he can operate early December when classes are over and I'm about to retire," he tells me.

I exhale a breath of relief.

We attend the wake of a prominent town elder whom we've known for years. The line into the funeral home is very long and so slow that a middle-aged couple in front of us turns around and starts a conversation. They're giddy with the description of how *they* want their funerals conducted. "A full Irish one and an open casket. And absolutely," continues the woman, "I want the undertaker to make up my face to look mighty attractive. Of course a full Mass and afterwards a gathering with plenty of whisky and beer."

"Wow!" I exclaim. "Well, all I want is for everyone I've known to come to our house and have one heck of a party." Dave agrees, and from the look of shock on their faces, you'd think I'd just dropped dead on the spot.

"You do believe in heaven?" says the woman whose eyes have widened abnormally.

"Well, that's a good question." I pause. "I hope there's a heaven and if there is, quite frankly, my chances of admission are about fifty-fifty. And I repeat my long-held conviction that the belief in heaven was begun ages ago to control people. Heaven for the obedient, and the disobedient can burn in hell. I've now shocked the couple twice and they turn away, abruptly.

It's dark on the way home and I drive at night for the first time in a while. Suddenly I understand why elderly people stop driving after the sun goes down. I find that I can't see clearly because of the blinding glare from the lights of oncoming cars. Is my night-time vision going to pot? Maybe I should wear dark glasses. Someone once told me how she got her eyes adjusted with laser treatment and it really helped her night driving. And she swore it was painless. I must ask my ophthalmologist at my next appointment.

"Yes," he tells me, "I highly recommend this procedure for you, and I can do it tomorrow as there's a cancellation."

And it *is* painless. Only one eye needs zapping along with clicking noises and sparks flying everywhere. Doc Henry shoots the laser beam into me about ten times and a nurse holds my head so tightly I couldn't move it if I wanted to. Now I can't wait for darkness to arrive.

As soon as night falls, I zoom down our steep driveway to the road and drive to the end of the straightaway and turn. There's not a car in sight. I sit there for five more minutes and nothing appears, so I continue two miles to the main road and park a short distance from the traffic lights. When I see the lights change I drive back on to the road. After a couple of seconds a stream of cars moves towards me and lights galore sink into my eyes.

Success! The glare has gone. And just as well or I might have driven into a pole right outside the Catholic Church, or on to the brand-new pristine front lawn next door.

Will John and Jennifer buy Lot 2? Dave's so happily laid back about it all. I'm becoming more and more wrought-up. We need to lighten our farm work. Just maintaining the two old barns takes time. Vines quickly find their way through cracks, birds and bats find their way inside and soil the floors. And I can see the grass and weeds growing up and up at breakneck speed.

What is more, I don't feel *with it* today. Am I beginning to fit the first-class mould of an SC? Is that why I just left some address labels in the post office? I'd paid for them and now I can't find them. This morning I went back to the counter and nice Gene grins. "You didn't leave them here. Feeling scatty again?"

"I guess so and I can't believe you've remembered that neat word, Gene."

Not a soul has seen my labels.

Because I find they have been in my purse the entire time.

And I haven't seen my watch in twenty-four hours.

Help! Are all these moments the signs of serious senior citizenship?

Many of my young friends tell me they are also making similar slips. Or are they white-lying to make me feel better?

My citizenship hearing is tomorrow. Surely they won't deny giving it to an old lady with a clean police record. Well, there are quite a few speeding tickets spread over forty-nine years. And I still have to know all the correct answers to ten questions, selected from a hundred that I've been studying. I must also demonstrate that I can speak English. I'm sure I can pass that English test with a hundred percent score. Then, if I fail to answer all the ten questions, I'll still get a fifty percent average – a pass! The immigration lawyer, whom I consulted about the citizenship procedure and how I could become a dual citizen, had said, "Good try, but that sort of fifty percent won't fly."

Thank goodness my watch turned up on the tack room floor. Looks as if I never secured the buckle's tongue into the leather strap's hole.

I leave home with a briefcase full of the required documents. *Please bring, if still available, all previous passports, alien registration cards, marriage certificate(s), (evidence of all previous marriages and divorces!) birth certificate and those of your children (if any) and of your present husband, tax returns covering the past three years, two new passport photos …*

Mindful that the traffic is often bad and it can take much longer than fifty minutes to reach Boston, I leave with an hour to spare. I ring the traffic report number on my cell phone and they say there's an incredible backup for miles and miles as you enter the city. Something is going on in the Convention Centre. Chancing there'll be no police around I hit ninety miles per hour on the first clear part of the Turnpike.

I reach the traffic congestion and along with several other scofflaws use the breakdown lane and weave in and out of vehicles. I giggle at the thought of a cop's face when he asks me where am I going. "To my citizenship hearing, sir."

The Massachusetts General Hospital's parking building is not full. I have no idea where else I can park. To be on the safe side and look as if I have a medical appointment, what with video cameras cropping up everywhere these days, I get out of the building and quickly walk through the main hospital doors. I sort of wander around, saunter back out and grab a taxi.

"The John Fitzgerald Kennedy Federal building please." My driver has me repeat it twice. He's from the Mauritius Island and is not fluent in English. It takes a minute for me to recall something from sixty years ago … Mauritius Island … off the East Coast of Africa and the home of the extinct flightless dodo. The gentle spirit of the dodo, and its lack of fear of the early settlers, were interpreted as stupidity and hence today's meaning.

That scrap of recall is an encouraging sign! We speed up Cambridge Street.

Inside the Federal Building three determined security officers appear to be faithfully on the job and I have a long wait while they deal with a dubious-looking woman in front of me. Suddenly, without any bells and whistles, they tell me to pass on through the barrier as they empty out the contents of the woman's large purse. Now to Room

Number One, an endless walk, starting beside a sad courtyard with an extraordinary piece of black art shooting off in ten different directions, and below it is a bed of aged roses, desperate for water.

Room Number One. Almost full. I'm told to slide a document, that I received in the mail, through a slot at counter number twenty-four. There's no sign of anyone on the further side. A roving official indicates for me to take a lonely seat in the back row.

And I wait and wait and wonder how many times I've already looked at my watch. My appointment is for 1pm and along with a host of instructions came a note in capital letters: *DO NOT ARRIVE MORE THAN HALF AN HOUR BEFORE YOUR APPOINTMENT. The room can get crowded.*

There's now standing room only. In the front of us are many counters, some unmanned, and behind me are booths with active interviews going on. A TV is tuned to CNN but no one can hear it and there's a notice daring anyone to alter the dials. I watch one frustrated applicant try to turn up the volume and nothing happens.

Being at the back of the room and close to one of the interview rooms I can hear the loud voice of one of the examiners. It wafts out of the open doorway and the poor woman being questioned starts to cry. She can't answer a single question. She gets one more shot: "Name me two long US rivers."

"Mississippi."

I try to force my brain to recall a second USA river. My stomach knots and I find that I'm grinding my teeth. Sudden relief … the Colorado, and the Connecticut. For good measure I add the small Farmington River and I know its name for the only reason that son Paul's house is located right above it.

After three-quarters of an hour I hear my name shouted out. It's the first English-sounding name that has boomed across the room. I move into the booth and a skinny middle-aged man with an uneven moustache greets me pleasantly. It's fifty-five years since I last sat an exam. *Or* swotted so hard for one.

The first question raises my freshly plucked eyebrows.

"Are you really seventy-five years old?"

"Yes, sir."

"Okay. What is the colour of the stars in the US flag?"

"White."

"*Who becomes the President if the present one dies?*"

"The Vice-President."

"*How many members are there in the House of Representatives?*"

"Four hundred and thirty-five."

"*What are the three branches of our Government?*"

"The Judicial, the Executive and the Administrative." For a moment the interrogator can't decide on the next question. My heart's taking a beating.

We're away again.

"*How many changes or amendments are there to the Constitution?*"

"I think there are twenty-seven."

"*Correct. What is the Supreme Court's law of the United States?*"

"The Constitution."

"*What is the Bill of Rights?*"

"The first 10 amendments of the Constitution."

"*Can you name thirteen original states?*"

"Connecticut, New Hampshire, New York, New Jersey, Rhode Island, Massachusetts, Pennsylvania, Delaware, Virginia, North Carolina, South Carolina, Georgia, and … Maryland."

"*Which countries were our enemies during World War II?*"

"Germany, Italy and Japan."

"*Who was the main writer of the Declaration of Independence?*"

"Thomas Jefferson."

"You've passed," the man grins. "Congratulations and I hardly need to test your ability to speak English."

I smile to myself and recall how Dad had me take *elocution* lessons at boarding school. He was such an Anglophile, and heaven help us if we spoke with a twang or incorrect English. Apart from quoting tons of Shakespeare (hardly a contemporary language) I got pretty good at correctly speaking sentences like: 'How now, brown cow,' 'Go down town, Rover, and fetch the cows some food,' and 'I live in a beautiful country called New Zealand.'

I query the examiner about what would happen if I'd failed?

"You would have to return and be questioned again and if you failed a second time, you'd be requested to go before a committee."

It's no wonder I had to work very hard for this test ... the history of the USA covered a bare week of my New Zealand education. By contrast we spent several years covering our own country's short one hundred-year-old story. Learning some of the highlights was great fun for a teenager ... how fierce Hone Heke vanquished a number of tribes, and all about the Englishman Edward Gibbon Wakefield who planned the colonisation of New Zealand in 1841. The man was notable for being an heiress abductor and a convict. After being steeped in the history of our own two islands, we used up a school term on Britain and a few weeks of European history. Woefully, we then spent that one last week covering the history of the USA.

Next comes another long walk to room number 175A and I'm again seated with about seventy other restless people. I truly wonder how on earth I passed all the questions. At a recent dressage show with Minty I forgot a movement in one test and forgot to halt at X on entering in the second test. To think that I've ridden those two particular tests so many times over the past two years ...

This new room is very hot and there's no drinking fountain and nothing to read. I sit next to a pitch-black elderly man and try to engage him in conversation, but he doesn't speak English and has an interpreter who can't be bothered helping him. Officials keep popping in and out of the room and shouting out yet another name, often apologising for their pronunciation. After an hour I'm ushered down an endless corridor and shown into the second to last room. A young woman, with an amazing stream of long blond hair, greets me warmly and I have to raise my right hand and swear to tell the truth and nothing but the truth. So help me God.

"I do."

Her name is Karen and she's nice and polite as are all the officials so far, no matter what the colour of the skin or ethnicity of any of us applicants.

Now for more questions.

"Have you ever had a drug problem?"

"No. I've never even tried them." And the thought flies through my head that I must sound very pure and demure.

"How many children do you have?"

"Three."

"Are you aware of any more that you might have?"

"No." I try to stifle a giggle.

"Maybe children in another country?"

"No." Surely this is more a question for a man?

"Have you ever been a member of the Communist Party?"

"No."

"Have you ever been involved in any terrorist activity?"

"No." (Unless you ever saw me lose it with my wild teenage sons.)

"Have you ever tried to overthrow a government?"

"No."

It goes on and on and on and I begin to think with all those "no" answers that I won't convince her of my honestly. So when she asks:

"Have you ever had an alcohol problem?"

I say "No." But I think it might look better if I show her that I *can* be a bit of a rebel. "Well, back in my university days I did pass out once."

"Have you ever been arrested?"

"No."

I giggle to myself and briefly recall my false arrest in Paris. In 1958 Flick, two other friends and I were travelling through Europe in Flick's very old car. We arrived in Paris and booked into the cheapest Montmartre hotel we could find.

Way before sunrise, the four of us walked along a very dark street to get our coffee and croissants. Shortly we were to leave for the boat to cross the channel back to England. I finished my breakfast quickly and returned along the ill-lit street to the hotel. The front door was locked and my room key didn't work. I didn't have a clue what I should do, and just stood there, swinging this huge key with an attached block of wood. Suddenly two gendarmes came sweeping towards me and fiercely grabbed both my shoulders. I had no idea what they were saying and I just kept on repeating 'Je suis Anglais. Je suis Nouvelle Zelande.' After a while they calmed down and I managed to tell them that I had slept the night in this hotel and that my friends were still down at the corner café and I had to hurry and pack as we needed to catch the ferry to England.

I was let go and one of the men tapped out a code on the front door bell. It buzzed open. It turns out we were staying in a 'house of very ill-repute.' This definitely confirmed all the suspicious noises that we'd heard and all the comings and goings throughout the night.

"Have you ever been denied admission at a USA border?"

"No."

"Have you ever voted illegally?"

"No."

Then Karen asks me why have I waited forty-nine years before becoming a citizen. I thought that the best answer would be a very true one … that I loved the USA and wanted to live here, but my heart would always be in New Zealand, with such a large family and so many friends still there. I squash some welling tears. I must be a bit wrought up, and I'm tired. Last night Dave and I stayed up very late watching the presidential debate between Barack Obama and John McCain.

The questions continue to come and come and Karen now wants to know if I'd forgotten to add any organisations on my application to which I belong or to which I have belonged. For good measure I say, the Equestrian Federation of New Zealand. I belonged to it for the years I was riding in sanctioned horse trials and had to have permission from my home country in order to compete in the USA, just in case I had been banned from competing in New Zealand for some serious riding infraction.

Then Karen widens her eyes to the bursting point. "I can't believe that you have remembered the dates of seventy-five trips out of the USA."

"Oh, I don't have that sort of recall," I laugh. "I began recording the trips in the early 1960s when my dad paid for me and my children to fly, with loads of large non-disposable diapers, to New Zealand." She doesn't think the diaper reference is very funny. And I don't think she has a clue what a huge terry-cloth diaper looks like. "I wanted to record each trip for the children's future interest," I continue. "When they grew up and went by themselves, I just continued to write down every one of my trips."

Next Karen checks my two new passport photos, looks up and smiles and says that I have passed and welcomes me to my new status as an about-to-be-American citizen. She hands me an official-looking document on which she has written 50/20.

But it's not over yet. I'm back in the waiting room that is now so stifling that a weak fan has been brought in. I am told to wait. And I wait and wait until I am called to sign my passport photos and get my swearing-in instructions. I write my name on both photos (very legibly please) and am told to appear at the Hynes Auditorium in the city of Boston on November 5 at 9am. (Guy Fawke's Day!) The instructions include the following. *Expect to be at the ceremony for SIX hours. Eat a hearty breakfast, please.*

I'm also handed an official Purple Sheet and on the very day of the ceremony I'm to honestly answer all the following questions:

1. *Since your hearing, have you been widowed, divorced, married or remarried?*
2. *Have you been convicted of drug trafficking?*
3. *Have you helped an illegal alien cross the border?*
4. *Have you had any violations of the law … including traffic violations?* (This question has really caught my eye, and I must drive like a little old lady … like me!)
5. *Have you become an alcoholic?* (Oh please – and the ceremony's in five weeks' time?)
6. *Have you committed a terrorist act?*
7. *Have you joined the Communist Party?*

And so on.

Time flies and the citizenship swearing-in ceremony is tomorrow. It'll be an endless day with getting in and out of Boston and spending those six hours at the Hynes auditorium. So there's much to do today and I'm rushing hither and thither. I drive home on a country stretch of Route 140 bordered with nothing but endless woods. It is sign-posted at an annoying forty miles per hour. My speed increases incrementally. I do love to speed, but whoa a bit, Liz. I have crept up to seventy-five mph.

The wail of a siren.

Question 4 floods my head. Since your hearing … *Have you had any violations of the law … including traffic violations?*

I look in the rear-vision mirror and a police car is bearing down

238

on me, the multitude of blue and white lights flashing. I pull over, sick inside. To think of all that I have been through to become a USA citizen, well, actually a dual USA/New Zealand citizen. Will this infraction disqualify me? Will I have to start all over?

My purse has slid to the floor. Quickly I unsnap my seat belt so I can lean down and reach it and I open the glove box to find the car's registration. Now I'll get a heavier fine when the officer sees that I'm not wearing my belt. I sit back up, and lo and behold, the police car wails right past me and disappears around a corner. I'm so stunned I sit behind the wheel motionless as more sirens pierce the air. An ambulance, two fire trucks and more police cars flash by.

Saved.

Finally. I'm by far the oldest person around and I'm about to be one of more than three thousand streaming into the Convention Center. I look for the end of the three-deep line and it disappears around a distant corner. An officer, big badge, big shoulders and big grin suggests I crash the line. I half-heartedly object but it is very cold and windy. The officer just pushes aside a pipe barricade and launches me towards the front of the queue. No other citizen-in-the-making seems to mind. Everyone is more focused on keeping bundled up and getting out of this frigid day.

Attendants keep shouting, "Form two lines please! Aliens with the important Purple Sheet must stay in the left line. Everyone with the important Yellow Sheet please keep to the right lane." Then follows the repeated request. "Please folks, hold your Sheets out *unfolded* at all times and have your green card handy."

Up the escalators we squeeze, get herded along an endless corridor, snake around a planter and traipse back along the same corridor. By now I'm chatting with a well-dressed man from Nicaragua. He's a banker and lives in a high-end Boston suburb.

More corridors and more escalators and someone shouts out that we're to check in at the numbered table that corresponds with the number on our purple or yellow sheet. I reach my table number 3 and someone quickly reads through my responses to the fresh questions. I'm still eligible. I'm told to throw my old precious green card (coloured blue and pink for the past twenty years) into a farm bucket.

At last we are ushered into a gigantic auditorium, with more than three thousand chairs. Architecturally it's a very pleasing room, crowned with a stage, lectern, the USA flag and the flag for Massachusetts. Everywhere is the hubbub of different languages. The Nicaraguan and I have gone our separate ways and I'm directed to a seat and introduce myself to my neigbours.

There's very attractive black Cindy from Ghana who works in a famous Boston hotel. We chat about the conditions in her country, and a black woman from Cameroon joins in. Another woman is from Scotland and guesses that I'm a Kiwi. She's a bit of a residual hippie in her granny glasses, no make-up and long skirt and equally long plait, but I like her immensely. She turns out to be a professor at a top university. "But you know, I don't really want to be a USA citizen. I'm doing it for the sake of my children." I don't want to sound dumb, but I can't see how it can make any difference to her children. Although our Richard had an involved time getting a clearance to do security research when they found out that his mother was a foreigner.

Next to Scottish Shawna is a man from the Dominican Republic who melts when I tell him about my visit to his island and the wedding of the century. And now it becomes wait, wait and wait. When I first sat down it was 10am.

An announcement. "The judge will start the proceedings at noon. Anyone needing to go to the toilet please proceed at once. Take your purple or your yellow sheet with you. Keep it *unfolded* at all times. IF you are in the toilet and you miss the swearing-in, *you will not be granted citizenship."*

Cindy and I join yet another long line and clutch our purple sheets. A nearby man is impatient. "Hey guys, we were recommended to have a substantial breakfast. Why not suggest we limit our fluid intake as well?" There's no pushing, but an uncomfortable crush as we form a straighter line and hand in our sheets at a desk with three attendants. I'm given a very large red card with 147 written on it and am directed to door B. "Please return through door B."

The ladies' room is packed but it helps the time go by except for the deteriorating air quality. Back through door B and into another long line for the return of our purple sheets, Again and again we are reminded, over the PA, "Without your purple or your yellow sheet, forget it, go home and start applying again."

Midday comes and goes and still no judge has appeared. Announcements are made one after the other.

"The toilets are now closed."

"No one can leave the auditorium."

"There are over three thousand of you heating up this auditorium. Please strip down to the minimum of clothing." Shawna and I giggle at this double entendre.

"The judge is now on his way."

"Like he has just left New York?" Cindy quips as we try not to squirm on our foldaway canvas chairs.

12.15pm.

12.30pm.

12.40pm and finally ...

In comes the judge, followed by other dignitaries and they climb on to the stage. The herd relaxes and we watch the presentation of the two flags, those of the USA and Massachusetts. Now the judge ushers up two black men from two remote African countries. "These two fine gentlemen are about to receive their citizenship. But first we must honour them for serving in the USA Army." Three thousand murmurs of approval fill the auditorium.

The judge coughs, scratches his neck, adjusts the collar of his jacket and begins what I'm sure is his standard monologue. "May I welcome you all to this great honourable occasion. Young and old. You are about to become citizens of the great United States of America. Let me remind you about our rights as citizens, our responsibilities, our loyalty to the Constitution and our willingness to bear arms for our country, whenever called upon ..."

Me, bear arms? I picture myself with an AK40 shooting at insurgents who have just landed on a Massachusetts beach. I recall Dad's vivid description of how his home guard unit in New Plymouth was going to stick it to the damn Japs when they landed on Fitzroy Beach. But half of Dad's group said to hell with the Japs. They were going to run up to the mountain and hide in the bush. If I have to bear arms it may be more convenient to shoot at the enemy as they march up our new steep, farm driveway.

The judge is not in a powdered wig or gown. He has a powerful voice, but looks like everyman. Finally, he instructs us to stand, raise our right arm and, "Say after me. 'I (your name) do solemnly swear to uphold the Constitution of the United States of America ...'" I had been warned that in subtle words we will have to renounce our country of origin. Shawna and I mouth these words.

My right arm becomes sore from being in the air for so long and from all my rotator cuff injuries. I prop it up with my left hand. The judge ends at last with, *"Look at all the happy faces I can see."*

We remain standing and recite the Pledge of Allegiance. I learnt it last week from my grandsons. *"I pledge allegiance to the flag of the United States of America, and to the Republic for which it stands, one Nation under God, Indivisible with Liberty and Justice for all."*

Three thousand American citizens are now told to stand and wave their little flag as their country of origin is called out. Albania, Algeria, Argentina ... Brazil gets a huge number of stand-ups and cheers as does China. New Zealand is called, and a lone shrinking five-foot-two-inch seventy-five-year-old woman with fake hair stands up and waves her little flag. Alone. Cindy, Shawna and the Cameroon lady clap vigorously.

At last we can file out, one by one, row by row, purple sheet holders first and then yellow sheet holders. The flock is orderly until I am back at Table 3. Impatience overtakes us new citizens and the jam has me waiting twenty minutes for my citizenship certificate. The PA urges us to hurry please hurry ... I move off down this corridor and that corridor, down two escalators and through a mob of the new citizens' families and friends waiting in the lobby where they have watched the proceedings on a huge screen. Outside I face the early winter cold and I'm in a taxi within a minute. We drive over historic Beacon Hill to the Massachusetts General Hospital and I recover my illegally parked car and pay a hefty parking fee.

The next day I go to our local post office and apply for my very first American passport. I'm off to New Zealand straight after Christmas.

Chapter Twenty-Nine

Can You Swear You are Elizabeth Mary Benney?

I wake up dispirited ... a woman who falls off horses, lacks the discipline to ride without stirrups and put up with the discomfort, a woman who is losing her energy level – and, damn it, even her passion level is dropping. And she aches all over in the cold, but there's nothing like a couple of Advil pills to take care of that. I roll out of bed and will myself to stand up straight. Dave is a solid nine-hour sleeper. I can do no better than six or seven hours and it never feels enough as I'm working harder than ever with horses, garden, cooking ... and *maintenance*. It'll be a big relief when poor Dave finally schedules his hip replacement and retires. He will feel like a new man and wait until he sees my to-do lists!

Brother Richard says I *think* I'm working harder, but I'm actually slowing down. It just takes longer to get anything done. "Rubbish," I inform him. Still, something else bothers me. For the first time in my life I have to fight the urge to lie down for an afternoon snooze. And I'm dropping things more frequently and my finger dexterity continues to decrease. Is it from fatigue or the worsening arthritis in my hands? The usual victims are cups, glasses and plates. And many times they shatter. This morning I break my best thin-lipped coffee cup. It's odd that I can't stand drinking tea or coffee from a mug. Richard and I laugh that we have this same idiosyncrasy. Although I did once hear something on the radio that drinking from thin-lipped cups increases the flow of oxygen into the mouth and this improves the flavour of the drink.

While I dislike thick mugs, I really loathe getting jokes and useless advice in emails. They drive me nuts. And often they threaten you with bad luck if you don't forward them to ten other people. I always delete each and every one and I'm still waiting for the bad luck.

This morning, having woken up feeling like an antiquated matron, for no reason I open one suspicious-looking message. It is obviously doing the rounds and it infuriates me, although yes, I do read it:

A is for arthritis.
B is for back pain.
C is for cardiac problems.
D is for dental decay.
E is for eyesight and trying to read the top line.
F is for fluid retention.
G is for gas that one would rather not talk about.
H is for high blood pressure.
I is for incision scars you keep hidden.
J is for joints that jump out of their sockets and refuse to return.
K is for knees that crack when they bend.
L is for libido and what happened to sex?
M is for memory and I forget what comes next.
N is for neuralgia and pain in the nerve endings.
O is for osteoporosis or fragile bones.
P is for prescriptions. And I can't count how many.
Q is for queasy … is it fatal or flu?
R is for reflux … one meal turns to two.
S is for sleepless nights, counting endless sheep.
T is for tinnitus and it's not music in my ears.
U is for urinary troubles … too much or too little flow.
V is for vertigo. That's dizzy, you know.
W is for worry. The list is endless.
X is for X-ray and what might be discovered.
Y is for another year you're left here on earth.
Z is for what zest you may still have left.

I've survived all the symptoms that my body's deployed,

And I'm keeping a dozen doctors fully employed.

The last line's not bad but I wonder why I lack the nerve to tell everyone I know to please stop sending me this junk.

We finally have great Lot 2 news. John and his wife Jane have decided, at last, that they want the land, and their lawyer and Robert our lawyer are working on the purchase and sale contract. But Peter, the buyer's lawyer, never seems satisfied with any agreement and there's growing confusion over the wording of the document. This is because we're giving the buyers our septic system's leaching field and in exchange they are paying for our brand-new replacement system.

Then our easement requests confuse both lawyers. We want to use our old driveway in emergencies. I picture myself driving home and ice has covered the new driveway. I'm ninety-five years old and I have to walk a thousand feet up the hill lugging bags of food with dog in tow. We also want an easement so we can keep our superior TV and Internet cable service, part of which travels under Lot 2. Any cable up our new driveway would carry a different service and one that everyone says is awful.

The lawyers finally get this very 'unusual' (their quote) deal figured out and now Peter starts quibbling over a sentence here and there. I have to believe that he's protecting his clients. So it's back and forth and all at great cost to us and to the buyers. Then it becomes endless hairsplitting over single words. I lose my sense of humour. "You're both becoming a thesaurus," I moan to our lawyer. "And Robert, tell Peter that I'm off to New Zealand in three weeks and to hurry up."

Robert is off to Hong Kong and finally finishes all our paper work at thirty-five thousand feet above the Pacific. I email Dave's and my appreciation and write that I've had fun trying to picture what Peter looks like and what sort of character he possesses. Is he handsome and of noble bearing? No, he's old, withering and weathered and has a yellowing beard coursing over his corpulent belly. He has the flabbiest of handshakes and there's no question that he's a misogynist.

Closing day. At last. Robert's still in Hong Kong, but assures us that everything is taken care of. Dave and I arrive at a lovely early Victorian house full of law offices. We're just inside the front door when an astonishingly virile and very good-looking young man blows down the stairs to greet us and crushes my right hand in welcome.

"Hi. I'm the lawyer for John and Jane. Just call me Pete."

The proceeding goes well with much laughter and before we apply many of our signatures we must swear that we are who we say that we are. I'm first to go and Pete tells me to raise my right hand. "Do you swear you are Elizabeth Mary Benney?"

"Well sort of yes and sort of no," I respond. Raised eyebrows. Shocked silence.

"Let me explain," I begin. It's a story I can rattle off. "When I was eleven years old, I desperately wanted a middle name. My parents never gave me one. I think because my father never had a middle name, and since he was the tenth child born into his family, they say that they ran out of names. So I rode my pony, Monty, into our small town's courthouse and tied him to a lamppost outside the old building. I was ushered into the actual courtroom where the judge was sitting in all his finery of gown and powdered wig. He looked down at me and said, 'What can I do for you, little sweetheart?' "

"I want a middle name."

"'Really? And what do you want that name to be?' "

"Mary."

"'Do your father and mother know about this request?'"

"Yes. Well, my mother does. My father's away on business."

"Smiling broadly, as he keeps peering at me from behind the big bench, he says, 'Okay, Elizabeth, you can have a middle name and it is to be Mary. This will cost you two shillings and sixpence. Pay the clerk on your way out.'"

"I galloped home quite beside myself and to this day, some sixty-three years later, I have always used Mary as my middle name. It's on my School Certificate, my university degree, my passports, my marriage certificate, in fact it's on everything that requires a full name. My sister Jill said she remembers vividly how thrilled I was and she also recalled that the charge was two shillings and sixpence. But neither of us could remember if I were given any documentation."

By now I really have Pete's attention. I glance at him and pause. He must be a busy man and would surely like me to stop talking but, "Keep going, Liz. This is quite a story."

"Well, when I was in New Zealand last year and I was staying in my old hometown, New Plymouth, I decided to visit the courthouse where my name change was confirmed. I was curious if there were still some documentation filed away. The old historic building has been pulled down and the new one has none of the charm or the lamppost where I had tied my pony. I explained my situation and had the employee intrigued. However, all matters of births, marriages and deaths are now housed in Lower Hutt and I was given the phone number. Of course I ring them minutes later on my cell phone. They ask for a fee of twenty-five dollars via my credit card and said they would post me all the information about who I really am."

"And who are you, Liz?"

"I'm just plain old Elizabeth Benney. It's interesting, but I was telling this story to the husband of one of my best friends. Alan is a retired judge of the Supreme Court and said, 'Liz, there's no way you could have got a passport with that assumed name.' Well, I did. I imagine someone was careless and didn't thoroughly check the Mary part against my birth certificate. So, Pete, I have no middle name. I'm a fake, a fraud and a sham. The old New Plymouth judge just indulged me."

"Well, this story is a first for me," Pete laughs. "I guess you'd better sign away as usual."

"Before we start," I say tentatively, "I apologise for taking up so much of your time. I really should relate one more very quick story so you can understand where my verbosity comes from. And how I should never go gabbing on and on."

Dave gives me a shut-up look.

"Just last Monday I went through a box of papers from my childhood. My brother sent them to me after Mother died. To my astonishment she had kept every one of my school report cards. I picked up one from 1943 when my sister and I were sent to boarding school. I read down one report card to the comments at the bottom that were always written by the headmistress. This is what she wrote: *Elizabeth is very active, resourceful and cheerful, but far too talkative and likes to be the centre of attention.* It was signed Irene Wilson, MA. That's it, Pete. So from now on I'll try and heed her words, written when I was just nine years old!"

Pete rocks back his chair and hoots out, "Great story, Liz. *Of course* you can't help being loquacious." And it shoots through my head that I've never heard that word actually spoken before.

After fixing our signatures – Elizabeth *Mary* Benney – I tell film star Pete how I had often imagined what he would be like. "I had convinced myself that you were an old hoary man with a flabby handshake and that you hated women and that they were born to be seen and not heard and of course one and all belonged at the kitchen sink." He doubles up with laughter. "And you're no misogynist," I add.

We drive home. "Hey, Dave, let's celebrate with dinner out. We're down to the *maintenance* of only twenty-five acres." The rest is in forest and it will take care of itself except for keeping the trails and my galloping track cleared.

And now my trip to New Zealand is only a few weeks off. I will use my old passport when I leave and return on my brand-new one. My immigration lawyer had said to me, seriously, "*If* there's a hijacking and you have a New Zealand passport and because you are ..." he had hesitated, so I added, "a little old lady I'm more likely to get off."

"Well, I suppose you can look at it that way, but with a passport for a small country like yours, I bet you'd be one of the first off the plane."

Chapter Thirty

Re-Living the Past

The usual last-minute frenzy and Dave's, "Got your passport? Got your tickets? Got your money?"

"Hey, I'm *not* incompetent," I laugh, then remember how reasonable is his question. When I was off to New Zealand two years ago we arrived at the airport bus stop and I remembered, with the worst hot flash, that I didn't have my immigration green card. Legally it's supposed to be on my person twenty-four hours a day, but of course it is safer locked in the safe. We had raced back home and I was stopped for speeding. I waved my plane ticket and passport at the officer and told him where I was headed while I managed a pretty good poor-old-soul act … "Wow, you're going a long way, ma'am. Hurry and go for it!" He slapped the roof of my car and for a moment I thought he was going to say, "Follow me and I'll use my sirens."

Rather than have a ten-hour wait for my long Pacific flight from San Francisco, I've opted to stay overnight and spend the next day sightseeing. First I want to visit Alcatraz prison. The hotel desk clerk checks his computer and all boat trips are fully booked. Why not take a chance? I taxi to the departure wharf.

My driver comes from Armenia and parks right outside the entrance to the boat dock. I hand him the correct change and tip and he leaps out of the car and runs around to open my door. A pre-pubescent kid, dressed in a ranger's uniform, rushes up to my driver, grabs one of his shoulders with one hand and with his other hand slams the door in my face. "There's *no* parking in this spot. Move your ass, immediately."

In slow motion my driver's face bulges red. Again he starts to open my door, but the kid quickly presses against it. Driver backs off a foot, very slowly rolls up his sleeves, scowls and bares his gnarled fists. The kid's shoulders sag against my window. "I'm allowed to disembark passengers right here," my driver screams as a large crowd gathers. His shouting gathers steam. "I've been letting passengers off at this spot for *forty* years. Before you were born, little critter!"

The kid backs off and I open my door and get out like a handicapped Senior Citizen. The ranger stares at me, mortified. He begs my forgiveness and I tell him not to worry. "Oh, you're an overseas visitor, too. Sorry, sorry."

I reach the ticket office for the boat trip to Alcatraz and persuade a young Filipino employee to sell me a ticket. "Don't tell anyone, ma'am." And I'm on the boat and off across choppy water to the old prison.

We're given headphones and can tour at leisure while the tape describes the prison's history in detail. I must say the place is a palace when compared with the cruel Old Newgate Prison in Connecticut. Newgate is way under the ground in pitch-dark dripping tunnels and alcoves, all originally built to extract copper. In 1773 it became Connecticut's first prison and in it were confined serious criminals, burglars, horse thieves, counterfeiters and forgers. Later in the century poor Tories and Loyalists were held here during the Revolutionary War.

Fourteen hours are ahead of me to Sydney and we're very late taking off at 2am Boston time. A passenger had checked in but wasn't on board and everyone's luggage has to be unloaded to find and throw off his bag.

Half asleep, I recall some of my long Pacific flights. One of the most notable trip had three of us sharing seats number 12A and 12B. "Let me introduce you to Mum!" said the woman on the aisle and she gently caressed a very fancy tin container sitting on the consul between us. "Mum came from New Zealand and wanted her ashes scattered along the Tongaporutu beach."

Next is a three-hour layover in Sydney and a further flight of three more hours across the Tasman Sea. Suddenly I hear my name announced over the P A system. "Paging Mrs Benney, Mrs Elizabeth Benney. Please come to the lost and found counter." I'm clutching my purse and my backpack so what's up? I'm handed my New Zealand passport. "You left it on the security belt," and I get the increasingly familiar *poor old soul* look.

Auckland at last and Seng is waiting for me. Richard's sitting in the car in a handicapped parking slot. It's out into the countryside and to Richard's and Seng's charming old house and enviable garden. We sip tea at the verandah table, shared with the two cats. Black and white Albert and I really hit it off. Several years ago he arrived at the house, unexpectedly and wouldn't stop staring at Richard through his bedroom window. After two days Richard couldn't bear the sight of those beseeching eyes, so he fed him. But since his own cat, Morris, was jealous of other cats Albert was taken to the SPCA and donated along with fifty dollars. Back home Richard's conscience started to prick. Immediately he and Seng returned to the SPCA and asked that the cat be given back. "No way," he was told. "You must wait until we have evaluated him *and* you."

A week later, they both passed the test and Albert was returned for a further timely sum of seventy-five dollars. To everyone's relief Albert and Morris turned into great friends.

The three of us talk about Richard's upcoming Parkinson's operation. I can't believe how much he has deteriorated since my visit seven months ago from Hong Kong. Richard is only sixty-one years old and the first signs of Parkinson's appeared when he was around forty-five. We all thought that the small tremors were the result of too much partying. Now the progression has led to the dyskinesia that has his shoulders jerking in all directions. We worry about his making it to Brisbane in Australia for the operation. Electrodes, with attached wires, will be placed in the brain and Richard will be awake so he can answer questions and move parts of his body as requested. No doctor wants to chance any part of the brain being mistakenly put out of action.

During a second operation, the wires from the electrodes will be hooked up to two stimulators, like pacemakers, in the chest. Then the big moment when the switches are turned on. Will Richard be able to live a pretty normal life? His neurosurgeon is very confident.

The three of us visit friends, my ex-sister-in-law and some cousins, one who actually came to our wedding in Massachusetts. Her husband was supposed to give me away, but his mother died the day before and he had to fly back to his native England. So Dave substituted his room-mat, Lew. He and my wedding ring turned up at the very end of the ceremony as Lew's car had been towed away for being in a non-parking area.

It's now off to Wellington and a superb view of Ruapehu, Tongariro and Ngaruahoe. When Jill and I were in our early teens at Tupare we watched one of Ruapehu's huge eruptions. The best view was from the top of a high gum tree in a pasture up by the road. We teetered as we thrilled to the giant plumes of fire, molten boulders and towering thick smoke from the volcano. And then a neighbour spoilt it. He was driving his cows along the road and yelled at us to climb down, immediately. "You'll kill yourselves, you bloody fools!" Of course we stayed up in the tree. Mother found us a bit later. "You know I can trust my darlings up there, but better come down. Mr Ramsay rang and he is all upset. He's afraid that a branch could break and it'll be the end of you both."

My great old friends Nev and Ruth-Mary greet me in Wellington and take me to see some of my early haunts. I can barely recognise Queen Margaret College and my old enlarged classroom. Gone are the windows that went down to the floor and through which I saw my very first American. At that time New Zealand was an R and R location for the men fighting in the Pacific. Four Yanks drove up in a jeep. Full of joie de vivre they piled out and came right though the open windows. Our teacher, nicknamed Buster, was corpulent by 1943 standards and the Americans rushed up to her desk, hugged her and asked her out on a date. It looked as if her face would detonate with the rising heat. It was the best moment of my year at the school and my first taste of long flat strips of chewing gum the men gave us. We'd never seen anything like it before. The only gum we'd ever chewed resembled Chiclets.

The next week some of us boarders were being driven along the Hutt Road. A jeep full of waving American soldiers and towing a trailer passed us at sky-high speed. It hadn't gone a hundred yards when the trailer flipped off, turned upside down and careened across the railway tracks, coming to rest on the stony bank of the harbour. Little did I dream at that moment that after my twenty-fifth birthday I would spend my life in the USA.

We drive up to Karori to see my other old Wellington boarding school with that somewhat over-blown name, Samuel Marsden Collegiate School for Girls. How I hated those three imprisoned years, clad in green from the top of my head to exactly three inches above my knees. Until quite recently I never again wore anything green. Looking back, I know it's unfair to blame Marsden School for all my unhappiness. As it turns out those long three tedious years were a blessing in disguise.

"How was it that you didn't go back to Queen Margaret College when you were expelled?" Nev asks.

"They decided to do away with boarders. I'd been signed up since birth to be enrolled as a high school student. When the boarding part closed down I remember thinking what a marvellous break. Then everything went to pieces."

I don't recall that Samuel Marsden (1765–1838) was ever mentioned to us students, or why our school was named after him. But now I can guess, as more and more historical facts have been uncovered. He was an English parson who migrated to Australia and ministered to the new population. He also became a farmer and employed convicts who'd been thrown out of England, often for petty crimes. Marsden became known as 'The Flogging Parson'. Even by the standards of his day, he inflicted cruel punishments and gloried in them.

Samuel Marsden eventually sailed to New Zealand where he introduced Christianity. On the strength of it he was memorialised in the school's name when it was founded in 1878.

How I wish I'd known all about Marsden's background when I was incarcerated here from 1949 through 1951. How I'd love to have announced to all the staff that I knew about Samuel Marsden's Australian heartless life and how denigrated our school should feel.

Now as we continue up a new entrance to the school, I tell Nev and Ruth-Mary how I decided to commit suicide the night after I first arrived. I was seething at Rose Allum, my headmistress at New

Plymouth Girls' High School, for expelling me. I was livid at Dad for going along with her. I became more and more emphatic that I would punish Dad and Miss Allum and fill them with everlasting guilt. I knew that Mother would be very upset at my death, but I rationalised that after my suicide she would be freed of all her concerns about me. Like my being bottom or almost bottom of every class, my insolence in class, my breaking all the rules, my defiance and the fact that I would never graduate from high school and would end up 'working my whole life in Woolworths', as they used to warn me.

Three storeys straight down from my tiny cubicle bedroom was a hard patch of bitumen paving. I pictured the horror on everyone's face as they looked at my mangled, bleeding body where it landed right below my window. Yes, I'd show them all. I kept on looking down those three storeys, my thoughts flashing all over the place. Did I have the guts to jump? I was still trying to get the courage when a *huge* earthquake struck Wellington. Panicking I dived back into bed, snuggled under the blankets, blocked my ears and squeezed shut my eyes. And waited. I was in a brick building and Dad always said that such construction wasn't nearly as good as wood for withstanding New Zealand's big earthquakes. A large one would crumble this building.

The building kept on standing and I heard sirens keening all over the city. I decided to live after all, although the thought of punishing Miss Allum occasionally crossed my mind and how she would live with the miserable *guilt* for the rest of her life.

"You know," I tell my friends as we gaze up at my old window, "of course my suicide plans were pure drama. I was far too chicken to jump from any window, and the holidays back at Tupare, riding and riding, were far too much fun to miss at the end of the awful long terms."

A few days after the earthquake I wrote a broken-hearted letter home. Dad passed it on to my poor bed-ridden mother. I decided I would make them feel really rotten and so guilty, but shame on me for never considering Mother's stressful illness and being away in hospital. Mother kept the letter and gave it back to me many years later. I still have it.

And here it is, mistakes and all, exactly as I wrote it on 12 February 1949. I was just over 15 years old.

Dear Mum and Dad,

Thank you for your letters. This is a filthy place. The meals are rotten and we have two half hours homework every day and over the weekend 3.

We had the awful earthquake very badly and several kids paniced.

It is Sat. today and I have nothing to do. Most girls are playing but I am just sitting in this cubical and have been doing so for nearly 3 hours.

I have nothing to read as the library will not open for another 2-3 weeks. It's awfully dull here. Please Dad remember to send me the paper cutting of the horse show results. I haven't taste a fresh piece of bread yet and no one could have any tea this morning because the milk was sour, and yesterday we had for dinner stuff like sick which I had to eat as there was nothing else.

Miss Wilson (house matron) is nice. Thank you very much for the food hamper. I was very pleased and if I eat a choc about half an hour before each meal I lose my appetite and therefore don't mind eating my meagree share of food.

There is usually quite a bit of bread but if I eat more than about 1 piece everyone teases me sort of and I know they disapprove because this morning one girl said, 'Do you remember Janie, didn't she eat, she always had two or more slices of bread.'

It rains everyday and hasn't stop blowing once. For the last 3 nights I have frozen for we only have 1 blanket and a sort of sheetish blankitish thing.

Next week I have to get up at 6.15.

I haven't seen the hills yet because of the mist. Until today I was made to sit with the 3rd formers. (I am a fifth former.)

Well I suppose I had better go and find someone to do something with or I will be told off. Please write quickly with the show news.

With love,
Elizabeth.

When I re-read the letter, many years later, I apologised to Mother for writing something so mean. Her response blew me away. "Russell and I didn't believe a word of it. We shrieked with laughter!"

As we drive out of Marsden's front gates I look up at an old house on a nearby hill. I can't stop grinning to myself. It still amazes me that I was permitted to spend a Saturday night here with my friend Ginger. I was constantly being grounded and in detention because of bad behaviour. On this one occasion, not only was I allowed out for the night but also I had a date! I'd met this gorgeous guy, Bob, at one of our school's tea dances. He was one in a load of dance partners (who were all strangers to us girls) driven to Marsden from Scots College on the other side of the city. Oh yes, our dance had to start in daylight. And end in daylight! Bob danced with me most of that late afternoon and begged me to go to their Scots College ball, held at night. And I finagled it.

He picked me up at Ginger's house and I was dressed in my long blue and white taffeta gown, one inch off the ground and modestly covering my shoulders. And in broad daylight we went in the *tram car* to Scots College. Oh the stares of the other passengers. Bob also brought me home in the tram and guided me in the dark to Ginger's front door. I could take you to that spot today where he paused and *kissed* me. I'm sure it was also his very first kiss. It was so hasty he hit part of my mouth and part of my chin, and he was gone. I didn't care … I was totally out of my mind with joy. I was no longer s*weet sixteen and never been kissed.*

I never heard from Bob again.

Early in the evening I fly for thirty-five minutes to Nelson in the South Island. I collect my bag and look for Marg, my friend and hostess. She's nowhere to be seen. All at once a blonde blur rushes through the door and races across the floor. Another follows. It's Marg's beautiful daughter, Penelope.

"Sorry, sorry, Liz. The foal escaped from the pasture. He's fine, thank goodness." We eat at a superb restaurant overlooking the sea. Three different people wait on us and I marvel at how New Zealand is becoming so multi-cultural. There's a girl employee from Austria, a man from Sicily and a man from Warsaw. Much confusion when we're told that the specialty of the evening is White Bread. It turns out to be whitebait, that tiny gourmet fish the size of a two-inch length of string. Each one has pitch-black dots for eyes and the complete bodies are fried in batter. They taste blissful.

Yet on to another flight to Christchurch where I spent my memorable student days. My friend Flick has a dinner party for old friends – and how the spirit of our youth lingers on. The next morning Flick and I reminisce about our O E and how her old car kept on breaking down so we resorted to hitchhiking many miles through Germany, France, Denmark, Belgium and Holland. We had one rule – never accept a ride with more than one man. And when we did, on two desperate occasions, we had to fight off their advances.

Later that day I fly in a very small plane to Wanaka. We become a paper dart in the descent. The woman across the aisle from me throws up and we land with a jarring impact. Seat belts aren't enough. I'm at the back and notice that all those in front of me are also hanging on to the seat in front of them. Jill and John meet me and I can see from their relieved faces that they witnessed our landing.

Jill shows me a corner of New Zealand that is new to me. It's over the golden tussock-clad Lindis Pass and down the Waitaki River Valley, across barren land interspersed with rich irrigated fields. There are the remains of stone crofts and a rich history from the days of the early settlers. We're on the edge of New Zealand's only desert and yet without warning we're suddenly in an area of normal rainfall. I picture two nearby farmers, one struggling to tame the desert and the other watching his grass that never stops growing.

Oamaru on the East Coast boasts of being New Zealand's only true Victorian town. Its stunning architecture brings back brilliant memories for me. Three of us decided to cycle around the southern part of the South Island. I had just finished my last year of boarding school bondage and off we set from Christchurch. No bikes had gears in those days, or front brakes, and many of the roads were unpaved. Oh those first few hours of cycling, our high level of energy and our independence! But it didn't take long for it to become rotten hard work as we struggled along gravel roads and up hill after hill. Just before Oamaru we found the perfect solution. Hitchhiking.

It worked, and we travelled with our bikes on the backs of many farm trucks for the next ten days. By the time we arrived in Queenstown we had run out of money and were heartily sick of youth hostels or sleeping on the bare ground. We were also starving and pinched peaches from someone's garden, very careful to take just the ones that were hanging over a fence and on to the side of the road. We argued that of course the fruit was on public property. I convinced myself that it was not like the peapod I stole from the Chinese man's store in Hawera. We telegraphed our parents who wired us money to complete our enterprising adventure. By bus.

We now drive south along the coast from Oamaru and stay in a motel with unusual regulations prominently displayed.

No fish to be cleaned in your unit.

Complimentary tea, coffee and milk provided for your <u>first</u> cuppa. What about the second cuppa?

Visitors must *be off the property by 10.30pm.*

Extra beds used unnecessarily will be charged at $5 a bed.

Wet beds will incur a minimum charge of $10 depending on how wet they are and the amount of damage caused.

We dine in a hotel called The Kink in the Road. The land around it is dead flat and just past the hotel is a futile dogleg bend in the main highway. We read that a dog lifted his leg on the surveyor's equipment and messed up his readings. It's all great fun until I'm reminded of my progressing late stage of life. Jill says, "Don't be offended but I must tell you that there's a drip on the end of your nose!"

I check my shirtfront – no food has landed on the fabric. Yet!

Chapter Thirty-One

Squeezing in More

With my trip nearing an end I return to Wellington and pick up a rental car. I want to squeeze in as much as possible of my old haunts and memories. A thought keeps on looming … how many more times will I be able to fly home?

First I will visit Otaki and see the old sanitorium where Mother spent so many on and off years between 1943 and early 1954. Oddly enough no one can remember how many different times she was admitted. Even Mother couldn't remember when once we asked her, but I suspect she didn't want to recall any of that part of her life.

Jill was now with me at Marsden, but didn't enter the school in disgrace. During my last year and almost every Sunday the two of us were permitted to miss chapel, church, chapel and boredom and drive to Otaki with Fred, the husband of Mother's recovering roommate.

Fred picked us up early from Marsden. Of course we were draped in uniform green, but we had our civilian clothes cleverly hidden underneath. First Fred would stop at his sister's farm in Waikanae and Jill and I would wildly gallop two of her ponies along the farm's oceanfront sands.

Today I drive into Otaki and get directions to the sanitorium from an engineering company. There's a new entrance and I park and locate the familiar hill. Near the top Mother would be waiting for us just outside one of the patients' little huts. We were not allowed anywhere near the sick women as the tubercular bacillus is highly contagious, but we would shout to each other, up and down the sloping lawn. All the huts had open fronts, almost like run-in shelters for horses. We all knew that endless fresh air, no matter what the weather, and total rest was the uncertain cure for the disease before antibiotics saved so many lives. Now the huts are all gone.

Glancing up the hill I look at the main administration building. It looks unchanged and the whole place gives me the shivers. Until today I had never really put myself in Mother's place. How on earth would restless, type-A me cope with such a disease? How would Jill cope, and my brothers? And how did Dad cope? How Mother must have worried about us and especially her unruly elder daughter and her young son, John, being tossed between special homes, relatives or living at Tupare if Dad were able to find suitable housekeepers. And later young Richard was added to her sad distress.

Should Mother have defied the doctors in 1947 while her TB was briefly inactive and Richard was born? None of us regrets his birth! But I picture her anguish when the illness struck yet again on the very day after Richard's birth. During our visits from Marsden, Richard was three years old. The war was over so Dad was able to find housekeepers with varying degrees of dependability. And except for the holidays I was away from them and our predictably hostile interactions.

I stand at the bottom of the hillside, now long overgrown with native bush, but I recognise the contours. I ache for Mother as I recall how we had to stay two hundred feet away while she stood above us beside her hut. After we'd shouted out every bit of news we could think of there came the inevitable blowing of kisses, the waves – and tears. On the way back to school Jill and I would say little. Was Mother close to death? Please give her a chance to win this battle and live, I would pray.

And she did win! Actually 1953 started as a bad year. Mother was very close to death when it was discovered that the drug streptomycin, in combination with another drug, could cure tuberculosis. For five days a week, Mother was injected with the antibiotic and had to swallow a thin pill the size of the lens in a pair of granny glasses. She became so used to the needle that she let beginner nurses practise on her. It took another long year, but miracles do happen. Mother lived, and the bacillus bacteria never attacked her lungs again.

I had planned visiting Inge, my close old Marsden friend, but sadly she had died two months previously from the pervasive bone cancer. She never felt sorry for herself and never once griped about her condition. Another Marylon. And another great friend gone. I hope I'm not a complainer if I develop a terminal illness or become incapacitated along the way. But I'm not so sure. Even a simple cold puts me in a rotten mood.

Now for a rapid visit to my old friends, Doff and Steve. Every summer they're in their family cottage on the banks of stunning Lake Taupo. Steve is the same Steve who arrived in New York the day I flew in from London to see Dave, way back in 1958. How utterly crazy was our unleashed tour of the East Coast, with Dave and me sleeping in the old Buick and Steve outside in his sleeping bag on the hard ground.

And too soon it is yet another goodbye, mindful of the creeping years and the unspoken thoughts – will we all see one another again? I drive through endlessly changing landscapes towards New Plymouth. Finally I see cloudless Mt Egmont, the name – to be politically correct – now changed to Mt Taranaki. The majestic mountain sinks deeper and deeper into my heart, the closer and closer I drive – the stately and stable symbol of my outlandish and nonconforming childhood.

Home.

Family and endless parties, reminiscing and visiting my favourite haunts, especially Tupare.

I wander around the glorious gardens and recall where, so many years ago, for sixpence an hour I weeded and weeded for those required daily sixty minutes. Dad had uncanny radar on us, and we dared not cheat. Today I'm a weeding authority and whenever we have help in our garden I drive them nuts. Half the time these well-meaning gardeners don't know much and look at me blankly when I tell them that the roots of weeds *must* all come out with their heads. "Otherwise they will shoot up again, practically overnight."

I stand in front of the kauri tree where Mother's and Dad's ashes are scattered. Dad died in his ninety-second year. He was a man of incredible vitality and reminded me of my immigrant forebears – full of energy and bursting with initiative, innovation and artistry. And what a raconteur. I could listen to the same stories time after time and still double up on the floor. And the parties we had at Tupare … the battering of the piano, the gin, rum, whisky and beer flowing. And the late hour when no one wanted to go home and the food had run out. "No problem," Dad would shout and dramatically dash into the kitchen and bring out the sandwich crusts on a silver salver.

Richard loves his gin and rum. When he was a teenager, he would eye the cellar, full of booze and double padlocked. I can't believe that Dad, the engineer, was so stupid as to forget about the hinges on the door. Richard and his friends oiled them and with no effort could lift off the door and raid the hard liquor. They would siphon off the top half of a bottle of gin and add water to make it look untouched. To the remaining half bottle of rum they would add cold tea. Dad drank only whisky, which they left undiluted. Dad never found out and we quail now when we think of the guests' comments on their way home. "That cheap old bastard, serving us such disgusting and weak drinks."

On one of my old trips back to New Plymouth I visited Dad every day in a nursing home where he was suffering from the onset of dementia and Parkinson's. During each of my visits he would be sitting in a wheelchair, his chin on his chest, never showing any sign of recognition. Still, I talked on and on about my life in America, Dave and the children. It was talking to empty air, every visit – but you never know if some of the news is being absorbed. At the end of one of my visits I popped into the nursing home on my way to the airport. As usual Dad was in the wheelchair, unresponsive to anyone entering his room. "Hi Dad. It's Liz," I spoke loudly; "I've come to say goodbye as I'm off back home to America." To my astonishment he laboriously lifted his head, looked me in the eyes, tried to smile and said a sort of "Bye, bye, bye," while moving one hand a couple of inches in farewell. He died shortly after that last visit.

I suppose there are worse things than regressing into silence. Still, if I ever become unresponsive, hey everyone, please keep giving me all the news – you just never know. I also question if dementia is inheritable. I guess that being genetically close to Dad, Richard and I are candidates to become *non compos mentis* but being able to absorb a little news may be better than what Maurice Chevalier called the alternative.

Mother was fifteen years younger than Dad, and lived for twelve more years. Most of that final period was in her new house in town and right above her beloved Tasman Sea. She had a housekeeper in an attached apartment and of course one day there was going to be another of my final visits. She suffered a stroke and lived the rest of her two years in a nursing home. I often wonder if the stroke was caused by Mother's excessive use of salt. She would consume at least a heaped teaspoon with every meal. We would chide her about it and she would just laugh. Was her salt intake connected to her long time on the streptomycin drug that fought her tuberculosis? She had little sense of smell when it was all over, and undoubtedly her sense of taste was also affected.

Nine years ago, saying goodbye to Mother as she lay in that nursing home was wrenching. She was able to talk and move her right arm, no one ever heard her complain, and she never had anything but a smile on her face and an interest in everyone else's lives. How she loved flowers, and when she began losing her sight we took her giant sunflowers. When Jill married and moved to the South Island, someone said to Mother, "Oh how sorry I am that your daughter's going to live so far away." Mother chuckled, "It's great news. I have a daughter who lives near *Boston*." With help from United's mileage-plus awards I managed to visit four times during the last year of her life.

I gaze at the kauri tree and think of all the memories that lie scattered with the ashes. I wonder if I'll be the first of my generation to go. "Aw hell, Liz," I say to the tree, "put that thought away." I'm not at all afraid of death but I have so much to do before I reach the last stop.

My New Plymouth friend Margaret and I drive to visit the farm where she grew up in the very remote district of Kohuratai. The mountain is stunning today, stark against an infinite blue sky and with streaks of snow tapering down to the six-thousand-foot level. We recall how I climbed Egmont that day with her brother, David. And how I didn't want to marry him at that point … I was too absorbed in my somewhat eye-popping university life. And what a lucky break for him. Did he deserve this scatterbrain? David, sadly, died of cancer in his forties.

We drive through the rich pastureland and suddenly reach the limit of Egmont's eruptions. You can mark the line when the rich volcanic soil turns into the blue papa. Now rugged land stretches before us, a beautiful area of steep saddles or hogbacks with deep valleys in between.

Margaret was educated through the Correspondence School until she boarded at New Plymouth Girls' High School. Miss Allum also gave Margaret a raw deal. She was put into a home science class that pretty much majored in cooking and sewing. She is rightly bitter that she never had the chance to learn French and Latin. "Well, Margaret, I would gladly have swapped places with you. Although, to tell the truth I hated cooking and sewing just about as much as I hated French and Latin. But the former would have been easier to pass."

Retribution. Margaret made it to Otago University and eventually became a top professor in biochemistry.

The land becomes wilder and more isolated but there are amazing views from the tops of the saddles. On an unsealed road we wind down a saddle into the valley where Margaret's father farmed and her mother raised three children with no electricity. The old house has been replaced with a modern structure, but the stunning isolation of the area is unchanged.

Now it's on to a gravel road through the very remote Tangarakau Gorge, and recently the route has been named the Forgotten Highway. Margaret and I reach Ohuru where a man is standing beside an ambulance and we ask him where we can buy a cold drink.

"No shops open here anymore," he sighs. "All eleven of them are boarded up." We learn that the old coal mine has closed and there are only two hundred residents left in the town. But the good news is that city people are selling their homes for big money and many have started moving to Ohuru where houses can be bought for as little as thirty-five thousand US dollars. The nearest shops are three-quarters of an hour away in Taumaranui. "Are you busy with the ambulance?" I ask him.

"Well, in 2008 I had three calls for the entire year. In 2009 it really picked up from October to December and I actually had three calls. Someone fell off a motorbike, someone had a seizure, and an old lady, all alone on a remote farm, thought she was sick but really the poor old soul just needed company."

Soon it's the final goodbye to John and Lynda and then to Richard and Seng. I bury the thought that I might not see my younger brother again. The implant operation is not always successful. I wander through the well-designed international airport building and think back to the first time I flew out of this little country. The terminal could have been a small farm structure with an added tearoom, and sparrows everywhere pecking at food crumbs. So starts another long flight to Massachusetts and I squeeze back tears as the snaking coastline of beautiful New Zealand disappears behind the clouds below.

Chapter Thirty-Two

This Confounding Technical World

Home to a huge welcome from Dave and an ecstatic barking dog, and home to jet lag, thank you letters, cooking … and maybe even jumping! Within fifteen hours I get pulled over for speeding. I'm driving to our small post office to get the mail and from nowhere a cruiser sweeps out of a side road, siren blaring and lights flashing. Our sweet Rocky is very protective of me and barks his head off as I hand over my licence and the car's registration.

"You know you were doing over fifty miles per hour and this is a thirty miles per hour zone!" he shouts as Rocky tries to drown him out. The officer takes my documents and saunters back to his cruiser.

I sit and wait and stew.

Ten minutes later I'm handed a warning. "Thank you, sir," I beam. "You know last night I got back very late from New Zealand. Old driving habits are hard to break, but at least I was on the correct side of the road just now." (He doesn't get it.) "If you have any question about my integrity," I ramble on, "you can ask Officer Bruce about me." Bruce is second in command in the police force and is our former farmhouse tenant. His wife was the great woman who never complained about having only one functioning burner on the stove.

I think to myself, yes I *was* speeding, but immodestly I consider myself a jolly good driver regardless of the odd fines. And regardless of the fact that SCs are known to *think* that they're great drivers, I really *know* that I *am* a great driver!

Not long ago I gave up my heavy driver's licence or Class II as it's called here. I'd had a permit to drive big trucks since I was sixteen, and I never, ever actually passed that driver's test. Dad had a cumbersome 1935 three-ton Ford V8 truck and I learnt to drive it, double-clutching and man-hauling the steering wheel. The New Plymouth inspector came out to Tupare to test me, but he and Dad were far more interested in talking about breeding dogs. Suddenly the examiner looked at his watch. "Oh dear me. Must run. The old woman wants me to take her somewhere. Elizabeth, I'm sure that your father has taught you well." And he wrote out my licence on the spot. Later it was automatically transferred on to my Massachusetts licence. I seldom needed it until I started riding in America. The stable owner, where I boarded my horse, lost his licence for drunk driving and here I was, qualified, and legally able to drive his horse van with an attached trailer carrying four more horses.

A few days later I bump into Officer Bruce and he grins. "Yes, I heard all about your infraction."

I drive home and my luck changes. I need to write my thank you letters to New Zealand and my computer keyboard has frozen. I try gently tapping a few keys, then bashing a few keys. No luck – and my fingers become more and more out of control. Dave's at work, but he's always too busy to worry about the intricacies of computers. What's a secretary for?

I ring computer-whiz Tonia and there's no answer. She and I have Log-me-in, a brilliant technique where Tonia can open my whole computer and display everything on her own lap top and I can watch her move my mouse arrow and get things working again. At the same time we're communicating on the phone and Tonia is the one and only boss. "Mother, take your hands off your mouse. Let *me* do it!" At last she rings me and I explain the malfunctioning keyboard. "Mother, it just needs a new battery." I had no idea it was battery-operated.

Batteries. I'm constantly installing them in every size and shape – my computer mouse, the keyboard, my cell phone, watch, (a professional needs to change this battery), camera, telephone, radio, blood pressure unit, scales and the energiser on the electric fence – on and on. What did we ever need new batteries for at Tupare?

Torches, and torches alone.

A few days later my computer won't work and Tonia's in Los Angeles at a meeting. I ring my server and I'm told to boot the thing. "I have booted it," I tell him. Yes, I think to myself, I'd like to boot it with one of my riding boots. A technician can't come to fix it for two days. "It'll be Wednesday, ma'am."

"About what time?" I ask.

"Between eight in the morning and five in the afternoon.

"Please, could you narrow it down to maybe during the morning or during the afternoon?"

"No." And the phone clicks off.

How can I manage without my computer for two days?

Two men eventually arrive. One is in training. They fix the problem in less than thirty seconds. One of the attachments of my modem has disconnected. Forty dollars please. It's tough having grown up before the days of fancy technology. Today I have one headache after another trying to figure things out and I'm always in an impatient mood. Is it from growing up without advanced technical experience that now has me lacking in modern savvy skills?

I think back to our first answering machine. The steps in the guidebook made no sense. After a lot of hits and misses I managed to install a message and found out how to play it back – then my vanity took over. There were too many um, um, ums and two many pauses when I struggled for the next word. Now, how do I delete it and start over? Finally I got it right but it was too long. And does one really need to add, *Please wait for the beep?* It was 1989 and we'd just bought the farm and everyone was putting cute and not so cute messages on their machines. If it had been a simple task I might have recorded back-ground music of *Old McDonald had a farm*.

Next it was the formidable task of figuring out my first cell phone. The instructions clearly assumed that you were an experienced technician. To make it worse, I had purchased an international phone with even more options. To this day I have covered just fifteen of the eighty pages of instructions. For a large investment I can make calls, receive calls and retrieve my messages. I won't report how many times I've had to return to the store where I purchased the phone and nice

Chris has helped me. He's great at *show and tell* and I'm just as great at forgetting how he showed me and how he told me. Some of my requests must have driven him nuts. How common are these problems among people of my age?

"I need to delete things, Chris, and I can't figure out the instructions."

"For no reason the cell phone has started vibrating if I have an incoming call and I like *sound*. Please can you show me how to change it?"

"I can't remember what to press to see the number of the person who just rang me and left no message."

"How do I recognise call-wait? In fact do I have it on this phone?"

"What do drafts, multimedia templates, browser msgs and quick notes mean …?"

"And Chris, you must understand that I grew up with *operator telephones* and the technical world can be very baffling." He doesn't get it.

"Hi Chris, nothing's working."

And then Chris tells me, "Because it's time for a new phone."

Now whenever I'm half-way through the store door it's, "Look who's here! Liz's in another mess." And I have to confess that my teenage grandchildren can figure out anything and everything, and they even text messages at unbelievable speed.

On my first trip to New Zealand with my phone duly charged I arrived and tried to ring one of my brothers. The phone was dead. Then try to remember how to make internal calls or overseas calls or have people overseas or in New Zealand call me. I now carry the instructions with my passports. For example, if I'm in New Zealand and want to make a call to someone in New Zealand I must dial 0 and then bring up the + sign, then dial 64, then the city code and then the local number. And at international rates.

Of course I was back seeing Chris on my return to Massachusetts and he let out a belly laugh. "Didn't you read the instruction manual? You must *always* turn off your cell phone when flying. Or it will spend the whole time trying to find a server. This runs down the battery, Liz!"

Forget about all the instructions for contemporary washing machines and dryers, microwaves and even the iron ... When I think of all the options we didn't want but had to pay for. All I really want to know is how to turn something on and how to turn it off.

Forget about the options on my digital camera. I grew up with the simple box brownie. Just click. But after much practice I can take fairly good shots on my contemporary camera, and Tonia patiently taught me how to transfer them on to my computer and send them away on email.

Click on My Documents.

Click on My Photos.

Choose the photo and right click on it.

Click on Edit.

Click on Image.

Click on Stretch/Skew.

Change the Horizontal 100% to 50%.

Change the Vertical from 100% to 50 %.

Click on Okay.

Click on Save.

Click on the chosen photo and drag it to a waiting email. And hope everything works.

Whew.

I don't know how she does it but, right out of her head, patient Tonia reeled off these instructions. Of course I wrote everything down in my important notebook. Losing this notebook would send me into a major dither – 'a state of flustered excitement or fear' says my dictionary. (I must have been born with a dithering inclination, as my very first nickname was Ditherer.)

My indispensable notebook contains all the passwords I could never commit to memory ... our security system, the ATM, my bank account on line, my two email accounts, my doctor's email access, my Visa account, on and on. About the only thing I don't need to write down is my mother's maiden name.

Deleting photos on my camera is another issue. I try to delete one shot and end up deleting the jolly lot. One day I'm determined to figure out the video on the camera and how I can set the camera and run myself into the picture. And I will find out what are recorded pixels, quality levels, white pictures, sensitivity, EV compensation ... and on and on. I'm so thankful that I'm reasonably good at something – jumping horses. Or is it that I *was* reasonably good at jumping horses?

Forget about ever finding my way around my computer. I'm just so indebted to savvy Tonia so I don't ever have to talk to India or the Philippines, which is where the people you ask for help all seem to be based.

Then there are the options in my pick-up truck. I just wanted it to pull my horse float, but when we bought it nine years ago many trucks were being installed with the options you find in upgraded cars. The idea was that families were going to be into trucks, but the SUV outmoded them. Still, I have yet to figure out most of the selections. When we bought the truck the salesman programmed it so that the seat slid back whenever I went to exit the vehicle. The minute I turned on the engine the seat would automatically slide forward to a pre-programmed position. But after a near-crisis, it doesn't work.

Truck repairman Mike arrived one day to check a strange noise in the engine. He got into the front seat, turned on the engine and the seat did its automatic forward slide towards *my* pre-selected position. Now I am five foot two inches high and Mike is six feet five inches tall and with such long legs it looks like they hang out of his armpits. The seat wouldn't stop moving forward and his legs were getting more and more scrunched up against the dashboard. "Shit!" he yelled. I don't know what he did but commotion ensued and he finally got the seat to stop. It has refused to function automatically ever since. Even a technician thought he had it going well, but by the time I got home the thing was back to manual only.

Very simple appliance purchases have also given me hassles. We needed a new toaster, just a plain one with two slots for two slices of bread. I bought a good brand, drove home and tried it out. There was no heat. Back I drove to the store, some forty-five minutes away and a Turnpike fee as well. It was kindly exchanged. Got home and this one was also broken. Back I went, yet again, and thankfully there was a different salesperson in the toaster department. Home again and I couldn't believe that this *third* toaster didn't work. I checked the plug and it was active.

Maybe I'd better check out the instruction manual, I thought. Oh no … *I* was the damaged goods. There it was in large black letters on the first page: *When toasting just one slice of bread, always use the slot with the arrow. This is to save electricity. The other slot will not heat unless two pieces of bread are in place.*

I look around my study and under my desk. Wires and cables of every shape, size and colour go from outlet to outlet. To my gratification I have actually mastered a printing machine, a fax and a scanning machine but heaven help me if they ever become disconnected.

Not long ago I gave son Richard my eight-year-old car. He hopped in and started studying everything. "What's this knob for, Mother?"

"I've no idea. I've never noticed it before."

"Oh, it's a lumbar adjustment for the seat."

"And this little lever on the steering column, Mother. Any idea what it's for?"

"I've no idea. I've never noticed it before."

In no time Richard has it figured out. "It moves the steering column forwards and back."

I can't believe I had no answer for three more questions.

I think about Tupare's old family runaround Vauxhall car. We all learnt to drive in it and could use it any time we wanted *if* we first did an hour of weeding as well as the daily-required one hour. All the car had were windscreen wipers, a horn, three forward gears, a reverse gear and lights. For indicating a change of direction, we would push a small knob on the steering column, either to the right or to the left. Out would pop a little directional signal with a tiny light bulb inside an orange glass case. One day I tried very hard to change gears by calculating the tone and speed of the engine and not using the clutch. I managed well for two or three changes and then successfully stripped the entire gearbox. Dad thought it was from the old age of the car. I wish now I had confessed to him, years later of course, and cleared my conscience.

When my technical world fails me yet again, how I miss those uncomplicated olden days. And to think that a long time ago I wanted to be a civil engineer …

Chapter Thirty-Three

Family Round-Up

The construction of our new modern septic system has started and how these sophisticated designs have changed since my youth. Sixty years ago, in the homes of some of my childhood friends it was often a bitterly cold walk from the house to the corrugated iron lean-to with the toilet straddling a fly-bitten hole in the ground. Cut up sheets of newspaper for the toilet paper hung from a string.

I think about my horsey friend Maddy, the one who helped me spook the other students in the fake tapu cave. Maddy's house had the characteristic outdoor toilet on their farm. I often stayed with my friend and we slept on thin mattresses on the floor, helped milk the cows and make hay. But more extraordinary for me was that her father had never married her mother and had long ago disappeared from their lives. Maddy thought that he came from Spain.

Equally outrageous was that her mother was again *living in sin,* and with a man of the *cloth.* He had left Britain and discarded his parson's clothes when he arrived in New Zealand and was trying to become a dairy farmer on a poorly equipped rented farm. To be part of the lives of such renegades wowed me. But how dare they lie when Miss Allum forbade Maddy and me a day off school to ride in Friday's classes of the Hawera A and P Show? Well, we were permitted to attend, but we had to have all our schoolwork up to date and signed by each of our teachers. I managed to obtain two signatures … for gym and for cooking. Maddy got one signature, for French … she had lived in France for a while.

Miss Allum never mentioned the situation to us again. Of course the busybody had forgotten about Maddy and me, what with running a large school of girls.

The day before the start of the show I returned home in the school bus on this perfect Thursday afternoon. I bathed Pollyanna and finished packing up my clothes and tack as an hour later my mare was leaving on the back of a neighbour's lorry for Hawera. Miss Allum's demands were well out of my mind.

The phone went. Mother answered and came on to the terrace where I was standing. Her face was drawn and she had just come home from yet another long recuperation in Otaki.

Oh no.

"Elizabeth, that was Rose Allum. We're both ashamed of you for trying to deceive us and go to the show when you knew very well that you didn't have the signatures from your teachers. I gather that *none* of your academic work is up to date."

My world was busted.

Now I would have only two classes on Saturday. But adding to my outrage was that Maddy's mother had got the *parson*, of all people, to tell Miss Allum that Maddy couldn't go to the show anyway because she had come home from school very, very sick. Sick? She won a stack of ribbons on Friday.

Sue arrives at work all bug-eyed. "Brian has proposed to me!" she cries with happiness, and dances all over the stable aisle.

"Oh Sue, I hope you said yes."

"Without a moment's hesitation. And he has given me a beautiful ring. Quick, look."

"I wonder if the bigamist will hear about it."

"Well, I have to email his parents to see if Karl was ever baptised, because Brian is Catholic and I'm Protestant and it will mean a lot about how we plan the ceremony."

"I guess he didn't ask your father for your hand in marriage?" I laugh. "That was the *de rigueur* requirement in my day."

"Really? What if the father said no?" she jokes.

"Well, I'll tell you about that big moment in my life. Dave flew out from Boston and joined me at Tupare. When Dad was in his study at the end of the day, Mother, Dave and I decided it was *the* time. I think Dad knew what was up as he asked Dave to shut the study door behind him. Of course Mother and I stood outside and listened to the clink of glasses being filled and the conversation turning very general. Finally we heard Dave say, 'Russell, do you know why I'm here?'

"'Sure,' replied my father, and went on talking about the garden. Finally he raised his glass and said, 'Well, Dave, good luck and congratulations. She's a good kid, but can be very independent and all I can say is thank God she's now your problem!' Dad must have guessed that Mother and I were listening through the door, and called us in to celebrate."

Sue appreciates this, and I hurry outside to bring in the horses and bump into our tenant, Letitia. She's only two weeks off delivering her second child. "In what hospital are you having the baby?" I ask her.

"Oh, I'm delivering in the bath upstairs. A midwife will help me."

A baby in our stable apartment's bath? All I can think of are the many assorted tenants who have previously used that bath. "We'll fill the bath with very warm water," she continues, "and when my contractions are coming full-swing, it'll be so comfortable and easy."

Holy smoke.

I think about my three times of giving birth and when the contractions started. I can't imagine anything that would have eased them, except being completely knocked out which was the popular American way when I delivered Richard's eight pounds four ounces in 1961.

I'm told that a bath delivery recreates the amniotic fluid for the newborn. From my point of view, haven't billions and billions of babies, dating back millions and millions of years to the baby chimps in the course of evolution, been born in the conventional way? I don't say it, but I certainly hope we won't hear ambulance sirens on the big day.

This whole birthing procedure still holds questions for me and when I see the husband outside this morning I catch him getting into his car. "Hey James, I'm just curious and I don't want to be an alarmist, but what if the baby's head is stuck outside the birth canal and the cord has ruptured inside. Wouldn't the baby drown?"

"I don't know, Liz." He looks a bit alarmed, and now I wish I hadn't asked.

New baby aside, we have a growing problem with these tenants. It almost looks as if James and Letitia are taking over the farm. They wanted a vegetable garden and we suggested where the plot could get the most sunshine. Unlucky for us, the increasing size of the vegetable garden means that it can now be seen from our house ... along with bundles of stakes, hoses, barrows, buckets, spades and sheets of plastic covering who knows what. We had no idea we would start looking like a market garden. Then a colossal load of wrapped bundles arrived on the back of a huge truck and they're all lying at one end of the stable aisle's floor. We're told it's a swing, a playhouse, a slide and 'other great things'.

"James," I exclaimed, "this is a horse farm and not a pre-school playground." However all is to be assembled way out of sight behind my indoor arena and in back of the tractor garage. Meet two very tolerant landlords. And from now on, no tenants with children!

For weeks the tenants have parked three cars on the farm and Letitia still doesn't drive. Now it looks as if Letitia's mother and *her* car have moved on to the farm, and for how long? Who knows?

A month ago I did have words about this expanding parking lot. "We don't want to look like Walmart's," I said. James replied that two of the cars are supposed to be towed away for good. But the question now is: *when?*

Added to all this tenant-expansion I find one of the horse stalls crammed with junk. We said they could store their outdoor grill in it. Finally, I went up to the loft the other day. James had locked himself out of the apartment and I had a mass of keys to try to find the correct one. I flipped when I reached the top of the stairs into the apartment. Half the huge space where we kept the hay and shavings during my horse-boarding days is now filled with junk, and I mean *junk* ... tools, lawnmowers, suitcases, toys, boxes, barrels, bicycles, ladders ... you name it.

I'd not been upstairs in many months. After old Jax died, Dave and I had a small stable built and it was attached to the house. With its three loose boxes for my three remaining horses I joked how we were now a fake 19th century New England farmhouse. There were two moments that decided we should build. I went to feed the horses one morning and there was a seven-foot drift of snow blocking the stable door. And not many days later, Dave went to hay the horses at 7pm and found an inch of ice coating everything on the farm. The temperatures were way below freezing. It doesn't take much to imagine what could happen to a Senior Citizen in the middle of winter. I read my own obituary: ... *Mrs Benney, ninety-seven years old, was found dead on an ice-encrusted path at her farm. It was assumed she was on her way to feed her horses. The cause of death was determined to be a broken hip and hypothermia.*

When I gasped at the state of the old stable's loft I almost exploded. "Golly, James! This is awful. Are you a collector? I don't believe how you can live this way. It's disgusting." (See how one can say these things after reaching the age of seventy?) "This area doesn't go with the apartment," I continued. "Sure, if you need to put the odd article against the back wall, okay. But this horrendous mess has to go." He promised me that it would all be removed shortly. He's waiting for a dumpster and his father to help him.

What is more I sense that they're finding me an increasingly irritating landlord. But at the end of every month there's always a rental cheque, albeit lying naked on the concrete floor just inside the garage door.

Today's becoming full of bizarre moments. A friend rings me about a true story. She has a neighbour with a pet chook, and a coyote caught it. The family Labrador scared away the predator and he dropped the hen and fled. The owner scooped up the hen and rushed her to the veterinary clinic. Diagnosis. She's in a state of extreme shock and her heart rate is way above normal.

Prognosis?

Indeterminate.

I tell this story to my own vet when I take one of our cats to have his teeth cleaned. David says that he has seldom treated pet hens, but the other day he did have to X-ray fifteen of them. The owner had lost her diamond ring in the chicken coop and was sure that one of the chicks had swallowed it. And the X-ray results? Negative. I forgot to ask David if the birds had first been tranquilised, as one usually does to an animal before an X-ray.

Next I get an email from son Paul and a photo of a good-sized black bear in his garden. The animal had just pulled down the bird feeder, stuffed himself with seed and is lying on his back, sunbathing and with a contented grin on his face. Paul is going to design an indestructible bird feeder. He has already had a confrontation with the same black bear when they came face to face at his garbage can around the side of his garage. "Mother," he tells me, "I turned the corner and suddenly our faces were six inches apart. I could smell his bad breath. He got as big a fright as I did and we both flew through a hundred and eighty degrees, the bear banging over the steel lid of the can."

Later in the day I'm outside talking to James and his wife. "We think the baby will come in about an hour," she tells me. "My contractions are three minutes apart."

"Then I guess you've filled the bath?"

"We're thinking about pumping it up right now," James says.

"What? Pumping up what?"

"We decided to get a special birthing bath. We didn't want to pump it up too soon or the cats might scratch and puncture it."

So our bath is not involved, thank goodness. They have rented something that looks like a little kid's pool but with high sides. It will be filled to more than two feet deep. Off they go inside and half an hour later I see two strange cars tear in and screech to a halt. The midwife and a student of midwifery.

Later we learn that the new little boy came before any of the family could reach the apartment to share in the show. But their two-year-old loved the whole procedure and kept trying to float his boats in the water. All went really well, but the hot water ran out before the bath was full enough and it didn't feel as warm as Letitia would have liked.

Forty-nine years ago, forty-eight years ago and forty-five years ago, there was no way that even Dave was allowed into my hospital delivery room in the States. Now if the children had been born in New Zealand, when the Parents' Centre movement began in 1952 with its campaign to have fathers support their wives in maternity hospitals when in labour …

278

I get a ring from son Richard, wondering if we could occasionally employ grandson Luke during the upcoming summer holidays. "It's time he had a taste of employment, Mother."

"Of course. There's certainly plenty of farm work. We'd love to have him and Jonathan too."

And I think back to my first job, as a sixteen-year old. Dad announces that holiday employment will be good for me and he went on and on about how I need to become a responsible member of society and get a taste of the *real* world. And here I am, just back from my first miserable year at Marsden and making horse plans galore. Three of us are even going to ride around the mountain, tethering our horses at night and sleeping on the ground in our sleeping bags. We can never make it in just the two days of a weekend off work. Dad gets the very reluctant me employed by Ivan Watkins Company where he is a director. Along with many products they produce the new and soon controversial poison spray, 245 D, which kills the gorse and blackberry rampant on so many of New Zealand's farms.

Bicycling to work isn't too bad since Tupare is closer to the mountain than the town and it's all-downhill for four miles, usually with a tail wind. Cycling home uphill and into a head wind is another story. On the first day I'm shown how to use the telephone switchboard. Masses of plugs have to be shoved into various holes and switches pushed forward or back to make the connections. It's quite fun until I'm censured for more and more mess-ups. Some people are highly embarrassed when I connect them to the wrong people. So the boss moves me into a room with hundreds of pamphlets advertising the new miracle 245 D. These are to be wrapped in brown paper, tied up with string and addressed to all the many distributing companies and farmers around New Zealand.

Two days later I watch the postman toil into the office with an enormous canvas sack over his shoulder. "Gor blimey. What a shambles. Whatever nut was in charge of preparing these pamphlets for postage mightily screwed up. Tied them with a granny knot, she did, and almost all of them fell apart." Actually I had tied them exactly as I was shown.

So I'm further demoted to making tea and coffee and running errands for everyone. Then with nothing to do late one afternoon I stand in an empty secretary's room and idly turn the handle of the franking machine. Around and around. Little do I know that every turn equals the cost of a stamp that could be printed by the machine on to an envelope.

I'm sent packing, but not packing pamphlets this time. *Sacked*. To compound the ignominy, Dad tells me how he spent his very first-ever pay cheque on a present for his mother. I can still remember the amount I was paid – two pounds twelve shillings and six pence. And every penny of it left my hands.

The phone goes and it's brother Richard. "Liz, I've just had a ring from Doc, my Parkinson's specialist. He tells me that the new National Government wants to save money and that our New Zealand doctors must start performing the electrode procedure in this country, and you won't believe what he has proposed. Would I agree to be that first-ever patient done in New Zealand? So I say, 'Honestly, I don't know. For a starter, who will hold the manual, Doc?' I find out later that Doc has the Australian team coming over from Brisbane and they'll perform just *my* operation here and show the New Zealand doctors how it's done."

We discuss it at length and how arduous the trip to Brisbane would be for him. Seng also agrees with me that Richard should stay in New Zealand and *go for it*. Nothing could possibly go wrong if the Aussie team are present.

A day later he rings me again. "The Aussie team will do most of the work except the New Zealand surgeon will do the actual drilling into my head. Doc said that this part of the operation is a pretty routine procedure. So I'm going for it."

"Great decision, Richard. It's hard to believe that it's finally going to happen."

He asks about Dave's hip.

"It's becoming more and more painful and he promises that he'll see the orthopaedic surgeon soon. I'm sure the joint needs replacing as it's mirroring how his left hip deteriorated in 1999. You know he left that one so long it became bone on bone before he decided that he'd better have the operation. Can't you hear Dad's and Mother's words, Richard? '*Rise above it and don't complain.*'"

The next day Richard scans me a letter he has just received from the Movement Disorder Clinic.

> You have been booked to undergo Deep Brain Stimulation surgery on Wednesday 12 August 2009.
> *Please note that if you are taking aspirin, dispirin or cartia this should be discontinued 10 days prior to the surgery.*
> You will be admitted by medical and nursing staff to the neurosurgical ward (time to be confirmed) before your operation and seen by the Australian neurosurgeon. You will have a preliminary MRI scan at Auckland Radiology Group on Monday 10 August at 1415 hrs.
> You will be asked not to take your Parkinson's medication after midnight prior to the surgery.
> On the day of the operation you will be taken to the theatre admitting ward and the stereotactic frame will be applied to your head. Local anaesthetic is injected into your scalp and the frame is screwed into place. You will then be transferred to the Radiology Department for a CT Scan. Following this you will go to the operating theatre to undergo the procedure.
> You will be given some sedation whilst two holes are made in the frontal part of your head. After this you will be woken in order to assess the effect of the stimulation via the probes placed in the target area in the basal ganglia, deep within your brain.
> Doc will ask you to perform several activities including speaking, moving your hands and feet and reporting on your vision. Once the correct area for stimulation has been located you will again be sedated whilst the electrodes are secured in place and the scalp incisions are closed.
> You will wake up in the theatre's recovery room and then be transferred to the High Dependency Unit in Ward 83 for overnight care. Your Parkinson's medication will be recommenced. At this stage the wires which are at the ends of the electrodes will be outside of your head and secured in place by a bandage. A post-operative CT scan will confirm their placement. Two to five days later you will return to theatre for placement of these electrode wires under the skin. They will be placed under the scalp and track under your

skin bilaterally down behind your ears, down your neck and under your clavicle where they will be attached to a stimulator beneath the skin on your chest. The stimulators are about the size of a stopwatch.

Your hospital stay will be about 5–7 days. After discharge you will be able to go home.

You will need to return to Neurology Clinic Day Stay daily for about a week for adjustment of your stimulators and Parkinson's medication.

Ongoing management will include outpatient visits to the Neurology Department approximately six weeks after the surgery and then as arranged by Dr ...

We look forward to catching up with you next week.

Yours sincerely,

Lorraine,

Movement Disorder Nurse Specialist

My poor dear brother ... And he is to be the very first New Zealand patient.

Chapter Thirty-Four

The Big Operation

It's the day before the big operation and I ring Richard to wish him good luck and ask how he's coping. "I'm fine, Liz, but poor Seng's a mess. He's so worried." I talk to Seng while Richard turns off the kettle. "How are *you* doing?"

"I'm fine, Liz. But poor Richard's a mess. He's so worried."

"You know," Richard says, taking the phone again, "the Aussie neurologist asked to meet me and from listening to him I have a great feeling of confidence. He said 'I've done over three hundred of these Parkinson's operations and only two were a problem.' I was longing to ask him what had gone wrong, but I honestly preferred not to know that maybe those patients had died. I also met the anaesthetist and a bunch of nurses. A grand group and I feel very positive to be worked on by them all."

Of course one never knows about the outcome of such a huge operation and I want to end our conversation by saying, "I love you, Richard. You've been the best brother anyone could ever wish for," but in my mind it sounds a bit too final, maybe like a death knell.

"Tons of good luck, little brother!"

Twenty-four hours later Seng phones. "It's all over and Richard's currently in recovery. The team of doctors and nurses feel that everything went so well." Dave and I let out a cheer and I tear up with relief.

The following day Seng reports again. "Richard is really alert and told me about some of his experiences. The doctors kept on asking him question after question, to be sure vital parts of his brain were not being compromised. One of the questions, asked over and over again, was, 'Where are you, Richard?' And he would correctly answer 'Auckland, New Zealand.' After a while his sense of humour took over. '*I'm in New York, New York.*' The whole operating room exploded. They also made him count to fifteen and count backward. So he told the group that he was hopeless at figures and how he had failed School Certificate three times; but he passed this new test well."

Since the brain is still swollen, there will be more adjustments over the next few weeks and Seng tells me that he will be shown how to use the remote control. "Richard thinks it's so funny that I can now control him electronically."

Two days later I ring Seng as Richard will probably have had the second operation in the series. All is still going well. "He's going to write it up for you," Seng tells us. "This operation wasn't as long as the first one and the wires that were hanging out of the electrodes and bandaged around his head from the first operation were threaded through the skin and connected to the two batteries or stimulators in his chest. This time he was completely knocked out."

The next night I crash into bed and the phone goes. "Well, Liz, there was a bit of a problem with one of the electrodes, so poor Richard had to be put under anaesthetic yet again, but it went okay and he's recovering well."

Nine days later Richard is home. Seng phones and I tell by his voice that all's going well. "Want to talk to him?"

"Hi Liz. Well it's all over and I can't believe how different I feel. I'm dictating the whole event to Seng to email everyone." I don't say anything, but Richard's voice has markedly changed. He's talking slower and with a lot of slurring. I can understand him most of the time. "By the way," he continues, "has Dave made an appointment with his orthopaecdic surgeon yet?"

"Yes! Can you believe it?"

I open my emails and there is Richard's account of the operation as dictated to Seng.

Dear friends and family,

The date was 11 August around 1pm when I was admitted to the New Auckland Hospital. Was met at the reception of ward 83 by a tall elegant woman called Lorraine. She's the Movement Disorder Specialist Nurse to my neurologist, whom we all call Doc.

It was a bit like checking into a slightly tired Holiday Inn. Lorraine had organised a private room for me, for which I was very appreciative. Seng hung around until 7pm and left me there by myself. I went to sleep being awakened at 6am to get ready for my operation. As this Deep Brain Stimulation was the first ever done in New Zealand I was a sort of VIP. In spite of cousin Rowan Nicks' comment that, "You should never be the first!" I had decided to chance it. *As some of you know, Rowan is Mother's first cousin and a pioneer in heart surgery and an awful old egoist at ninety-seven years old and still travelling the world to attend medical conferences!* However we had Mr B, a great chap from South Africa, as surgeon with his young female assistant, five anaesthetists and some there for experience. The head chap called Nigel was Scottish and we bonded immediately. There was a collection of nurses and students observing the procedure and a professor of neurology from Brisbane (where they usually sent the NZ patients) called Peter, who also set up the unit there and helped set up this one in Auckland.

The first nightmare was having this 'crown of thorns' screwed to my head with spikes that pierced the skin and went deep into the bone. They used some local anaesthetic, which helped marginally for this, which I wore for four hours. I was then six hours on the slab and it was a far bigger operation than I had told myself. And one needs to be awake to signal the placement of the electrodes. They used a type of anaesthetic that kills the pain but doesn't really knock you out. There must have been nearly twenty-five people in the operation theatre, standing room only, coming and going during the procedure.

Apparently women come in for brain surgery with two

hundred-dollar perms only to have part of their hair shaved and bright orange iodine poured all over the rest, making them look like orange rats. A giggling little Asian nurse told me I had the same effect without the perm. Lorraine stood close by to hold my hand. And then the surgeon started to drill my head. I was a little nervous about the drill, (a hell of a nervous actually), and when it started it was identical to Joe's, my builder's concrete cutter. The noise was deafening and the smell was like Seng´s BBQ spare ribs. The surgeon and his assistants were cursing one of the fixtures for not fitting properly and then they dropped a screw into my brain and retrieved it with some difficulty with a suction machine. (It sounded like a vacuum cleaner.) This is not uncommon, apparently, although I was AWAKE and could hear everything. Then a piece of the electrodes dislocated itself and fell on the floor – they thought. They later retrieved it from my neck!

The electrodes were placed in the brain on one side then the process was repeated on the other side, the drilling accompanied with absolutely no pain but the noise and vibration were very disturbing. The surgeon instructed his assistant to vacuum up the bone dust. I actually fell asleep twice. The crowd came and went with Lorraine holding my hand. Then I couldn't see for an opaque plastic sheet thing over my brow that was filling up with a mixture of brain fluid, blood and iodine, ending up running down my neck. It turned out when I lifted the canopy it wasn't Lorraine's hand I was holding at all but the delightful professor who was taking it in turns with the girls from the anaesthetist group. I felt flattered, and I must say the general staff were all good-humoured, thoughtful and caring.

Before all this procedure I was wheeled into the CT scans after the crown was on my head. Somehow they find the spot with the help of sounds from brain waves and when they played the recording, it sounded like me playing my drums in the 1960s. The technology is *drum-founding!*

After this I was again wheeled into a recovery ward full of members of the animal kingdom breaking wind, coughing, machines beeping. Fortunately I like animals!

There was an impromptu Samoan hymn sung some beds down

the ward, which was rather moving.

The day after my recovery, I was wheeled again into the surgeon's operating theatre with a much smaller entourage 'only for four hours this time'. The wires from my head were all placed under the skin via the back of my ears and down both sides of my neck to just below the collarbones. They were then attached to the battery-operated (Itrel Neurostimulators 'IN') – one on each side of my chest. One of the female anaesthetists suggested putting them where my abs should be, whatever they are. That operation was very successful but when they wheeled me back to Noah's Ark I was told the first op had a little problem. They thought that the electrodes were perfectly placed, but the right hand side was a little too far into the brain and due to the changing pressure in the brain it had moved and I needed another op to pull the wire up 2mm. Bugger!

Back to the operating theatre two days after the second op, and I was greeted by all and sundry in the pre-op rooms and in the corridors like an old guinea pig. This was only going to be thirty minutes. I told my Scottish anaesthetist, "We must stop meeting like this," and he put me under a general anaesthetic.

The afternoon after my third op, my neurologist Doc came and adjusted my IN, tapping on my turgid stomach, and with a smile said, "It's full of corks, Richard. Lose some weight and watch that wine!" After he turned on the electrodes with his remote control, I immediately stopped shaking and to cut a long story short I found myself walking unaided, eating without spilling anything, my back pain gone, my dyskinesia and freezing almost stopped. I'd say that I can move eighty-five percent normally and Doc hasn't finished tuning me yet, which will be done daily over a couple of weeks with 7.45am appointments each time at the public hospital. I'll have to get up at five in the morning, three hours earlier than normal.

I can't tell you how relaxing it is not shaking at all. All I am worried about is that Seng's been given a remote control to turn me off and on. This is actually to reset my systems in case of interference from outside magnetic influence such as airport security etc. He will have the ultimate control!

Later, an audience with about thirty neurologists watched me

287

doing my tricks, even running down the corridor, (but not as well as my cat Morris's dancing), to their amazement.

I must thank you all for being so concerned and considerate with your messages of support. And my special thanks to Seng and my old friend, Murdoch.

Richard II.

This afternoon I get a ring from New Zealand and Richard's laughing his head off. "Yesterday I told Doc how I drove for the first time and hit a hundred and twenty kph. He was dismayed. 'Oh Richard!' he was shouting. 'This always happens with a patient. They think they're driving carefully like they drove when they were so handicapped. They don't realise how well they're feeling and do not recognise the speed at which they're driving. *So Richard, don't drive for three more months!*'"

"Are you obeying him?" I ask with scepticism in my voice.

"Well, yes. Sort of. I'm just driving down to the village and back."

I ask what else he and the doctor talked about? And Richard tells me about the very mild dyskinesia that he is still experiencing and also a strange sudden muscle freezing. It has been occurring when he goes through doorways. Suddenly his body just stops and even though it's for a brief moment, he's so scared of falling over the way he did before the operation and broke those four bones, but Doc has tweaked the batteries and says the symptoms will go in a day or two.

The freezing happens about four times a day and usually when he's tired at the end of the afternoon, but otherwise he feels almost a hundred percent. Answering more of my questions he says he's also to stay on two Parkinson's pills a day for now, and that Doc has pushed the batteries up to 3.25 or something around there and they can be charged up to 4.5 so there is still room for even more improvement.

"The dyskinesia is really nothing," he tells me. "And you should see me run up and down the stairs. To think that before the op I was afraid to use them! And guess what? *North & South* magazine wants to do an article on me and I've had rings from radio stations wanting to do interviews."

"Will you?"

"I don't know. I don't want to be on the radio. I find I'm sometimes slurring my words as if I've had too much gin. It's a side-effect of the stimulator being adjusted higher. Have you noticed it?"

"Frankly, yes. But it's a small price to pay for everything else that's so positive. What about the magazine interview?"

"Yes, I've accepted the *North & South* invitation. They need me to go back to the hospital and don a hospital gown and all that for photos. Make it look as if I'm still a patient."

A few days later I get an email from Richard, dictated to Seng:

'I'm now at the end of the tweaking stage and things feel great.

It's common for patients to forget how disabled they were, as I realised when I saw Doc this afternoon. He told Seng to turn off one of my stimulators. It was a test run.

Straight away I slumped into my chair and writhed uncontrollably. I must say that I feel very vulnerable realising that a couple of very expensive electrodes are all that are keeping me upright.'

But he carried on with an uproarious account of how their costly six-year-old fridge had blown up, and their troubles getting a replacement.'

I reply:

'Your crises match ours on Tahuri farm. But I think you have an advantage. Men get a better break when dealing with service people than women do. You're lucky you're not a Senior Citizen. It gets even worse.'

Chapter Thirty-Five

The Last Jump

Dave arrives home from a visit, finally, to his orthopaedic surgeon. I rush outside to get the prognosis. "What did he say? Did they X-ray?"

"The X-rays show that the hip joint's now bone on bone."

"Oh poor you – no wonder it hurts so much. Heck, Dave, this is awful. When's the operation scheduled?"

"I've put it off until the end of the year. It's to be done on December 12. The doctor just couldn't believe that I've already left it this long, but I told him I want to finish my last term ever at MIT and before my retirement begins the middle of January"

"But December's four months off!"

"I can take it. Stop worrying. There's a good prognosis."

"You can lead a horse to water, and all that," I sigh. I make myself a cup of tea, sit and ponder the future. Inevitably we'll have health challenges and it's not as if we live in a Boston condominium with one cat. The future suddenly looms as so uncertain. What does it hold for Dave? His father had a stroke and his mother developed dementia. Dave's younger brother Warren died soon after birth, but no one would ever tell us what happened.

Mrs Benney once told our children that Warren was a little angel and that God wanted him, but that was as far as she would go. For genetic reasons Dave and I have always been curious. Earlier this year when I was in New Zealand, I rang the office of Births and Deaths and asked if they could provide us with a death certificate for a Warren Benney who died sometime around 1934 and is buried in the Te Awamutu cemetery. Three weeks later we received the certificate and it was a shock to us both ... Dave's little brother died on Christmas Day in 1934 of meningitis and spinal bifida when he was only four days old.

Thankfully spinal bifida is not an inheritable condition and is caused by a lack of folic acid during pregnancy. And what does the future hold for me, the clone of my father? Dementia and Parkinson's? Oh well. There's really not much I can do about it.

Poor Dave, but he will feel great after the operation and six weeks of rest and therapy and being waited on hand and foot. How lucky that the outcome is so good and he will have the same eminent surgeon as before. "It'll be very routine, Dave," he had told him. The doctor has a farm in New Hampshire and he and Dave had a great time talking tractors, hay making, fertilising ...

Dad had three different operations on both hips. The first was just a realignment of the head of the femur and the socket of the hip joint. A few years later it was again becoming painful, bone on bone, and they repeated the operations, but used the plastic parts that were current at the time. It worked well for several more years and then the plastic wore out and a third operation was performed on both hips. A newly developed and strong composite metal was installed. "You'll soon be running again, Russell," the doctor told him. And before long he *was* running, all over the place as he approached his eightieth year. There's a story told by his aunt who was well into her nineties, still very spry and walking down the main street in New Plymouth. She was almost totally blind but was able to perceive a person running madly along the footpath with a dog following closely behind. "Russell, Russell, that's you, isn't it?" And sure enough it was my father who seldom went anywhere without his dog, even to business meetings. "Who else would it be?" she had laughed.

I think about my own hips. They have never given me any problem, yet. I'm a physical double of my father and lead a very similar active life. Why have my own hips been so trouble-free? My orthopaedic surgeon once told me that an active riding career acts as a counterbalance to classic hip degeneration. Riding strengthens the muscles in the area and they in turn hold the joints together. When I was first pregnant and went to an obstetric doctor I'll never forget one of her first comments: "My goodness, Elizabeth, you have the most remarkably developed muscles in such unusual places."

A couple of weeks ago Kathy decided to try just *one* more date after the last one turned into yet another disaster. On parting he'd announced that he'd been warned to avoid women involved with horses! Things now couldn't be going better for her. Jim has good manners, he's accomplished, makes no demands and is interested in Kathy and not just himself. She arrives to give me a dressage lesson and we're in my indoor arena as it's pouring outside. I've been giving Minty Adequan shots for his old stiff joints and he feels like a youngster. There's a small jump on one side of the arena. A friend has dragged it out of the storage room to start teaching her horse the fundamentals. It's set as a cross-rail and the middle of it is a mere six inches high. Every time I ride past the jump, Minty refuses to take his eyes off it.

Our lesson ends. "Kathy, now that I'm done, I'm just going to jump Minty over that tiny cross-rail. He still misses jumping so much. Me too," I laugh. Of course I'm in my dressage saddle and my stirrups are way too long for jumping, but hey, a six-inch cross-rail is nothing. I could probably do it without my stirrups … ha ha.

Minty was bred to jump, and his talent and experience far surpass his dressage. I look at the tiny jump and I'm filled with a cocky confidence. Of course one wouldn't lose the skills after sixty-six years, it's just the old body that let me down that one time at my trainer's farm. And that fall was over a *high* and very *wide* jump. I was probably getting a bit fatigued after jumping several courses. I certainly had no problem jumping the three little beginner jumps that Paul re-set that fateful day. And, to be immodest, they were faultless jumps. What's more they were five times higher than this trivial cross rail.

"I'll just trot it," I tell Kathy. "The old boy certainly knows how to get across this height with the minimum of effort."

Minty indisputably knows his job from so many years of competing, both in the hunter show ring and in eventing. Even a four-foot obstacle to Minty is no big deal and he's so safe and so honest. In fact not long ago when we had no more boarders, my mares were in a field out of

Minty's sight. He missed seeing other horses and jumped out of his pasture over a three-foot-high cross-country jump that was built into the fence-line during my eventing heyday. So I nailed on a rail at about three foot nine inches high. Over he went again and cantered off to his 'girls'. "Now, Minty, this'll keep you in," I muttered to him as I secured the rail on the very top of the fence line. It was four foot three inches off the ground. Minty took one casual look at it, picked up an easy canter and jumped it in impeccable form. But instead of galloping off to find his mares, he stopped on the spot. I could read his mind from the quick glance that he gave me. "Quick, guzzle this delicious lawn that needs cutting."

Now I say, "Okay, Kathy. Here goes."

We round the corner.

Minty's eyes lock on to the tiny jump.

His ears prick.

His body tenses just a little with anticipation.

He keeps up his lovely rhythmic trot.

How well I know the exact feel of his approach.

Old times are here again, even if I *am* in my dressage saddle with the stirrups four inches too long for jumping.

Okay, Minty, I know that you'll be perfect and tomorrow I'll put my jumping saddle on you. And we'll go a little higher and …

We're at the perfect take-off spot.

A deluge of adrenaline pours through Minty.

With the release of long frustration it compounds into one heck of a mammoth leap. He soars over those six inches as if they're set at an Olympic height.

I lose my balance.

I'm lying flat on the ground.

Off Minty canters to the end of the arena, stops, and gazes at the prostrate me swearing my head off. I use every dirty word that I've ever heard in my entire life, most of them for the very first time, and it's a long while since I've ever been so raging mad. I'm sore and I'm humiliated but I wiggle and my legs and arms don't feel broken. Kathy should tongue-lash me. She says nothing but I catch a glance of her face registering abject horror. Is she responding to my fall or to my language? Probably both.

So this is it.

The Last Jump.

Ever.

I struggle to my feet, convinced now that *finally* my long jumping career has really ended … with me lying on the ground a second time. I can't believe that my body did this to me. Of course I hurt all over my left side and especially around my rib cage and in a day or two I know that the whole area will turn pitch-black. My face feels spared this time and I can cover up the rest of the evidence with late autumn clothing.

Soon I start suffering horrible spasms around my heart. I check my blood pressure and it has spiked way up. I go into a tailspin and email my doctor. He replies that from all the symptoms, especially the spasms, it sounds as if I've broken or at least cracked a rib or two. And he's sure that I know how to handle such a fracture! I'm not to worry about the blood pressure unless it stays up. Pain can make it go haywire. To my description of how the accident happened, Doc writes: '*Have taken note of your recidivism, Liz!*'

A few days later I read a very interesting article. It has been proven that whenever you experience sudden pain, swearing your head off really helps. It increases the heart flow and releases endorphins that are pumped into your system to help lessen the pain. The article cautions that the everyday overuse of swearing will result in the loss of its effectiveness in a genuine physical crisis.

So, Mother and Dad, I know how badly you wanted me to be 'a little refined lady' but it's okay for me to swear! Occasionally.

I seem to have had more than my share of genuine physical crises over the years. I *swear* I'll be more careful from now on, or my time left to reach one hundred and five will be cut short.

On this day I accept, at last, at very last, that I will never jump again. And I think how odd it is that the word *swear* can have two such diverse meanings.

Chapter Thirty-Six

Getting My House in Order

I need several weeks off riding while my ribs repair, and meantime thoughtful Dave looks after this old cripple living on pain pills. Soaking in a hot bath is helpful, and I wish I had one of those old people's bars above the bath to help haul myself out. On second thoughts, no, let it wait for the distant future. One of those emergency alerts that hang around the neck can also wait for the *very* distant future.

Ah well. Time will mend me to a certain degree. I'll soon be seventy-seven and Minty will be twenty. Then we'll have just one and a half years left before we ride that test for the combined one hundred-year-olds.

I ring Richard and he answers in a very low-key voice. "What's wrong?" I ask, "You sound really down."

"I've been awake since 1am. You won't believe what happened. I've had terrible dyskinesia. I was a squirming eel out of water and fighting a losing battle to live. I just managed to take a Parkinson's pill and it didn't help much so I woke Seng. He grabbed the remote control and one of the bloody batteries in my chest had turned off one side of my head. Seng turned me back on and I'm fine now, but it really shook me up."

"What on earth triggered this?"

"I've no idea and it's Saturday today. Seng's going to email Doc, but I doubt we'll hear from him before Monday."

"I'll ring you your time Tuesday. I'm sure it'll turn out to be nothing."

"Yeah, the replacement of the battery-run stimulator? Another operation? I dunno. I was feeling so great and pretty well normal. I guess I must *be prepared*."

"What a good Boy Scout," I joke and he laughs. "Have you talked with the doctor about reducing the slurring of your words?"

"I will later this week when I have an appointment, and you know it's not abnormal for some patients after the operation. Doc may reduce the strength of the stimulator a bit and that's supposed to help."

I don't tell him about my fall or my chest pains.

Keep everything in proportion, Elizabeth.

Two days later I hope to hear a good reason for the battery failure. Richard answers my phone call with laughter that pricks my eardrum. "You won't believe what caused the malfunction. We rang that nurse, Lorraine, yesterday as we couldn't wait for Doc to answer our email. She asked if I'd been anywhere near magnets. 'I sure have,' I tell her. 'When we replaced an old refrigerator I spent ages cleaning the magnets from its door. I rubbed the backs of them all over my chest.'"

And that's what triggered the shutdown of the stimulator. I can't believe that rubbing little magnets on his chest had such a reaction. But it is great news. I was prepared to hear Richard was back in hospital for more surgery.

"When does the article in *North & South* come out?" I ask.

"It arrived yesterday and Seng has posted you a copy. The article's not bad, but I look pretty haggard in the front-on photo."

We hang up, and I make a resolution.

Be prepared.

And especially as Dave thinks he will be dead long before me. "Do you think I want to live to be *one hundred and nine*," he grins, "so that I can boast that I've outlasted your one hundred and five aim?" If it so happens that Dave does outlive me, of course the children will make sure he's well cared for.

But for now I've decided that this SC must:

1. Plan who will care for my horses if I expire before they do.

I need to write out a detailed record of their shots, feed schedules and individual quirks, especially cocky Minty's. He can't stand being out in the rain. And he must be fed first or he'll bang a hoof on the stall door. Years ago tests showed up his many allergies … so he must never be fed any corn or oats, but barley is an excellent digestible grain. When he was eleven years old he had a serious reaction to the annual rabies shot and could die if he ever receives another one. Interestingly, my vet Lol checks his titer every year and so far he's still protected. One wonders why the state of Massachusetts dictates that horses be legally vaccinated every year.

The children will willingly take care of the cats and dog.

2. I must face the taxing task of marking on a map of the farm where every electric line is buried and enters into the house, the stable and the outbuildings. The same with the telephone lines, the Internet cable, the intercom cable, the water lines and the Dog Watch line that great underground wire that we installed for Richard's golden retrievers who spend three weeks with us every summer.

The Dog Watch line gives the dogs a small zap if they try to cross it and run away. Of course there's a click-click warning as they approach the tape. Then there are the water and electric lines to the eight waterers or troughs, and the masses of underground drains here and there and everywhere. On second thoughts, all this can wait until Dave's hip is working again and I know he will help me.

3. Have the children finally choose what they want from our possessions so I can finish putting names on everything.

Paul wants to know what is the most expensive item in the house!

4. Throw all my old shoes, my old stained clothes and those with colossal holes and rips into the dumpster.

I can't chance the children giving them to the Salvation Army and insulting their faithful volunteers.

5. Clean out the safe, clean out the basement, clean out the garage, clean out all the kitchen cupboards, clean out all the many other cupboards in the house and stables, the drawers and shelves, clean out the attic, clean out my tack room and grain room, clean out the detached three-car garage, clean out the jump storage room beside the indoor arena and watch out for mice!

Whew … well, I'll tackle some of the above one of these days.

6.If I have a terminal disease, will I follow Marylon's courageous example and ring my best friends to say goodbye?

I'll think about it, if and when such a fatal illness should strike.

7. I must impress on the children they are to announce that I died when the moment arrives.

How I hate those euphemisms *she passed, she passed away, she passed over, she passed on* (she passed out!) or *she went to greener pastures,* and, even worse, *God took her.*

8. If any of you decide to put my ashes around the kauri tree at Tupare, please make sure you pack the container in a suitcase when you fly to New Zealand.

It is *not* to share the two seats designed for two passengers sitting next to each other. Important. Please remember that in *no way* am I to be put into a coffin and buried.

I've just read the following in today's *Taranaki Daily News:* 'The dearly departed now require a bit more real estate to rest in eternal peace. New Zealand's obesity rate is forcing funeral directors, coffin manufacturers and even gravediggers to upsize their preparations for the recently deceased. There is nothing worse than seeing a person jammed into a small box.'

And few things are worse than seeing more pristine land dug up, sanctified and weighted down with a heavy engraved stone.

Says me!

9. In my Rolodex, I must put checks beside all the people I adore.

And when my time finally comes, the children will know to send them the following message: *Do drop by Tahuri Farm to posthumously and humorously celebrate the great life of Liz Benney with champagne and chocolate cake.*

Insert address, date and time.

And please take really good care of Dave.

Hopefully he will be attending!

What's all this hurry?

I've got twenty-eight years left!

POSTSCRIPT

During my teen years I kept a notebook in which I wrote sayings that appealed to me. One of them is still a favourite: *There is nothing more certain than the uncertain future.*

Dave's hip replacement is still scheduled for 12 December 2009, a week after his final term ends forever at MIT. He doesn't show any emotion about his official retirement starting on January 15 but I know it's the end of fifty-three years in a profession he loves and will sorely miss. But he has been given a very pleasant new and smaller office and will become an emeritus professor, driving to Cambridge about once a week. For a long time now he has tried to *rise above* the hip distress but no amount of stoicism will help bone rubbing on bone.

Today is 12 November and I raise my glass of wine, "Hey, Dave, one month to go until the operation, until relief. And only two more weeks, ever, of MIT classes. What a blast you're going to have!"

And the uncertain future strikes, without any warning.

Because of his hip pain and restlessness, Dave has been sleeping in the spare bed in his study. We always get up at 5am and a week later I hear him calling me at 4.45am. "Liz, Liz, Rocky's hungry and there's no dog kibble. Where's his food?"

"What?" I say to myself. I fly downstairs and the huge bag of dog food is in its usual cupboard. What is more, Dave is dressed and announces that he's off to MIT. "See you tonight," he waves.

"Whoa, wait a minute. It's only 5am. You never leave this early."

"I've got a meeting at ten."

"But it only takes an hour to get to work and what about your breakfast?"

"I ate it at ten last night and went back to bed."

And he's out the door, satchel in hand.

In my gut I know that something is very amiss and immediately email our doctor, Dr C, at the Massachusetts General Hospital in the city. He rings me at 7.30. "Liz, I must see him immediately."

"I know he'll object, but I'll try and move this stubborn horse."

"And you come too, if you can."

I ring Dave and catch him in his office, still two hours before the meeting. "Dave, Dr C wants to see you immediately."

"What rubbish. I'm *fine*. There's nothing the matter with me."

"Dave, eating breakfast at 10pm, being unable to find the dog food, leaving for work at 5am …"

"I know, I know …" and his voice tapers off.

"Dave, something does seem a bit out of kilter. We all love you too much to overlook this kind of odd behaviour. Please listen to me. Dr C is a very busy man and he wouldn't want to see you unless he was concerned. He wants me to come as well."

Silence.

"Well, okay," Dave finally replies, quietly, "I'll meet you at his office, but I must make this department meeting and I'm teaching at noon. Leave me a message with the time of the appointment."

Dr C thoroughly checks Dave all over and asks many questions of us both. He's non-committal and orders immediate tests starting with an MRI.

The following night at 8 o'clock the phone goes and it's Dr C. "Liz, I'd like to talk to both of you together." I ask him to please wait a minute as Dave's outside with the dog. Already I know that the diagnosis is significant. When I had to have my mammogram repeated and it scared me stiff, the nurse told me that *if* something serious had turned up, I would have had an immediate *personal* call from my OBGY doctor.

Dave picks up another phone. "Dave, Liz," says Dr C, "it's not too bad, but you've had a stroke. There's a blood clot in the upper right section of your brain and some bleeding as well. And you're to have an electrocardiogram and an echocardiogram." He goes on to say that he wants even more tests done and he'll prescribe blood-thinner medicine. He is kindly and very matter-of-fact.

I wonder how a man who is almost eighty years old, who has seldom had a cold and with nothing but an appendix, hernia and the first hip replacement operation in the past, is now taking all of this. "Dave," continues Dr C, "I'm afraid the hip replacement must be postponed for six months. We've got to monitor this situation before the ordeal of an operation."

We both reel at all this sudden news. Of course one expects aging problems, but our conscious and positive minds have always buried such thoughts. But no matter what one's age when the first problem strikes, it's certainly unnerving. I try to cheer up poor Dave. "Hey, you know what? You're not showing any paralysis and your speech is fine. Just think what might have happened."

"It's interesting," he responds, "but you know, lately I've found that my mathematics has lost its sharp edge. I couldn't figure out why."

I fly to the Internet to get the exact explanation of both procedures. An electrocardiogram is a test that measures the electrical activity of the heartbeat. And for an echocardiogram, an instrument called a transducer transmits high-frequency sound waves towards the heart and an echocardiography machine converts these impulses into moving pictures of the heart. It allows doctors to see the heart beating, and to evaluate the structure of the heart.

I don't mention to Dave what I've found out.

The tests proceed and there's more alarming news with another evening phone call from Dr C. "I'm sorry to tell you but the tests show that you, Dave, have a hole between the left and the right ventricles of your heart. The hole should have closed at birth. Your heart is also slightly enlarged and there's some arrhythmia."

"Where did the clot originate?" I ask him.

"I can only hazard a guess. Maybe in the leg from inactivity because of the hip, or maybe in the defective heart."

Now Dave needs an appointment with the cardiac specialist and a stress test that he passes. But will they close the hole or not? It's a bit of damned if they don't and damned if they do. Dave and I vacillate between yes and no. Finally, Dave decides. "Leave it, please. I've lived almost eighty years with this hole and I can continue living with it!"

So we begin a new era of existence. We don't dwell on the past and we don't talk much about the future and Dave knuckles down until the operation date, which is now set for the end of June.

But oh no. He decides that he's really committed to attend a mathematical meeting at Qingwa University in Beijing at the end of June. Dr C says he can travel to China but he must fly business class. He'll be away one week, so the replacement is now postponed until the beginning of July.

Dave arrives home in good spirits. The meeting was huge and he found that many of his old students, some of them well in their sixties, were attending. Then the big surprise. The greater part of one day had been put aside to pay tribute to Dave's contribution to the mathematical world, his retirement and his eightieth birthday. There were many speeches of recognition and a huge banquet. I was astonished that this very modest man of mine was flattered and very moved by such a special event.

Things are looking up. We just want that new hip and life will return to normal.

Well, normal? Not so soon. Another elderly crisis knocks us down. Dave drives to a nearby horticultural nursery in his eleven-year-old manual Toyota pick-up truck, which he adores, and with nothing powered except the engine. Back home he alights, somewhat clumsily because of the handicapped left hip, and then the good hip twists as he reaches the ground. And the ground is way too far down for a man of Dave's age. How I have begged him to get a running board or a step installed – but try convincing this stubborn Kiwi.

He totters inside and says that his right hip is suddenly more painful than the left hip, which of course has been bone on bone now for months. Somehow we make it upstairs and Dave sinks into the chair at his desk.

Thirty minutes later he calls for me with panic in his voice. "Liz, Liz, I can't get out of my chair! Quick, help me please!" There's no way I can move him, even an inch. I run and get my old climbing sticks from when I nearly killed myself tramping the Milford, Routeburn and

Hollyford tracks. But he still can't move and the pain is even worse. "Dave, I'll ring Bruce. He's strong and will help." Bruce is the sergeant in our local police force and our good friend after he and his family were those superb tenants in the farmhouse for ten years.

Within minutes Bruce arrives in his cruiser. Another officer pulls in behind him. The second man grins at me with recognition. He's the policeman who last caught me for speeding. And let me off with the warning.

Together they still can't get Dave out of the chair. He is never one to complain, but we're very aware of his muffled expressions of pain. Bruce calls for an ambulance and it arrives with yet another police car in tow.

I fall outside the realm of reality. What on earth is the matter?

In the midst of my anxiety I'm fascinated to see how the three men and a woman use a sophisticated procedure for getting Dave into a type of sling and then lifted into a special chair. From there they're a practised one-ness, carrying him down the stairs. Dave is slipped on to a gurney and off the poor man goes to the local hospital. It is 7pm and I'm told that I can visit him at eight when they hope to have a diagnosis. X-rays are a certainty.

I ring Tonia and Paul, and leave Richard, on business in London, a message on his Blackberry. The hospital is only ten minutes away, a fact that reminds me of our old friend Alison. When we bought the farm she said, "I do so hope it's close to a hospital. It's essential that you live nearby now that you're starting to age."

"*Starting* to *age*? Hardly!" I had laughed. "And that is such a subjective observation, Alison. Sorry, but we want this farm and to heck with hospital localities."

How I value its proximity, twenty-one years later.

The hospital is crowded with fast-forward activity contrasting with people lying motionless in beds along corridor walls. "Today is the usual mad Friday," one of the nurses grimly announces and briskly leads me to the emergency/trauma area. Dave is propped up in bed with an IV in his arm. "What's being dripped into you?" I ask. He has no idea. He has privacy for which we are both grateful.

And we wait and wait for the X-rays to be taken. On the way in I had noticed a sign saying Triage area, and Dave certainly isn't an urgent case. Then the inevitable "I've got to go to the bathroom!" I find the bottle required, but neither of us knows how to manage this strangely shaped object. And it dawns on me that none of us young nurses-in-the-making at the Wellington Hospital, so many years ago, were shown how to use this urinal and practise on a male patient.

I go out to the corridor and ask a nearby nurse. "Your husband is such a sweet man!" she grins and cheerfully aids Dave. I don't really associate the word 'sweet' with a man, but it is meant sincerely and really moves me. Dave guffaws when I tell him.

Finally, Dave is wheeled off to X-ray and is soon returned to his room. And we wait and wait for the orthopaedic surgeon to appear. By 11pm I must go home as some of the animals haven't been fed. The nurse in charge says she will try to locate the surgeon. "Call your husband at midnight," she tells me, "and I'm sure he'll have a diagnosis by then."

Midnight. My phone call is not transferred to Dave's bed but to a nurse in the trauma unit." He's ready to go home! Come and get him," she tells me hastily.

"What!" I say abruptly with my voice rising. "I don't believe it." I'm already in my nightgown so I throw on some clothes and speed off.

Dave looks a bit perkier and is able to stand but walking is a major problem. I should ask for a wheelchair but the hospital appears to be out of control. Even at this hour, every seat in the waiting room is still filled. I help Dave lumber out to my car in the handicapped parking. Of course I've parked illegally, but what the heck. It *is* way after midnight and the slots were all empty when I drove in. The good news is that the old artificial hip has no fracture. The surgeon believes Dave severely dislocated it when he stepped way down from the truck. The doctor is too busy to linger and answer any questions.

We reach the passenger's side of my car and poor Dave can't get in. It's a staggering sight as we totter around to the other side of the car. Somehow I get him on to the back seat. At least Dave is filled with heavy-duty pain medicine. I heard from one of the nurses that he was an eight on the pain scale when he was admitted.

Getting him out of the car is a formidable task and finally the challenge of getting him into bed. Shoes off, clothes still on. Rings from the children, including Richard in London at Heathrow and about to fly home.

Is all this reality? I walk the dog outside, stumble upstairs and crash.

Morning arrives three hours later and I have a conflicting situation. I've accepted an invitation to ride Minty in a clinic, and tons of auditors are paying money to watch various riders throughout the day. I certainly don't want to go but feel a strong commitment. I make breakfast for Dave, help him to the bathroom and decide I might have made a jolly good nurse. I get the animals fed, make a quick drive to the drug store to collect Dave's prescription pain medicine, get the mares turned out, the stalls mucked out, Minty groomed, kitty litter boxes cleaned, then I pack up the float and load my horse. Finally I pull on my riding clothes and make Dave swear, three times, that he won't try to move out of bed. "I'll be back in less than three hours so try and hold off going to the bathroom. Okay?"

I'm only a minute late for the 11am demonstration and fortunately had loaded Minty all tacked up and wearing his white polo wraps and not his safety leg wraps. But he's a great old horse to ship. The summer heat is now intense with high humidity and I wonder how on earth I will manage to ride. I have this dead feeling and could lie down and sleep right here on the arena footing. But the old adrenaline floods me the minute I sink into the saddle. I don't know where it comes from, but I end up riding quite well and Minty is a star for the whole hour.

Dave managed to stay put while I was gone and now I help him dress in clean clothes, remembering the skills I did acquire when I took that nursing course at the Wellington Public Hospital so many years ago. And I make an appointment to have a running board attached to Dave's old Toyota and try to cheer him up. "Dave, only nine days now and the operation will all be over."

The countdown to the operation continues. We're down to seven days when Dave has to come off all medications. The injured hip is getting better, but without the pain prescription he's very uncomfortable in both hips. And his patience is understandably wearing thin.

Four days left to endure the bone on bone. Then the phone goes. I take the message. "Please would you tell your husband that his orthopaedic surgeon has had a personal medical emergency and is unable to do the hip replacement on Tuesday. The operation is now scheduled with an associate for 29 July."

Oh poor Dave.

Three more weeks to wait. Dave can go back on all his blood thinner and pain pills and once again stop seven days before the new operation date.

Finally. We're instructed to be at the hospital at 5.45am. We give ourselves over an hour to drive after starting the day at the ungodly hour of 3.45am. I feed the dog and cats and my willing stable helper plans to arrive at 6am to feed and turn out the horses. The orthopaedic hospital is considered one of the best in the USA, and we feel so privileged to be accepted there. Dave is his usual calm self as he is checked in as soon as we arrive and is whisked off for preparation.

I'm off home feeling strangely vacuous but within four hours the surgeon rings. It's *over*, at last. Dave has come through it all one hundred percent. But we are warned that the recovery will be slow. The operation should have been done a year ago and many muscles have started to atrophy. His body has resembled a Z from compensating for the pain. Ah well. We will cope.

The surgeon also said that Dave's heart has come through it really well. A cardiologist was on hand during the operation and Dave will still be constantly monitored with electrocardiograms. I ring the children, email our New Zealand family and enjoy a long cup of tea and a ton of shortbread biscuits. To heck with discipline.

Are we Senior Citizens looking at a harbinger of the future? What other parts of our bodies have surprising anatomical blunders such as poor Dave's hole in his heart? What other operations are there in our future? Maybe there will be broken bones, almost a given with the elderly. My mind spins with so many of the possibilities for Dave and for me. The uncertainty of the future has started to loom and I must stop dwelling on it.

POSTSCRIPT II

Right now, 1 May 2011, I'm ready to send back the page proofs of this book to my publishers for printing and the uncertainly of the future has struck again. Yet one more of our old friends has gone. Three weeks after I said goodbye to Nev at the Wellington airport last November, he died of a cerebral hemorrhage, to the great shock of Ruth-Mary and his many friends.

There are times when it hurts to have New Zealand ten thousand miles away, too far for us to honour yet another great friend at his funeral. But Doff wrote a moving account of the service in the Wellington Cathedral ... how all of Nev's family spoke so well and how their words epitomised Neville's remarkable character. His daughter Mary said that her dad had never spoken a cross word to her in his life. And one of Nev's grandsons, Sam, speaking so clearly in a beautiful child's voice, said, "There's not one thing I would change about my grandfather."

Then, on February 1 at 4pm my great indoor riding arena imploded and one of the large front doors even blew out fifty feet. It was superbly built and totally to code, and John, our builder, said there had to have been a tremendous build-up of snow on the far northern side.

Because of the many gigantic snow banks from our epic record-breaking snowy winter, we couldn't see that section of the roof. I quail when I think how I was riding Minty inside the building just three hours before the roof gave way. Would we have survived?

Soon after our arena's collapse, infinitely worse news reverberated around the world. The majestic city of Christchurch, where Dave and I met at the university, suffered another harrowing earthquake. We agonised through the following days of disbelief … the pictures of the tangled, irreparable buildings and the unbearable suffering, followed by the remarkable moments of Kiwi grit and fortitude. And the painful wait, before we heard that four of our family and our close Christchurch friends had survived. The quake struck New Zealand like a severe heart attack, leaving us to wonder how the city can recover and recapture the aura and beauty of her halcyon days.

But life still has some positives. On this superb May Day the reconstruction of my new arena is well underway and I'm able to say, unequivocally, positively and absolutely finally, that Minty and I have jumped our last jump together.

And does it bother me? Not one little bit.